FLORIDA STATE
UNIVERSITY LIBRARIES

OCT 21 1998

TALLAHASSEE, FLORIDA

Eastside Landmark

EASTSIDE LANDMARK
A History of the East Los Angeles
Community Union, 1968-1993

John R. Chávez

STANFORD UNIVERSITY PRESS
STANFORD, CALIFORNIA

Stanford University Press
Stanford, California
© 1998 by the Board of Trustees of the
Leland Stanford Junior University
Printed in the United States of America
CIP data appear at the end of the book

TO MY BELOVED MOTHER,
Andrea Quiroz Chávez,
A Native of Los Angeles

Acknowledgments

First of all, I would like to thank the staff of the East Los Angeles Community Union, without whose assistance this book might not have been written. I am particularly indebted to John Echeveste and David Lizarraga, who, despite apprehensions borne of difficulties with earlier investigations, permitted me access to much critical material at the TELACU Center.

I would next like to thank my colleagues who read and commented on assorted parts of the manuscript in its various forms: Bill Taylor and David Weber of Southern Methodist University, Al Broussard of Texas A&M University, Richard Griswold del Castillo of San Diego State University, and Mario García of the University of California, Santa Barbara. Larry Parachini, author of earlier studies of TELACU and community development corporations in general, has my special gratitude for his pioneering work, not to mention his encouragement of my own.

My research has obviously also benefited from institutional support of various kinds. The Henry J. Kaiser Family Foundation and Texas A&M University provided some financial resources, in the early phases of the research, for which I am thankful. Southern Methodist University supplied additional funds through the William P. Clements Department of History and Center for Southwest Studies. Particularly helpful at various stages of the manuscript were research leaves granted by SMU's Dedman College. Of course, the staffs of the many libraries and archives I used throughout the project deserve credit for their constant cooperation. Especially deserving is the staff of the East Los Angeles Public Library, an institution that has assisted me in various projects for two decades and whose manager the last few years has conveniently been my own sister Linda Chávez Doyle.

Other family members also provided assistance in various ways. My parents, Manuel and Andrea Chávez, and my in-laws, Gerry and Robby Poirier, subsidized this work by cheerfully providing housing during my many research trips to the Los Angeles area. Gerry's knowledge and supply of computer equipment made my work easier and more precise. Of course, my sister Carmela, my brother Manny, and the rest of my family both immediate and extended have my deep appreciation for their constant support throughout my life, academic and otherwise. Last but not least, my wife Lori and our children David and Monica have made everything especially worthwhile.

J.Ch.

Contents

Introduction: TELACU's Significance in Mexican-American History	1
1. National Precursors and Local Founders	15
2. The Chicano Movement on the Eastside	46
3. Nueva Maravilla and East LA Self-Government	77
4. The Master Plan and TELACU Industrial Park	107
5. Regional, National, and International Networks	137
6. Politics on the Eastside	167
7. TELACU Under Investigation	195
8. Resurgence of TELACU and the Eastside	223
Conclusion: TELACU's Larger Significance	253
Notes	267
Works Cited	293
Index	303

Maps and Illustrations

Maps
1. TELACU's Original Special Impact Area — 4
2. The Chicano Southwest — 144
3. The Greater Eastside — 244

Illustrations
1. *Orgullo de Nuestra Herencia/The Pride of Our Heritage* — xii
2. Thrifty-Wash/Lavadero Económico — 36
3. The Bell Plastics Building — 74
4. Nueva Maravilla — 100
5. TELACU Industrial Park — 128
6. The MAUC Center — 151
7. The Roybal Center — 166
8. The TELACU Center — 194
9. Tamayo Restaurant — 232
10. The Portals — 260

Eastside Landmark

1. *Orgullo de Nuestra Herencia/The Pride of Our Heritage.* Mural in ceramic tile by Frank Martínez and Joe L. González, TELACU Center, Commerce, Calif. Photograph by author, 1997.

INTRODUCTION

TELACU's Significance in Mexican-American History

Recovery of Historic Place

In 1968 the assassinations of Martin Luther King in Memphis and Robert F. Kennedy in Los Angeles seemed to confirm the general disintegration of American society. In that year the United States experienced social unrest on a massive scale. Decades of racial segregation, oppressive conformity, and war in Vietnam had bred the civil rights, counterculture, and antiwar movements. Violence exploded as frustration overcame moderation in those circles. Urban areas were especially hard hit by riots as many blacks seemingly abandoned King's ideal of nonviolence. In reaction to the failure of full integration in earlier years, ethnic separatism gained momentum.[1] Not only did many blacks reject integrationist ideals, other minorities called for "self-determination," as a solution to the problems of their communities. Among these other minorities were Mexican Americans, the Chicanos of the Southwest.

By 1968 in California, the Chicano movement had become a potent force, sparked by the grape strike and its leader César Chávez. By that year the movement had penetrated the cities, including the Los Angeles area, home of the largest Mexican-American population in the nation. Though Chávez like Martin Luther King advocated nonviolence, other activists, especially the youth of the urban barrios, were growing impatient. Influenced by black radicals, such as Malcolm X and Huey P. Newton, the Brown Berets and other Chicano activists advocated militant defense of their communities and self-determination in the conduct of their affairs. Thus, Chicano radicals hoped to counter police brutality, crime, poor education, poverty, and the other pervasive problems of the barrios.[2]

Despite the apparent fragmentation of society, many liberals sought to hold the nation together, even as they themselves were drawn increasingly to the left. Exemplifying this left-of-center position was the East Los Angeles Labor Community Action Committee, an initially obscure but ultimately significant Chicano organization founded by liberals amidst the dissension of 1968. Soon renamed the East Los Angeles Community Union (TELACU), this organization's liberal founders advocated self-determination, but also encouraged reconciliation with the "system."[3] This seemingly contradictory position contributed to an enigmatic image of TELACU—as an institution symbolizing recovery of the historic place of Mexican Americans in the Southwest, but also as a model encouraging national integration through socioeconomic development.

TELACU Defined

Established to improve conditions in the barrios on the Eastside of the Los Angeles area, the East Los Angeles Community Union has promoted Mexican-American recovery and self-determination holistically. It has provided social services, trained leaders, participated in electoral politics, preserved culture, and enhanced ethnic pride, especially by developing the economy of the Mexican-American community. A few years after its founding in 1968, TELACU became a federally funded community development corporation (CDC), a quasi-public, semiprivate institution that defies easy definition because it does so many things and takes so many forms. In early practice a federally funded CDC was usually a nonprofit entity established to improve the economic well-being of a "special impact area." To accomplish its ends, however, a CDC often had for-profit subsidiaries, businesses designed to provide local jobs, remove blight, and contribute to charity by making profits for the "nonprofit" holding company. This paradoxical form led some early observers to call the CDC an attempt at socialism through the use of capitalist structure. Be that as it may, this enigmatic structure allowed TELACU's major contribution to Chicano self-determination—economic development on a scale unmatched by any other Mexican-American community organization in the country.[4]

Interestingly, this development rests primarily on real estate, a fact that has permitted TELACU to impress its image on the landscape of the local community. Indeed, TELACU is attached to place as are few other Mexican-American organizations. The institution's founders designed it to serve a particular geographical area—Greater East Los Angeles, popularly known as the Eastside. Furthermore, as the CDC grew, it found real estate development the most dramatic way to serve the community. This activity has made TELACU visible in the barrio in a way possible for few other groups. It has constructed buildings and encouraged the renovation of many structures throughout the Eastside in a pattern that has left the community with landmarks to TELACU's brief history. Indeed, to a large degree the CDC has measured its success through the changes it has brought to the local landscape.[5]

The Eastside as Homeland

Though the federal government once confined TELACU to a clearly delineated "special impact area," the Eastside as a whole has vague boundaries. Most observers would agree that it includes at the least Boyle Heights, Lincoln Heights, El Sereno, and East Los Angeles; indeed, these communities formed most of TELACU's original special impact area. Others would add Highland Park, Commerce, Montebello, and even Monterey Park, each of which had sections in the original special impact area. Though not initially within TELACU's purview, Eagle Rock, Vernon, Maywood, Huntington Park, and Bell also merit consideration as parts of the Eastside. The latter thus embraces, to some degree, not only separate municipalities, but communities governed directly by the city and county of Los Angeles. This political fragmentation is nevertheless obviated by a high degree of demographic and cultural unity, for the Eastside shapes distinctly Mexican-American Los Angeles. TELACU's founders dedicated the institution to the recovery of this "homeland" in 1968.[6]

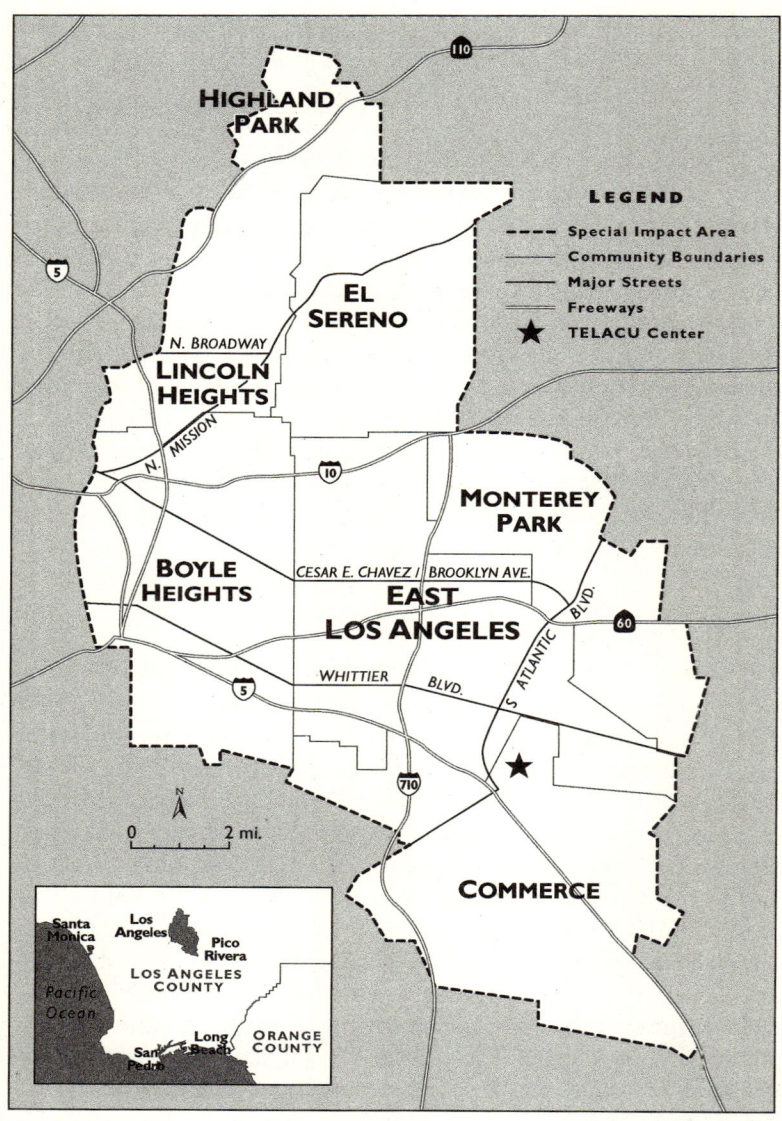

MAP 1. TELACU's Original Special Impact Area. Cartography by David Deis.

Introduction 5

If we consider Hispanic landmarks, the Eastside expands even farther. If we use population and culture as the defining criteria, the plaza area, the cornerstone of Los Angeles, belongs to the Eastside despite its location downtown. Also downtown are the Million Dollar Theater and the Grand Central Market patronized by Mexicans for most of this century. Whittier Boulevard, another perhaps less obvious landmark, stretches from central Los Angeles beyond the county to the southeast. Many Mexican Americans have followed this section of Spain's old Camino Real in their migration to the suburbs. Certainly, San Gabriel Mission, birthplace of the metropolis, remains a landmark of Mexican-American Los Angeles. Clearly, the Eastside has outliers—outliers joined to it by the Hispanic heritage.[7]

Though the landmarks of Mexican-American Los Angeles stand throughout the county, we find that heritage particularly identified with unincorporated East Los Angeles. This community shares a boundary with the city of Los Angeles, Indiana Street, the eastern edge of the pueblo's original Spanish land grant. To the north of East LA lies Monterey Park, to the west Montebello, to the south Commerce. East LA remains the heart of the Eastside and has the monuments to prove it—Soledad Church, Garfield High School, New Calvary Cemetery, and the Roybal Medical Center. Some, like the cemetery, decorated on the Day of the Dead (All Souls' Day), are old Hispanicized sites. Others, like the Roybal Center with its pre-Columbian-style frieze, are much newer. The TELACU Center, headquarters of the East Los Angeles Community Union, exemplifies the newer monuments.[8]

TELACU Center as Landmark

The TELACU Center stands just outside of East LA, in the city of Commerce, although its postal address is Los Angeles. Despite these complications, we find TELACU very near the heart of the Eastside. Featuring "a glass exterior supported by columns of black volcanic stone," the center was obviously intended to be a landmark from its dedication in 1983. Gracing the headquarters building, *The Pride of Our Heritage*, an epic mural, depicts Mexican-American history, particularly in the local area. Indeed, according to TELACU's president and chief executive officer, David C. Lizarraga, "TELACU Center stands as a monument to our corporation's commitment to building a better East Los Angeles...."[9]

The landmark TELACU Center, especially because of its "forty-foot ceramic tile mural," merits more than casual attention. The mural moves from the universal to the particular and back again. A blue sky embodying the supreme being forms an arch extending down the sides of the mural. Below the deity are Hernán Cortés, Malintzín, and Cuautémoc, the key figures in the Spanish conquest of Mexico. Farther down appear the Franciscan missionaries come to convert the Indians of California, a group focused on the founding of Los Angeles in 1781. A huge cauldron follows, pouring forth the intermixed descendants of Spanish and Indian that form the modern Mexican American. The lower quarter of the mural emphasizes Mexican-American contributions to the United States, California, and Los Angeles. Servicemen, farm workers, students, children, and representatives of TELACU itself fill out the lower panel. At the lower right, TELACU's first executive director, Esteban Torres, holds onto a globe with the American continents facing the viewer.[10]

The TELACU mural presents an image ubiquitous in Chicano thought since the late 1960s—a view of Mexican Americans as a people indigenous to their land of residence. The Southwest, California in this case, appears as a native land, rather than simply a land to which Mexicans have immigrated. While the Spanish missionaries appear as colonists, early immigrants, the significance of the cauldron in the mural must not be lost. In contrast with the melting pot of Anglo-American tradition, the ingredients in this cauldron form the mestizo of Spanish and "Indian" descent, not the intermixture of European groups implicit in the East Coast model. While Spanish ancestry gives Mexican Americans a claim to long-term residence in the region, ultimately the Indian biological and cultural heritage gives them their claim to indigenous status.[11]

Nevertheless, *The Pride of Our Heritage* remains incomplete historically. It moves directly from the Spanish colonial period in California to the twentieth century, bypassing the Mexican period

(1821–48), the Mexican War (1846–48), and the late nineteenth century. Omission of the war limits the scope of the mural compared with other works on the same theme, a general intellectual theme that has been called the "image of the Chicano homeland." That general theme depicts people of Mexican descent as belonging to the Southwest, and not alien to it, as so often presented in the mass media. In its simplest form the theme presents these people as long-term residents of the region; in a second, more inclusive form, the theme depicts them as natives. As we have seen, the mural incorporates both these forms. However, it lacks a third, more complex form of the image of the Chicano homeland—a depiction of the region as lost.[12]

Mexico's loss of its northern borderlands, as a result of the war with the United States, changed history for the region's Mexicans. In fact it created the Mexican-American minority. The absence of this historic loss from *The Pride of Our Heritage* reflects the conciliatory side of the East LA Community Union. Throughout its history TELACU has emphasized positive contributions to the community and minimized confrontation with the larger society. The servicemen in the mural's lower quarter clearly reflect this attitude of loyalty to the larger society. Despite the conciliatory motif, social conflict does appear in the mural's lower left-hand corner, conflict represented by the banner of the United Farm Workers union. On the whole, however, the mural leaves the impression that Mexicans had never lost California and Los Angeles and that Mexican Americans had always experienced equality in society.[13]

The significance of the mural's representation of the relationship between ethnicity and land should not be lost. Geographer David E. Sopher has commented insightfully that "Land on one scale or another serves as the chosen symbol of a people's being. . . ." The Southwest has served as such a symbol for many Mexican Americans since the United States officially acquired the region in 1848. Subdivisions of the region have served the same purpose on smaller scales, as we have seen in the representation of California and Los Angeles in *The Pride of Our Heritage*. In microcosm, landmarks such as the TELACU Center also serve as symbols of the ethnic identity of Mexican Americans. Because of its close involvement with real estate, TELACU as an institution has taken on the symbolism of land as well.[14]

An Imagist Interpretation

As the TELACU Center and its mural suggest, TELACU has carried out its construction projects in ways that deliberately emphasize imagery. Indeed, through much of the institution's history, TELACU's leaders have concerned themselves with its public image. Wishing to conform to the larger society, they have stressed not only beautiful buildings, but attractive offices, company cars, and business suits for the staff. But TELACU's ideas regarding land have been most significant because they have left the greatest physical impression on the community. While TELACU's leaders have had no formally articulated theory of imagery, they have clearly sought to make a mental, as well as physical, impression on the local community and larger society.[15] In this, TELACU has reflected the concern with image especially evident in business and government since the advent of television. Of course, artists and others have felt that concern for centuries.

More recently, a number of cultural historians and geographers, including Henry Nash Smith and D.W. Meinig, have examined the imagery of land in ways conducive to interpretation of TELACU's image making. Founded on Smith's *Virgin Land* published in 1950, the "myth and symbol" school of American studies posits that ideas about land form pictures in the mind, mental views, intellectual landscapes. These ideas, and concepts about space and place in general, usually take a form peculiar to one's own situation. For example, a Mexican-American Angeleno on reading the abbreviation *LA* might imagine a local seascape, such as the beach at Santa Monica frequented by Latinos. This picture would probably reflect the individual's personal experience in that locale, but would only be partially accurate if *LA* meant areas strictly within the city limits.[16]

Such mental pictures are images, combinations of fact and fiction, reason and emotion. For example, if a publicist mentions TELACU Industrial Park, we may imagine the TELACU Center (fact)

Introduction 9

with the mural on the wrong side (fiction). As we entertain this picture, we may realize "rationally" that the center occupies only a fraction of the park. But we may "feel" quite content with the perception since the full extent of the park is difficult to picture. The image of the center alone, though imperfect, adequately "symbolizes" the whole park.[17]

Such images strung together with a narrative resemble motion pictures, strips of individual frames moving rapidly through the mind. (Scholars with a literary bent have generally used *myth* to refer to these fuller, narrative images.) Specific mental landscapes form the background to characters and action, locations for our perception of historical events. Consequently, we might take San Gabriel Mission as a symbol of Hispanic history in Los Angeles, the mission's surroundings changing from rustic to urban as we considered historical events from the days of vaqueros to those of motorists. This "mythopoeic" (image-making) ability of the mind is what creative writers, advertisers, and politicians have always sought to tap in their attempts to influence their audiences. TELACU, more than any other Mexican-American organization, has sought such influence through imagery.[18]

The image the East LA Community Union has most sought to project is one of wealth and power acquired through integration into the democratic, free-enterprise system. While the CDC has always provided social services, its leaders have consistently denied its being an antipoverty agency or a charitable institution. TELACU's managers have increasingly presented the organization as a business corporation that belongs to the community. They have presented the CDC's direct social services as equivalent to any other corporation's community programs, by-products of its profitable ventures. The major benefit to the community claimed by the managers has been the employment created by TELACU's businesses. Politically, the CDC, like other corporations, has attempted to gain influence through contributions to the campaigns of politicians who have favored its interests and those of Mexican Americans. Consequently, as corporate headquarters, TELACU Center symbolizes the successful acquisition of wealth and power.[19]

The Colonial Image of the Eastside

Ironically, despite its more recent corporate orientation, TELACU's origins lie in the labor movement. And despite its conciliatory side, the CDC, as we have seen, also rests on the radicalism of the 1960s. The East Los Angeles Labor Community Action Committee was founded by Walter Reuther's United Auto Workers and eventually funded by the Office of Economic Opportunity, the federal agency at the core of the War on Poverty. While these liberal founding institutions certainly formed part of the "establishment" as conceived by the New Left in the 1960s, conservatives and some moderates considered them radical. The right had reason to be suspicious as some radical ideas and radicals found their way into federal programs. Interestingly, TELACU would rest on one of these ideas, a theory with separatist implications.[20]

This idea was internal colonialism, informally discussed by radical activists in the middle and late 1960s and formally advanced by scholars such as Robert Blauner and Mario Barrera in the 1970s. In the simplest terms these theorists argued that racial minorities in the United States existed in a situation analogous to that of peoples in Third World countries colonized by Europe. That situation was one in which the dominant European nations for their own benefit subordinated the peoples and lands of the Third World. Within the boundaries of the United States, the dominant Anglo-American majority exploited nonwhites in much the same way.[21]

The colonial relationship had originally been examined in broader contexts in a series of works by Third World thinkers, such as Frantz Fanon, Albert Memmi, and Paulo Freire. They in turn influenced thinkers in the United States, especially blacks, such as Malcolm X and Stokely Carmichael. American radicals advanced internal colonialism in direct opposition to traditional theories of inequality based on the experience of European immigrants to the United States. American racial minorities experienced inequality not because of conditions in some foreign place of origin, but because of involuntary and unequal incorporation into the United States. Furthermore, since the proverbial melting pot did not include minorities, they should seek self-determination, rather than

Introduction   11

integration into the nation. The colonial analogy seemed to allow little room for reconciliation with the larger society.[22]

Naturally, Chicano activists looked at their own history through the same lenses as their peers in the black power movement. All the major leaders of the Chicano movement—César Chávez, Reies López Tijerina, Rodolfo "Corky" Gonzales, José Angel Gutiérrez—in one way or another reflected the internal colonial analogy, either through contact with black activists or by way of Latin American thought. Unsurprisingly, Esteban E. Torres, Chávez's ally, Reuther's lieutenant, and TELACU's first executive director, applied the theory to his own community:

> East Los Angeles, like other Mexican-American communities, is but a colony dependent on outside forces that control the ownership and flow of economic resources. Because of that condition, such communities are rendered helpless to affect the social and political institutions about them. Given the ability to own and control their own economic resources, the community can then reverse the situation by attaining political power which then influences the attitudes of the social and political institutions. Moreover, it allows for eventual control, allowing for self-determination.

Despite the conciliatory message of *The Pride of Our Heritage*, TELACU's founders clearly established the organization with the colonial analogy in mind. They designed TELACU to win independence for East LA.[23]

Torres's comments reveal that behind the CDC lie more inclusive forms of the image of the Chicano homeland than depicted in the mural at the TELACU Center. For if East LA is a colony, according to the thesis, outsiders for their own benefit have expropriated the economic resources belonging to the area and its people. On a regional scale, activists argue, this expropriation began when the United States conquered the Mexican people and land that became the Southwest. This situation illustrates the third form of the image of the Chicano homeland, the view of the region as lost. This form presents a radical view of Mexican Americans because it depicts them as people disinherited—unequal members of the society. However, TELACU has frequently deemphasized this idea for fear of offending the larger society.[24]

Ethnic Recovery and National Integration

Most significantly, Torres stresses reversing the colonial situation and gaining self-determination. This reflects the fourth and most comprehensive image of the Chicano homeland, the image of the land as recovered. Torres and his allies established TELACU to help Chicanos secure their rightful place in the city, state, and region. *The Pride of Our Heritage* projects this aspect of the image of recovery because of its optimism. That Chicanos must recover from conquest, however, is not made evident since this would undermine the conciliatory spirit of the mural. Indeed, in this integrationist spirit, the mural reveals TELACU's attempts to help Mexican Americans play a greater role nationally and even internationally. As we have seen, in the lower right-hand corner of the work pose TELACU's leaders with blueprints of the future before them, Esteban Torres with the world in his hands.[25]

We could interpret this representation negatively, as crass self-aggrandizement. In fact, strong criticism has been leveled at TELACU for projecting an image of power and wealth, interpreted by some as corruption and extravagance. Critics have charged that TELACU's executives have simply succeeded in acquiring luxurious offices and fancy cars, rather than solving the real problems of East LA. These critics have charged that behind the elegant surface stands a structure that benefits the CDC's management, rather than the community. They have argued that rather than gaining self-determination for the community, TELACU has "sold out" to the world of big business and big government. In fact, the federal government and the *Los Angeles Times* leveled substantive charges of corruption, financial mismanagement, and campaign improprieties against TELACU in 1982. Ironically, convicted during the scandal was Joe L. González, the former board chairman and artist who executed *The Pride of Our Heritage*.[26]

Despite this, by establishing a visual presence in East LA, TELACU has not only demonstrated the importance of real estate for economic recovery, but offered Mexican Americans a renewed symbol of their being. This symbol is one of power, power based on ownership and control of land. In spite of its tarnished image, TE-

LACU reflects an important development in Mexican-American history, the gradual but increasing recovery of the Chicano homeland. TELACU represents a reassertion of the Mexican Americans' place in Los Angeles and the Southwest, but also integration into the nation. As such, for Latinos and other regional or ethnic minorities, TELACU also serves as a model of self-determined and equal participation in the responsibilities and benefits of the nation as a whole.

ONE

National Precursors and Local Founders

Visions of Recovery and Self-Determination

Despite the Stars and Stripes and the Bear Flag flying over its public buildings, East Los Angeles by the 1960s did not resemble the typical American community. Visibly different from the Anglo-American majority, the residents and their neighborhoods formed a *colonia*, a Mexican-American community perennially augmented from Mexico since the 1840s. In addition to the Coke, Marlboro, and Texaco ads along the commercial strips, storefronts displayed Spanish-language signs and Mexican wares, signs advertising Tecate beer and Pico Pica hot sauce. These and the *botánicas*, wedding boutiques, *carnicerías*, and other small businesses were symbols of the area's people that made their ethnicity even more evident.[1] By the 1960s the county had paved the commercial strips and most of the residential streets; indeed, the greenery had given way to asphalt and concrete to a degree considered extensive even in southern California. Nevertheless, to those familiar with eastern slums, the area could seem pleasant. No tenements existed here. There were mostly small two-bedroom houses, often two to a small lot, but with yards the envy of many a ghetto dweller in the East. Just the same, the poverty materialized in the peeling paint of porches, the cracking plaster of garden walls, and the tottering doors of garages. Indeed, poverty and its attendant problems pervaded East LA.

Despite its relatively benign appearance, East LA in the sixties faced serious difficulties according to almost every socioeconomic indicator. East LA's median family income of $4,800 compared poorly with the $13,000 of surrounding suburbs. Consequently, 45 percent of the area's population received some form of public assistance. For all men ages 16 to 24, the total unemployment rate in East LA stood at 30 percent. Much of this resulted from the high school dropout rate of 51 percent, more than double that of nearby Anglo-American schools. Given the low income level and high unemployment in the commuity, home ownership naturally fell below the 43 percent median for the city of Los Angeles. From 20 to 27 percent of families lived in overcrowded housing. Because of the absence of densely populated, high-rise apartment buildings, East LA did not look as poor as it actually was, but close inspection revealed that in some neighborhoods deteriorating or dilapidated structures made up as much as 60 percent of the housing.[2] In 1968 the East Los Angeles Community Union (TELACU) was dedicated to the recovery of this area.

Though established for the improvement of the community, TELACU from its beginnings acquired a mysterious image. This resulted partially from its unusual institutional structure. Since various outside institutions, especially the United Auto Workers and the Office of Economic Opportunity, contributed to TELACU's foundation and evolution, the founders of this community development corporation (CDC) aroused suspicion among other activists in the community.[3] Controversy also resulted from the various visions superimposed in TELACU's creation. These visions, involving the relationships between self-determination and reconciliation, between separation and integration, between collectivism and capitalism, and between place and people, were those of such prominent sixties' leaders as Elijah Muhammad, Walter Reuther, César Chávez, and Robert Kennedy. The varied interpretations of these leaders' visions by their lieutenants added to the complexity. The resulting structure evolved within a series of labyrinthine developments that would make TELACU an enigmatic symbol of Chicano, self-determined, socioeconomic recovery and integration.

Black Community Organizations

The structural origins of TELACU and the CDC in general lie as far back as those of the business corporation itself; the Massachusetts Bay Company would certainly qualify as a precursor of the community development corporation. TELACU's ideological roots date back at least to the late nineteenth-century economic nationalism of the *mutualistas*, the mutual aid societies of the Mexican barrios in the Southwest. But TELACU's more recent ideological origins stem from developments in black communities. As early as the 1930s, the controversial Black Muslims had applied a radical vision of economic self-help in their communities by setting up businesses independent of the white world. Though structuring their efforts in ways very different from those CDCs would adopt, the Muslims advanced the principle of economic nationalism to the point where in the sixties it would dramatically influence more mainstream organizations in black and other minority communities.[4]

Elijah Muhammad and the Nation of Islam

By 1960 the Nation of Islam was a controversial, but ongoing religious institution founded for the advancement of the "Black Nation." Elijah Muhammad, spiritual leader of the Muslims since the thirties, had by 1960 become the major proponent of black nationalism in the United States. Unlike Martin Luther King and other leaders of the civil rights movement, Muhammad rejected integration and favored separation of blacks from whites. If blacks integrated, Muhammad believed they would "still be servants of the white race." He believed that blacks should survive on their own. Consequently, the Muslims sought to instill hard work, thrift, and the desire to accumulate wealth in their individual members. Nevertheless, they also developed a "radical" concept of "communalism" to organize the economic activities of their temples. In this system followers regularly gave part of their income as alms for the support of the nation.[5]

Much of this money went toward the establishment of businesses operated for the common good. Malcolm X later described the purpose of the system thus: "Our businesses sought to demonstrate to the black people what black people could do for themselves—if they would only unify, trade with each other—exclusively where possible—and hire each other, and in so doing, keep black money within the black communities. . . ." In 1960 these businesses remained small—barber shops, laundries, grocery stores, clothing stores, bakeries, and small restaurants—but they would expand dramatically through the decade.[6]

Though centered in the industrialized North, the Muslims had temples in ghettos throughout the United States by 1960. Perhaps because of this, they did not develop a nationalism based on a specific place or region in this country. To some extent Muslims believed North Africa met the people's need for a homeland because it was the original homeland of some blacks and because of its long connection with Islam. Nevertheless, Elijah Muhammad did express the desire for land within the United States where blacks could form "a state or territory of their own." However, he more often advanced this idea in practical economic, rather than political terms. According to *Muhammad Speaks*, the major Muslim newspaper, one of the basic principles of the "program of economic rehabilitation and freedom for the Negro in America is the acquisition of 'some of this earth.' Thus ownership of land by Negroes is the key to development. . . ."[7] This clearly paved the way for similar thoughts regarding real estate by more moderate minority organizations such as TELACU.

Elijah Muhammad also spoke of the Nation of Islam as a "Nation in a Nation." By this he meant that the Muslims existed as a nation within the Black Nation, but also that the latter existed within the United States. In addition, by 1963 *Muhammad Speaks* had begun to refer to blacks in the United States as a colony. With a correspondent reporting from Africa during Algeria's civil war, that continent's anticolonialism clearly influenced the newspaper and its readers. Combining this current thought with the ideas of Marcus Garvey, the Muslims adopted and promoted the nascent internal colonial thesis, then also being advanced by the budding New Left. The thesis fit well into their beliefs in economic nationalism and self-help. Consequently, the Muslims began speaking of self-determination, despite the political, rather than religious connotations of the term. While the Nation of Islam did not rest on a specific land base, nor on a particular corporate structure, the Muslims would have a significant if indirect influence on TELACU and other CDCs. The Muslim stress on nationalism and minority self-determination would have great impact.[8]

Progress Enterprises

Structurally closer than the Nation of Islam to TELACU was Progress Enterprises of Philadelphia, a comprehensive self-help effort launched in 1962 by the Reverend Leon Sullivan of the Zion Baptist Church. Like the Muslim efforts, an important aspect of Progress Enterprises lay in its stress on the generation of capital by urban blacks for their own development. Sullivan, like the Muslims, came to the conclusion that economic problems largely caused the social problems of his community. As a result, he believed, "to have durable power black men must develop economic power." Both he and the Muslims encouraged businesses, certainly traditional institutions; yet the stress on community self-help and minority self-interest seemed radical because it suggested socialism and racial separatism. Despite this, Sullivan's approach remained integrationist, rather than separatist, and he encouraged accommodation, rather than confrontation with the system.[9]

Unlike the Muslims, Progress Enterprises incorporated in a manner that would serve as a structural model for many institutions later called community development corporations. Sullivan and the members of his church pooled individual monthly contributions (shares, not alms) into a nonprofit trust fund for social services and into a for-profit holding company. Both the fund and the company, nevertheless, rested under the nonprofit, tax-exempt umbrella of Progress Enterprises. While initial capitalization would later vary from one CDC to another, Sullivan's combination of nonprofit umbrella over nonprofit and for-profit ventures would remain the hybrid structure common to those CDCs most like TELACU.[10]

Significantly, Progress Enterprises embarked on a number of ventures involving real estate. Sullivan's organization purchased an apartment building in an all-white neighborhood in an effort at desegregation. This initial project clearly linked the drive for economic development to the goal of integration, rather than to the separatism advocated by the Muslims. Progress Enterprises followed with a million-dollar housing project and a shopping center. The first provided low-cost housing for the needy; the second provided opportunities for entrepreneurial training by requiring black management of the tenant companies. While Progress Enterprises would also venture into electronics and retailing, its base remained real estate. Seemingly, to Sullivan the path to economic power, at least on the local level, lay in the control of land. This too would be a pattern followed by CDCs like TELACU. Sullivan, however, made no direct early reference to land as a base for black nationalism, nor did he speak of blacks as a colony, as had the Muslims. His approach remained basically integrationist; he sought black economic power so that blacks could have greater access to the system. In this, Sullivan prefigured the conciliatory attitude of TELACU.[11]

Federal Programs

While minority communities engaged in self-help efforts, the federal government entered the picture tentatively with the election of John F. Kennedy in 1960. More important to TELACU and other CDCs than John Kennedy's election, however, was the appointment of his brother as attorney general. Robert F. Kennedy's ideas regarding community development corporations evolved from the time of his appointment in 1961 to his death in 1968. As part of the administration, he participated in several federal attempts to alleviate poverty, including the president's Area Redevelopment Administration and his own programs to counter juvenile delinquency. During the Johnson administration, Robert Kennedy and a key group of his associates, including Jack Conway (later directly involved in TELACU's founding), established the Community Action Program. This soon became the most radical and controversial component of the War on Poverty, a component reflecting the vision of Kennedy, rather than Lyndon B. Johnson.[12] Eventually, Robert Kennedy recognized that an integrated society could only come about when its distinct communities developed sufficient economic strength to interact on an equal social basis.

President Kennedy's Area Redevelopment Administration

In 1961 shortly after his inauguration, John Kennedy convinced Congress to establish the Area Redevelopment Administration (ARA), a forerunner of the War on Poverty. Kennedy's concern with geographical areas, rather than poverty and unemployment in general, made this agency distinct. These geographical areas prefigured the special impact areas later served by federally funded CDCs. The CDCs' interest in place and its relationship to people, especially in terms of economics, would hark back to Kennedy's concern. Kennedy had sponsored early versions of the Area Redevelopment Act during his time in the Senate. But during his presidential campaign, he became especially committed to the bill when he encountered dreadful conditions among poor rural whites in West Virginia.[13]

The legislative struggle leading to enactment of the agency focused on the advantages and disadvantages of supplying assistance to specific areas, rather than to the unemployed in the nation as a whole. (In addition, the issue of government intervention in the economy played a role, as we might expect.) National and local interests clashed over economic issues throughout the legislative debate.[14] This forecast later controversies over direct federal funding of community action agencies and CDCs, organizations serving localities, rather than the entire nation. Behind these controversies were fears that too much emphasis on the problems of local areas and their populations undermined national cohesion.

In general, concern with underdeveloped areas, called "distressed" or "depressed" areas in the early sixties, had evolved after World War II from the issue of unemployment. During the Great Depression unemployment had been a national problem, but as prosperity returned during and after the war, Washington only gradually realized that "labor surpluses" remained in certain areas. Recessions, which periodically struck nationwide, had hidden the fact that some areas never seemed to escape depressed conditions even after the rest of the country had recovered. These areas generally had industries that were dying or disappearing—Appalachia with its declining coal fields or Maine with its departing textile mills. President Kennedy established the Area Redevelopment Administration to help such areas recover economically. However, the ARA focused on small cities and rural areas; by contrast most CDCs later focused on big cities.[15]

The Area Redevelopment Act called for loans to nonprofit corporations to build modern factory buildings in depressed areas to replace declining industries. However, the idea of federal loans to companies willing to move or start up in these areas formed the core of the Area Redevelopment Administration. The act also contained the following provisions: long-term loans for new businesses, a public works program, technical assistance, retraining for the unemployed, and allowances for workers during retraining—all components eventually connected to CDCs. But the vision of the Area Redevelopment Act was limited to economics and did not include broad social issues. It did not encompass problems involving health care, education, housing, politics, or culture. These and other difficulties also contributed to an area's distress. The Black Muslims and Progress Enterprises had already shown that the problems of depressed areas required comprehensive approaches, a view that most CDCs would later share.[16]

The Area Redevelopment Administration had a short life. Not long after the agency opened its doors, opponents accused it of being slow, showing political favoritism, making unsound expenditures, creating unfair business competition, promoting cheap labor, supporting areas not depressed, being old-fashioned and narrow. Actually, the ARA was simply spread too thin to have any significant effect on the many geographical areas that it funded. Finally, the Economic Development Administration and the rest of the holistic War on Poverty replaced the ARA in 1965.[17]

Despite its brief existence, the Area Redevelopment Administration proved significant for the future development of CDCs because it stressed place in addition to people. In funding local regions, rather than the nation as a whole, the ARA had of course followed a precedent set by the Tennessee Valley Authority in the 1930s. Like the Tennessee Valley, the regions funded by the ARA overlapped the political boundaries of specific states and local governments. Moreover, the ARA distributed funds to private groups, as well as political bodies. While many of the funds went to rural, white areas, the practice of assigning funds to economically needy areas would eventually lead to greater federal expenditures in poor, urban, minority areas.[18]

Such areas would have more in common than poverty, however. Race and culture would tie them together, making the allocation of funds to such areas politically explosive, especially when this process bypassed local governments. Local politicians would feel threatened because more federal money would mean more local control by people traditionally outside the power structure. Of course, the Area Redevelopment Act of 1961 had projected no images of colonialism or economic nationalism. John Kennedy had hoped to provide jobs to poor areas so that poor individuals could help themselves. Nevertheless, his ARA eventually revealed that many of the "pockets of poverty" envisioned by its proponents actually resembled nations within the nation.[19]

Despite the limited results of the Area Redevelopment Administration, Robert Kennedy later cited its influence on his own thinking. He believed the ARA had illustrated the multiplier effect new businesses could have on job creation in poor areas. Because of this effect, he came to believe economic development would solve the problems of the inner city:

> The process of community development must begin on an economic base: a foundation of individual and community self-support, at last escaping from degrading and imprisoning dependency. . . .
>
> To have a maximum impact on the problems of the poor, the new enterprises must be established, the new jobs must be created, in the ghetto itself.

This was not the integrationist ideal of drawing workers out of the ghettos and into the suburbs, but an approach closer to that first advanced in the early sixties by the Black Muslims. By 1968 Robert Kennedy would be calling for "the building of self-sufficiency and self-determination within the communities of poverty themselves. . . ."[20]

The Committee on Juvenile Delinquency

Crucial to Robert Kennedy's thought was his chairmanship of the president's Committee on Juvenile Delinquency, formed in May 1961. Though the committee never actually met, it permitted a number of Kennedy's lieutenants to develop policy within his brother's administration, policy that would profoundly affect the structure of future poverty programs. David Hackett, a friend of Kennedy since adolescence, took charge of the effort. In that capacity Hackett called together a number of sociologists from the University of Chicago to implement their ideas on juvenile delinquency. Since the 1930s the "Chicago school" had advanced the theory that juvenile delinquency was not an individual psychiatric problem, but one that derived from the defects of the social environment. As a result, the Chicago school advocated restructuring neighborhoods to give youth greater opportunity. Organizers could do this by allowing poor youth to develop their leadership skills while designing their own projects.[21] This, of course, meant allowing the poor self-determination, an idea that would have a profound influence on Kennedy's thought and serious implications for many future programs.

By September 1961 Congress had allocated $30 million for Hackett's projects through the Juvenile Delinquency and Youth Offenses Control Act. Having lobbied vigorously for the bill in the House, Robert Kennedy played an indispensable role in its passage. (Hackett had taken him on several trips into Harlem, where direct exposure to ghetto life gave Kennedy a greater commitment to social change than ever.) Hackett established the first project, Mobilization for Youth, on New York's East Side. It was a "comprehensive attempt to prevent delinquency by unlocking opportunity"; it "included, among other things, public service jobs for teenagers, neighborhood service centers offering a variety of welfare services in one convenient place, employment of neighborhood people as subprofessionals in service institutions, and organizing residents into groups to solve their own problems." Hackett's group then applied the Mobilization model in cities throughout the United States.[22] Significantly, though this model focused on social services rather than economics, it stressed self-determination, empowerment of the poor.

By 1963 the idea of empowering the poor in general gained credibility among Kennedy's lieutenants because they saw their juvenile delinquency projects scuttled in city after city by local bureaucracies that had little desire to transform themselves or their neighborhoods for the benefit of the poor. Hackett and his group believed that they had erred in relying too much on professionals like themselves to implement their model, that they had not placed enough power in the hands of local residents themselves. The juvenile delinquency projects had had limited success because they lacked a constituency to challenge the local power structures that simply ignored the professional reformers. Hackett's reformers ultimately decided their approach had been too elitist; unfortunately, they had nearly exhausted their funds by the fall of 1963.[23]

Robert Kennedy's lieutenants would get a second and greater opportunity to test their theories because of the rising militancy of the civil rights movement. As black and white demonstrators clamored for the elimination of segregation and the recovery of black voting rights, intellectuals became increasingly critical of socioeconomic conditions in the country. Most influential among the intellectuals was Michael Harrington, whose *The Other America* documented serious inequities ignored for a generation. Influenced by this work and by the growing demonstrations for better living conditions among blacks, John Kennedy in late 1962 called for his administration to take up the issue of poverty. Robert Kennedy's juvenile delinquency specialists turned out to be the only people in the government with any real knowledge of the issue. Led by David Hackett again, the group began planning what would become the War on Poverty,[24] a comprehensive attack on problems the Area Redevelopment Administration had barely engaged.

President Johnson's Community Action Program

Before the war could be declared, John Kennedy was assassinated. The plan then passed to President Lyndon B. Johnson, who approved of it wholeheartedly. Hackett's team put together the Community Action Program, a series of demonstration projects based on the juvenile delinquency projects previously funded. Though the original model had only had limited success, the team hoped to salvage and transform the best projects experimentally into comprehensive antipoverty agencies. However, Johnson, anxious for bold solutions, discarded the experimental phase and launched the all-out war with unproven agencies. Both Robert Kennedy and Hackett worried over the haste and the changes made in the program they had initially envisioned. Kennedy, no longer at the right hand of the president, could not maintain the integrity of Hackett's initial plan. Nevertheless, both Kennedy and Hackett chose to support the Community Action Program, a controversial proposal for the recovery of local areas.[25]

The Community Action Program made up a major part of the Economic Opportunity Act of 1964, itself the major act embodying the War on Poverty. Congress stipulated that the program involve the "maximum feasible participation" of the residents of poverty-stricken communities. Though the drafters of the act did not know what this would mean in practice, in general they believed poor people should take control of their own neighborhoods. This would mean institutional reform since many of the new community action agencies, created by the act, would remain independent of local governments. These agencies would provide many of the antipoverty services that local governments had traditionally provided, but poor people would now more often make the decisions regarding the services they wanted. This was a radical provision because it threatened to deprive local governments and the class interests behind them of power they had traditionally held.[26] Congress had linked the idea of self-determination with federal aid to economically depressed areas. Somewhat unwittingly, Congress and President Johnson had linked the ideals of political self-determination and economic self-sufficiency.

The Labor Movement and Community Unions

In the heady period following President Johnson's declaration of the War on Poverty in January 1964, liberals outside government sought to assist the war effort by involving private organizations as

National Precursors and Local Founders 27

well. Naturally, labor formed the vanguard of this movement. As the administration experimented with specific program designs to fulfill Johnson's martial vision, labor unions and their allies launched a parallel attack on poverty by incorporating their own images of social recovery into national and local organizations. Of these, influential in the founding of TELACU was the national Citizens' Crusade Against Poverty (CCAP), an organization including such prominent leaders as Martin Luther King and Michael Harrington, and headed by Walter P. Reuther, president of the United Auto Workers (UAW).[27]

Walter Reuther, Jack Conway, and the Community Union

The CCAP's importance lay in its role as a major national organization behind the "community union." The community union emerged in concept and form, if not name, in late 1964. It was the brainchild of Walter Reuther and his lieutenant Jack Conway, formerly of the UAW, but then serving as head of the Industrial Union Department of the American Federation of Labor–Congress of Industrial Organizations (AFL-CIO). Reuther, head of the "militant" CIO before its merger with the AFL in 1955, believed that the labor movement by the 1960s had become complacent. He sought to reinvigorate its crusading spirit by organizing more workers in the traditional fashion, but also by organizing the workers' neighborhoods. He believed labor could alleviate the problems of poor areas by applying time-tested organizing techniques outside the walls of the work place. In other words he envisioned unions embracing entire communities.[28]

While Reuther generally receives credit for creation of the concept of the community union, Jack Conway put it into practice. Though a Detroit native, Conway had an unusual background for a union leader. He had received a Ph.D. in sociology from the University of Chicago and had taught at the University of Washington for two years before returning to Chicago to work in the personnel office of General Motors. While employed there, he joined the UAW in 1942 and served as Reuther's administrative assistant from 1946 to 1961. Conway then served as a deputy administrator of housing for the Kennedy administration and even took charge of Johnson's Community Action Program. By late 1965 he had left the government to head the Industrial Union Department. Conway's experience with the Community Action Program would clearly influence his own ideas of community organization.[29]

Borrowing from the structure of a community action agency, Conway imagined an action committee, but in this case comprised of union personnel living in the target area, a group of residents. This committee would organize a grass-roots membership, provide technical assistance in program design, and assist the community in negotiations with the powers-that-be. Beyond that, conceptual flexibility was necessary because the residents themselves had to give the community union its final form. Clearly, the ideal of self-determination had carried over from the Community Action Program. Given the source of the community union concept, it naturally received national support from the AFL-CIO, especially the UAW.[30]

The Watts Labor Community Action Committee

In early 1965 the Watts Labor Community Action Committee gave the concept of the community union concrete form in the largest black ghetto of Los Angeles. Paul Schrade, head of the UAW's western region, took charge of the initial effort and chaired an advisory committee representing seven interested international unions. Each union checked its rosters of local leaders and staff for those living in Watts and willing to participate in the new effort. About 350 individuals were identified and became the core, the labor action committee of the WLCAC. They elected officers; they formed an executive board and working committees. A local UAW member, Ted Watkins, became chair of the organization as a whole. Though Schrade and others outside the area established the first community union, they turned it over to local leadership almost immediately. Nevertheless, the stigma of outside provenance gave the new organization a controversial image.[31]

Initially, Ted Watkins and his supporters had planned to improve the WLCAC's image and gain the trust of residents by extending union membership to "all low-paid people" in the Watts area. Initially, they imagined the "community union" as a broad-based, mass organization. Local residents would frame the issues, elect leaders, suggest action, ratify decisions, and receive personal benefits. In other words, the residents would gain the self-determination that labor union members ideally enjoyed. However, at some point Watkins and his staff decided that such an ambitious plan was impractical. Instead, the labor action committee, originally intended as the core of the union, remained the whole with Watkins as the leader. Consequently, the Watts Labor Community Action Committee never adopted the full structure of a labor union, nor did it ever adopt the "community union" label. Watkins and his staff would seek to overcome the stigma of outside origin and elitism in other ways.[32]

Watkins decided to improve the WLCAC's image by designing programs together with people from the area from "the bottom up, and the inside out, rather than from the top down and the outside in." This permitted a limited amount of self-determination, less than originally conceived, but the influence of the ideal remained. The first projects were two locally designed youth manpower programs that affected about seven thousand people in the area. These programs apparently gained Watkins some trust in the community. Despite this, the WLCAC remained an outside organization in terms of funding, funding ironically provided by the U.S. Department of Labor. Though designed with self-sufficiency in mind, the WLCAC would find that goal illusive, and the need to accommodate various external funding sources would continue indefinitely. Nevertheless, by providing technical assistance in program design and negotiating for grants, Watkins and his staff did assist the community in concrete ways.[33]

Interestingly, the WLCAC met the requirements for soliciting federal funds because it became a nonprofit corporation under California law. Despite its nonprofit status, the WLCAC's new corporate image would have a decisive, long-term effect on the evolution of the organization. Ironically, the WLCAC would move away from its origins in the labor movement and take on the form of a business corporation. Despite the initial labor and social service orientations of the WLCAC, economic development would eventually become its major activity. As the WLCAC became more business oriented, it also became more accommodating in its dealings with government and the corporate world. The radicalism implicit in the community union concept tended to blend into the background of the WLCAC's new corporate image. The same phenomenon would occur with the East Los Angeles Community Union.[34]

The Citizens' Crusade Against Poverty

With the founding of the WLCAC, by 1967 Walter Reuther could boast that "A new concept of union organization has been developing in areas such as Delano and Watts, California. . . . This new organizing effort is called 'the community union.'" Indeed, by that time the general idea had also received concrete form in Chicago and New York. In most of these efforts, the leaders were prominent liberals dedicated to reforming the system, even as they adapted to it: César Chávez in Delano, Martin Luther King and Andrew Young in Chicago, and Robert Kennedy in New York. Except for the New York project, the United Auto Workers and the Industrial Union Department of the AFL-CIO had strongly supported the new efforts for change through self-determination. Moreover, the union brass had gained allies beyond labor through the Citizens' Crusade Against Poverty.[35]

Founded in October 1964, the CCAP formed a private front in the nation's antipoverty war. The Crusade joined together representatives of labor unions, the civil rights movement, social welfare organizations, churches, and academic institutions from throughout the United States. Eventually, local organizations of the poor were necessarily included. For the various projects of the CCAP, funding came primarily from the Ford Foundation though many other philanthropic groups also contributed. However, the UAW and the Industrial Union Department paid the essential administrative costs since Walter Reuther and Jack Conway had initiated the Crusade's key ideas. Thus, though the members of the Crusade varied in their particular aims, much of the funding found its way into labor's community unions.[36]

While the CCAP's programs were quite specific, its goals as a whole were necessarily general. As indicated by its representation, the Crusade's liberal leaders believed in a partnership between groups of the poor and groups dedicated to eliminating poverty. In addition the leaders had designed the Crusade partly as a watchdog over the War on Poverty; they wished to assure that public moneys did indeed reach the poor, and sought this end partly by monitoring legislation. On the other hand, CCAP's leaders had especially dedicated the organization to self-help for individuals and local groups. "We could best devote ourselves," wrote CCAP director Richard Boone, "to organizing and training poor people—increasing their bargaining power. . . ." As a national organization, the Crusade's key function would be "to get resources to poor people" so they could carry out the fight against poverty on their own. The economic independence of the poor was the fundamental goal.[37]

The most important specific activity of the CCAP became its National Training Program, an effort to prepare community organizers and technicians to assist the poor in their struggle for economic independence. Naturally, the community unions initiated by the UAW and the Industrial Union Department received most of this support for training. Besides the WLCAC, the National Farm Workers Service Center received such assistance. Founded by the United Farm Workers in Delano in January 1967, the service center related significantly to TELACU's history. The significance, of course, lay in the fact that the UFW and its center were Mexican-American organizations. The WLCAC and the others funded by the UAW and CCAP were black organizations.[38]

César Chávez and the National Farm Workers Service Center

The National Training Program provided leadership training, especially in community organizing, human services delivery, and economic development. The particular stress depended on the needs of the local organizations themselves. In the case of the UFW, the training program produced union organizers among its first graduates. Obviously, the UFW needed them to assist in the immediate battle then being waged against California grape growers. But also among the first graduates were technicians needed to staff the National Farm Workers Service Center, the component of the UFW most similar to the WLCAC. While the UFW per se remained structurally a labor union, the service center gave it the community component that led Reuther to include it among community unions.[39]

César Chávez had always conceived of the United Farm Workers as more than a standard labor union. In his eyes he and the UFW had to build a broader social and moral movement. With this in mind, they constructed a cooperative service center to help the workers, their families, and their communities. They located the center on forty acres of their own land and built it of adobe to symbolize the self-determination of the farm workers. The service center eventually established "a death benefit plan; a cooperative grocery, drug store, and gas station; a credit union; a medical clinic; a social protest theatre group . . . ; and a newspaper. . . ." In these endeavors former CCAP trainees provided critical technical expertise. For example, one graduate managed the credit union; another raised funds and developed programs with organizations sympathetic to the UFW. In helping staff the National Farm Workers Service Center, the Crusade gave the kind of assistance similar to that later given to TELACU.[40]

The UFW's service center would remain closest structurally to the community union concept originally envisioned by Reuther and Conway because of its broad-based membership. However, that membership derived from the occupation of farm labor, rather than a local geographical community. Consequently, rather than becoming a local neighborhood organization, the service center remained an appendage of the national labor union. Besides this, the service center continued to focus on human services, rather than on the economic development that became the forte of TELACU and other community development corporations. Nevertheless, the UFW's moderate but vital emphasis on ethnic solidarity would influence TELACU.[41]

While the United Auto Workers, the Industrial Union Department, and the Citizens' Crusade Against Poverty all obviously attacked poverty, significantly all their efforts targeted the problem in minority areas. This of course was in reaction to the civil rights movement and racial unrest of the 1960s and to the realization that poverty was disproportionately represented in minority areas. Though most of the efforts targeted black communities, the advent of César Chávez's grape strike in 1965 drew attention to the plight of Mexican Americans, not only in central California, but throughout the nation. Naturally, the labor movement found itself in sympathy with Chávez's strike and that feeling transferred to the ethnic group as a whole.[42]

The Founding of TELACU

Shortly after the founding of the Watts Labor Community Action Committee in early 1965, Walter Reuther, Jack Conway, and Paul Schrade began to consider a similar organization for Mexican-American East Los Angeles. They delayed this move while the United Auto Workers concentrated on Watts, especially after the riot in that area in the summer of 1965. During 1966, however, Glenn O'Loane, a local Mexican-American member of the UAW, constantly reminded the union of his community's needs. O'Loane worked at the Ford assembly plant in nearby Pico Rivera, in the same shop that employed Ted Watkins of the WLCAC. O'Loane consequently kept abreast of the UAW's efforts in Watts and pressed for similar aid to East LA.[43]

Glenn O'Loane and George Solís, Local Founders

Despite his Irish surname, O'Loane was the product of a Spanish-speaking family that went back generations in the Southwest. He had grown up in Alamogordo, New Mexico. While still in high school, he lost a job for participating in a union protest. After serving in the military during World War II, he settled at age twenty-three in Los Angeles, where he briefly worked for Boeing Aircraft. By 1948, however, he was working for the Ford Motor Company and active in the UAW. As a union committeeman, O'Loane described his job as that of a social worker, one who dealt with relations between the union and the community where workers lived. He once commented, "My thing was always social services, the people. You're dealing with little people, people with problems and on a one-to-one basis. I grew up in that environment and I enjoy it. It's an experience you can't buy." By March 1966 O'Loane had convinced the UAW to set up a new advisory committee, chaired by Paul Schrade, the committee that would establish the East Los Angeles Community Union.[44]

Following the pattern for the founding of the WLCAC, Schrade, with Jack Conway's assistance, brought together local representatives of about twelve national unions to serve as the advisory committee. Of these unions the most active in the founding of TELACU were the UAW, the Packinghouse Workers, the Amalgamated Clothing Workers, and the Teamsters. The rest showed only a passing interest and ultimately provided little directly in terms of personnel or resources. Naturally, the UAW spearheaded the effort.[45] Besides O'Loane, the UAW provided one other key participant from the local community, George Solís, an employee of General Motors. These two Mexican Americans became Schrade and Conway's major contacts in the community.

Though a native of Cheyenne, Wyoming, George Solís had resided in East Los Angeles since 1956. His father's employment explains his interesting place of birth. His father worked for the railroads, as did many other Mexicans throughout the West, especially the Southwest. Because of this, Solís visited Texas and Mexico often as a child on passes his family received through his father's employment. Drafted during World War II, he left Cheyenne permanently at age eighteen. After serving in the navy in the South Pacific and New Guinea, he lived in El Paso, where he took some college courses and worked as an inspector for the air force. Solís finally settled in East LA to be close to his mother, who had moved there previously. He found employment as a scheduler in the General Motors plant in nearby South Gate. From that point on, he became active in the UAW, especially in developing manpower programs, a task that occasionally took him to the union's headquarters in Detroit. This experience made Solís highly qualified for the advisory committee established by Schrade for East LA.[46]

Through 1966 and 1967 the advisory committee held many meetings at the United Auto Workers' regional offices on 9th Street in downtown Los Angeles. Regularly in attendance at these meetings were Schrade, O'Loane, Solís, Jess Avelar of the Packinghouse Workers, and Lucy Sánchez of the Amalgamated Clothing Workers. Representatives of other unions attended on and off. Initially, Schrade simply asked the committee members to go out into the community and get a feel for what the people needed. Nonetheless, he clearly had the WLCAC in mind when imagining the new organization. Indeed, Jack Conway himself made several appearances before the committee to discuss the community union concept. Throughout these meetings, Walter Reuther kept himself informed of progress, but never participated directly.[47]

By February 1968 the advisory committee had formally established the board of directors of the East Los Angeles Labor Community Action Committee (ELALCAC). Naturally, the directors came largely from the UAW and from those who had participated on the advisory committee. O'Loane was elected president and Avelar, treasurer. Ed Tovar became vice-president, and Ruben Imperial, secretary—both of the UAW. Besides Solís and Sánchez, the board included George Gruhle, also of the UAW, and David Lara, who joined simply as an East LA resident. ELALCAC then readied to open the first office of what would later be called the East Los Angeles Community Union.[48]

In February this office opened in a shopping center at the intersection of Kern and Hubbard in East Los Angeles. Glenn O'Loane became the first employee and initially the entire staff of the new office. Under the UAW's contract with Ford, he received a leave of absence from the auto plant to participate in union activities. Proving its commitment to the new organization, the UAW covered his salary and benefits entirely. However, compared with TELACU's later multimillion dollar budgets, its first was miniscule, only $150. With this the board gave O'Loane his first assignment, to gain the confidence of the community: "We had to assure the people that we weren't a big union movement coming in to take over but we're [sic] here to lend our help." Even as the new organization opened its doors, its outside origins threatened to give it a negative image.[49]

O'Loane immediately embarked on a social service program aimed at youth, a particularly important group in East LA because of the community's pervasive gang problem. Under the sponsorship

2. Thrifty-Wash/Lavadero Económico. The original TELACU office in a shopping center on Kern and Hubbard, East Los Angeles, Calif. Photograph by author, 1997.

National Precursors and Local Founders 37

of the WLCAC and the city of Los Angeles, ELALCAC arranged for six hundred youth, ages seven to sixteen, to spend a week in summer camps in the mountains at Saugus from July 8 to September 1, 1968. More importantly, ELALCAC provided summer jobs for fifty teenagers with funding from the Neighborhood Youth Corps of the Department of Labor. The youth worked helping senior citizens in East LA. O'Loane designed this program, not merely to get youth off the streets, but to put them back in touch with their elders for their mutual benefit.[50] In these efforts the package deals put together by ELALCAC proved structurally significant. Drawing on assistance from government as well as the labor movement, the organization was forming the complex network that would typify TELACU's activities from then on. Curiously, these first activities showed little sign of the self-sufficiency emphasized in the community union concept. Indeed, funding depended heavily on government.

Esteban Torres, First Executive Director

Even before the launching of these summer programs, however, the UAW had taken another critical step to strengthen ELALCAC. Paul Schrade, as chairman of the advisory committee, recommended that the board of directors appoint Esteban E. Torres executive director of ELALCAC. This proved a touchy situation since the recommendation came from outside and above the community, hardly an example of self-determination. On the other hand, the advisory committee realized Torres's exceptional qualifications, and he was a product of East LA. Of course, Schrade made the recommendation with the understanding that the board could reject the candidate or remove him at a later date if necessary.[51]

A native of the Southwest, Esteban Torres had extraordinary qualifications. Born in Miami, Arizona, he had experienced the hardships of the Great Depression. During the repatriation campaigns of that period, his father was deported to Mexico because of his union activities in the copper mines. His mother, employed by the New Deal's Works Progress Administration, moved to East Los Angeles with her children. Thus, at the tender age of three, Torres found himself in a broken family. On the Eastside he attended local schools, including Garfield High School, eventually East LA College, and finally Los Angeles State College. After serving in the army, where he reached the rank of sergeant first class, Torres in 1954 found work at Chrysler in nearby Maywood. He soon became involved in UAW activities, won union office, and eventually rose to the upper echelons of the labor movement.[52]

In the early sixties Torres moved to Washington, D.C., as director of Inter-American Affairs, a division of the UAW's International Affairs Department. In that capacity, he served as a special assistant to Victor Reuther, Walter Reuther's powerful brother. Because of Torres's ethnicity, language skills, and college courses in Latin American studies, he proved especially valuable in the UAW's international efforts. As U.S. auto manufacturers had established assembly plants in different parts of Latin America, the UAW had followed, organizing union locals in those areas. Torres directly involved himself in these efforts, as both an organizer for the UAW and a consultant to other auto unions. Traveling throughout Latin America, in labor and social democratic circles, he met many of the region's most prominent leaders, including the presidents of Venezuela, Costa Rica, and Chile. As a consultant and negotiator, he also worked in conjunction with agencies of the Organization of American States and the United States. The offer of his talents to ELALCAC certainly signaled the UAW's strong commitment to the socioeconomic recovery of East Los Angeles.[53]

Torres became interested in returning to the barrio in early 1966. At that time he had joined Walter Reuther and César Chávez in a trip to Mexico City. There in meetings with their Mexican counterparts, the union leaders discussed the employment of immigrant labor by agribusiness in the United States. In the process Torres learned much more about the conditions of Mexican Americans as well. More importantly, he came to share Chávez's vision of the United Farm Workers as a broad social and moral movement to uplift not only farm workers, but Mexican Americans. In addition, Torres accepted Chávez's vision of the UFW as a cooperative, benefiting workers and their families and communities. This cooperative vision, coupled with the "radical" ideas of Reuther and Conway, led Torres to return to East LA "to build a community union that could

National Precursors and Local Founders 39

act as a support arm to the farmworkers and to build a community organization that could harness its own economic and social power." Torres thus implicitly advocated self-determination, not only for the East LA community and California's farm workers, but for Mexican Americans as a whole. In May 1968 ELALCAC was officially chartered, with Esteban Torres as its executive director and self-determination as its goal.[54]

Community Development Corporations

As the labor movement established its community unions, Robert Kennedy, elected New York's junior senator in 1964, developed a distinct but parallel project. Having visited the nation's largest slum in 1966, Brooklyn's predominantly black Bedford-Stuyvesant, Kennedy vowed to do something about the appalling conditions there. Together with Republican Senator Jacob Javits, also of New York, Kennedy introduced an amendment to the Economic Opportunity Act of 1964, an amendment that established the Special Impact Program, legislation that would eventually lead to a profound transformation of the structure and vision of TELACU.[55] The significance of the new legislation and the resulting organizations derived from their clear goal of economic development, but from the perspective of business, rather than labor. A business perspective was clearly more conducive to the capitalist system.

Robert Kennedy and the Special Impact Program

In November 1966 Congress enacted the vague Title I-D of the Economic Opportunity Act, but Kennedy and Javits would gradually clarify the Special Impact Program as they put it into practice. Essentially, they sought a comprehensive approach to poverty that addressed the problem as one of areas, rather than individuals. The senators designed the new program to rehabilitate poor areas economically, socially, and physically. The program's new organizations would train residents for careers and deliver social services in a more coordinated fashion. Most importantly, private enterprise would have the opportunity for full participation in the War on Poverty. To embody this vision, in 1966 Kennedy established the

Bedford-Stuyvesant project funded by the Special Impact Program.[56]

In launching this project Kennedy organized two corporations to work as allies in the assault on poverty in Bedford-Stuyvesant—the Development and Service Corporation and the Restoration Corporation. The racial composition of their leadership demonstrated an integrationist, rather than a separatist approach. The Restoration Corporation had the responsibility of implementing development projects in the community; consequently, its board and staff comprised a wide range of black leaders, politically tied to Kennedy. The chairman, however, was a New York Supreme Court judge; the president, a former deputy police commissioner—hardly typical residents of the local community.[57]

This elitist, "top-down" arrangement appeared even more clearly in the D & S Corporation comprised almost entirely of white businessmen. On its board of directors sat Kennedy, Javits, and representatives of such corporate giants as International Business Machines and the Columbia Broadcasting System. Their role primarily involved fund raising for the Restoration Corporation. While few other organizations would copy Bedford-Stuyvesant's dual corporate structure, they would certainly note its source of funding. In 1967 it became the first "community development corporation" (a term not yet in common use) to receive federal funds for its general operations.[58] This would, of course, compromise the claims of self-determination made by the Bedford-Stuyvesant project and other CDCs.

While the dual corporate structure limited the community's actual control over the Bedford-Stuyvesant effort, the results looked promising. The allied corporations rapidly moved into economic development projects involving real estate, job training, and manufacturing. Within the next three or four years, the corporations convinced the city university to build a four-year college in the area, created a neighborhood park closed to traffic, began redevelopment of a four-block commercial area with an old-dairy-turned-office-building at its center, rehabilitated housing, trained construction workers, loaned funds to local entrepreneurs and home buyers, and established an IBM plant in the area. These were only some of the major activities; the Bedford-Stuyvesant corporations also carried out strictly social service programs.[59] While the dual corporate structure had little influence, its activities, especially in real estate, had much. Indeed, they became the model activities followed by all the community development corporations eventually funded under the Special Impact Program, including TELACU.

Despite the influence of Bedford-Stuyvesant, the concept of the community development corporation did not originate there, or with Kennedy and Javits. They originated federal funding coordinated with outside business participation in such efforts. Indeed, in the sixties several CDCs under different labels existed prior to enactment of the Special Impact Program. In addition to Progress Enterprises, a number of other "community development corporations" had formed independent of the government and of the new program. Among these were the Hough Area Development Corporation in Cleveland, the East Central Citizens Organization in Columbus, Circle Associates in Boston, and Yeatman District Community Corporation in St. Louis. Although all these organizations would eventually receive some federal funding, they began as indigenous neighborhood groups. They were designed to serve the poor and minorities, especially blacks; they were designed to promote self-determination. These organizations provided Kennedy and Javits with models for community development corporations, the ultimate vehicles of the Special Impact Program.[60] This program would not fully fund TELACU until 1972, well after the latter's founding and Kennedy's death. Nevertheless, Kennedy's vision greatly influenced the community union's development. Ultimately, the Special Impact Program would shift TELACU away from the labor movement toward a greater business orientation.

Robert Kennedy's death sidetracked the prospects of the community development corporation as a vehicle for national social policy. In his presidential campaign of 1968, Kennedy had made the CDC central to his proposed domestic policy. In his last campaign, Kennedy offered a seven-point plan to assist the cities: (1) jobs, (2) training for new jobs, (3) subsidies for businesses in poor areas, (4) education directly linked to jobs, (5) jobs linked to community social needs, (6) new careers developed from the urban redevelopment itself, and (7) community development corporations to coordinate the efforts of business, government, and the neighborhood to assure accountability to the latter.[61] Although the Bedford-Stuyvesant project had limited the control exercised directly by the community, Kennedy seemed increasingly to recognize such control as critical.

In *To Seek a Newer World*, the campaign book outlining his proposed policies, Robert Kennedy clearly envisioned economic self-sufficiency and political self-determination institutionalized through "Community Development Corporations":

> Everything that is done must be in direct response to the needs and wishes of the people themselves. To do this, it will be necessary to create new community institutions that local residents control, and through which they can express their wishes. . . . [C]ommunity corporations would ensure that what is done to create jobs and build homes builds the community as well. . . . not just the physical development of the community, but the development of its educational system, its health services—in short, all the services its residents need.

These corporations would apparently rest on real estate development, physical development that created employment, but they would also provide social services of various kinds.[62] Kennedy thus advocated the holistic approach based on economic development that TELACU and other CDCs adopted.

In the California campaign just days before his death, Robert Kennedy placed his proposals for community development in the context of his vision for American society as a whole: "it must be understood that the building of a truly integrated society depends on the development of economic self-sufficiency and security in the communities of poverty, for only then will the residents of these areas have the wherewithal to move freely within the society." Clearly, RFK saw integration into the larger society, rather than separatism, as the goal of his community corporations. But he also understood that minority individuals could hardly gain social equality in the larger society as long as their own communities could not provide them with the training and economic opportunities required for social mobility: "Those who speak of ending the colonialism of the ghetto must therefore recognize that the economic and social development of that community is at the heart of any policy of creating mobility." Interestingly, in elaborating on this point, Kennedy alluded to the colonial analogy advanced by the radical left, an analogy that implied independence, rather than integration. Despite the apparent contradiction, he dreamed of institutions that could bring about both community self-determination and national integration.[63]

Robert Kennedy was shot on June 5, 1968, at the Ambassador Hotel in Los Angeles. His death dashed the hopes of many in East LA, which voted overwhelmingly for him in the primary. Given Hubert Humphrey's support among Democratic power brokers, Kennedy had had little chance of winning the presidency. Nonetheless, he had offered practical solutions to the problems of the Mexican-American community and had exhibited unusual empathy with minority groups. Indeed, what Kennedy stated only weeks earlier in homage to Martin Luther King could have applied to himself: "He lighted corners of our country . . . [some] prefer to keep in darkness. He . . . threatened to upset . . . hundred[s of] years in this country in which Negroes and Mexican-Americans and Indian-Americans have been second-class citizens." Recognizing the subordinate status of minorities, Kennedy had realized that both their liberation and national integration depended on major change in the larger society.[64]

Present at the Ambassador the night of Kennedy's death were several other people involved with CDCs and TELACU itself. In his final remarks at the celebration of his victory in the California primary, Kennedy thanked César Chávez and Dolores Huerta of the United Farm Workers for their participation in the campaign. He also thanked Paul Schrade of the United Auto Workers for his support. Indeed, only moments later Schrade, accompanying Kennedy into the kitchen of the hotel, was seriously wounded by the same gun that killed the senator.[65]

Robert Kennedy's death did not, of course, mean the death of community development corporations. But no other major presidential candidate ever again offered to make them the centerpiece of domestic policy. Immediately after his death, a concerted effort arose to pass national legislation in that direction, but by 1970 that drive failed. The Congress of Racial Equality (CORE), a Kennedy ally, had initiated the Community Self-Determination Act, introduced in both the House of Representatives and Senate in July 1968. The Senate version of the bill gained the most attention. That bill proposed $30 billion for the nationwide establishment of "community development corporations," the term receiving its first official use in legislative language. Charles E. Goodell had introduced the first version of the self-determination bill as a member of the House. Appointed to Kennedy's Senate seat, Goodell reintroduced the bill in 1969 and 1970, but to no avail. Community development corporations, thereafter, remained tertiary weapons in the federal arsenal against poverty.[66]

An Organization for Chicano Recovery and Integration

Despite the eclipse of the CDC effort on the national level, TELACU was only beginning in East Los Angeles. Still a community union, TELACU under the leadership of Esteban Torres had by the summer of 1968 already begun moving from social service toward economic development. Before long the new organization had also become deeply involved in politics. The effort came none too soon, for political conditions in East LA mirrored the socioeconomic. Unincorporated and gerrymandered, the Mexican-American community completely lacked representation on the Los Angeles City Council, on the county board of supervisors, and in the state senate. The community also remained seriously underrepresented in the assembly and in Congress. This situation persisted despite the fact that of the area's 85 percent Spanish-surnamed population, 75 percent had been born in the United States. Such figures supported Torres's contention that East Los Angeles remained "but a colony dependent on outside forces."[67]

Torres's use of the colonial analogy reflected the radical side of the East Los Angeles Community Union. The colonial analogy implied the need for independence, for separation, of the Chicano community. It implied a struggle for self-determination, thus suggesting confrontation—possibly even conflict with the dominant society. Moreover, the emerging structure of the CDC seemed revolutionary; conservatives interpreted it as socialism through capitalist methods. But the controversial, multifaceted TELACU received criticism from the left too. TELACU's paradoxical, integrationist position—especially its accommodating corporate orientation—vis-à-vis the dominant society contributed to the enigmatic image of the organization. To left-wing activists, this position meant capitalism had coopted the organization from the beginning. They believed accommodation with Anglo institutions could eventually lead to integration and the disappearance of Chicanos as a people. Torres and TELACU had to reconcile the contrary visions that had led to its founding. TELACU had to superimpose these varied visions in an institution that would contribute to both Mexican-American recovery in the Southwest and integration into the nation.

TWO

The Chicano Movement on the Eastside

To End Colonialism and Recover the Homeland

When the East Los Angeles Community Union began operations in 1968, the United States was in turmoil. In the few months following the opening of TELACU's office in February, Martin Luther King and Robert F. Kennedy were assassinated, swelling the radicalism of the antiwar and black nationalist movements. The rising wave of radicalism included the Chicano movement. Though not yet known by that name, the movement begun by César Chávez inundated the normally quiescent barrios of East Los Angeles in 1968. Within weeks of TELACU's founding, massive protests against the Los Angeles school system had deluged the colonia. Similar demonstrations recurred throughout the following months, impelling Robert F. Kennedy to campaign heavily in the area just before his assassination in June. His death only deepened the anger and frustration of many in the community.[1]

In founding TELACU the United Auto Workers had sought to head off the riots and other disturbances that had already damaged communities throughout the United States. In doing so, however, the UAW sought to solve the underlying causes of turmoil, rather than simply the symptoms. Because internal colonialism seemed to fit the Mexican-American experience and offer solutions to local problems, Esteban Torres and other activists embraced the radical theory then being advanced in black communities. According to the colonial analogy, Anglo-Americans, in their occupation of what they called the Southwest, had subordinated Mexicans in a pattern similar to that experienced by Indians in the Spanish conquest of the same region and by blacks in the European colonization of Africa. As newcomers had colonized these regions, native peoples had lost control militarily, politically, economically, and in every other way. They had come under the control of outside powers for the benefit of outsiders. The consequences of these historical events persisted, establishing the modern relations between minority communities and the majority in the United States. Mexican Americans, like other minorities, remained a people dominated by the majority in every way, but especially economically.[2]

To end colonialism—to recover self-determination—Torres and TELACU argued that economic development had to take place within minority communities, such as East LA, for the benefit of their own residents. Such development would establish the basis for general social recovery and genuine integration into the larger society. Such development, however, would be a long-term process, and fuses in East LA were getting short. Economic development also implied reconciliation in a period when confrontation seemed to win the greatest concessions from the larger society. TELACU's attempt to merge the radical colonial analogy with a traditional message of economic development made the organization unattractive to militants. In addition, TELACU's complex structure, intricate transactions, and connections to labor made its public image somewhat mysterious.[3] Because of its commitment to long-term development, TELACU could not meet the demands for immediate action. Despite launching several enterprises designed to *decolonize* East LA, TELACU could not forestall the violence that broke out in 1970, a rebellion that emphasized separation, rather than integration. In the long run, however, TELACU would emerge from the crisis as a model for recovery of the community and rapprochement with the nation as a whole.

The History of an Internal Colony

The complex history of Greater East Los Angeles, like that of the Southwest, made it difficult for some observers to understand how Chicano activists could descibe the local area, let alone the region, as an "internal colony" of the United States. Were not Mexicans simply one other immigrant group in the nation's melting pot? How could they be native when they had not been born in the nation, the region, let alone the local area? The local history of the Eastside seemed to confirm such thought. Anglo-Americans had first developed and occupied Boyle Heights; Russians, Jews, and other immigrants from the Old World had first settled unincorporated East LA. It followed that Mexicans merely comprised the most recent immigrant group in the area; they certainly could not be a native group conquered and colonized by "newcomers."[4]

Spanish Colonization

Despite this perspective, the analogy of the internal colony had a basis in historical fact. El Pueblo de la Reina de Los Angeles began in 1781 adjacent to Yabit, a Yang-na rancheria, with local Indian converts as the nucleus of settlement. The first "Spanish" settlers included only two people claiming pure Spanish ancestry, the rest being a mixture of Hispanicized mulattos, mestizos, and Indians, a mixture later collectively described as "Mexican." The settlers came largely from Sonora and Sinaloa, south of the present border between the United States and Mexico. Thus, while the founding of Los Angeles resulted from Spanish colonialism, paradoxically the colonists on arrival had much Indian ancestry and soon intermixed with the local Indian population.[5]

The colonists had set out in staggered groups from San Gabriel Mission about nine miles to the east of the new pueblo site. Though founded in 1771, the mission had been relocated from its original site near present Whittier Narrows about ten miles southeast of the later pueblo. At the mission the process of *mestizaje* that produced Mexicans had already begun to incorporate the local Indian population before the founding of Los Angeles. Though the earliest legal union of this sort did not occur until later, sexual relations between local Indians and settlers occurred even at the mission's original site. These events would substantiate later Chicano claims to native status.[6]

In its imperial expansion Spain of course acquired Indians and their lands in both Sonora and California by force. Although Spain planned the mission system to incorporate the natives and their lands into the empire peacefully, troops always backed up the missionaries. Ideally, the missionaries would convert the Indians to Christianity and transform them into loyal subjects of the Spanish king. When acculturation had sufficiently progressed, the authorities would secularize the missions—divide them into regular Hispanicized communities served by diocesan priests. Though the system worked imperfectly, by the 1770s it had worked in Sonora to the point where the assimilated population supplied new colonists for expansion in California. Paradoxically, Spain used colonized people as agents for further colonization.[7]

On the way to the future site of Los Angeles, the settlers probably followed present Mission Road, cutting through today's Lincoln Heights on the northern fringe of the Eastside. The area between the pueblo and the mission, as well as much of the land to the south that would eventually form the Eastside, initially formed parts of the grants made to the mission and then to the pueblo under Spanish rule. In establishing the Spanish missions in California, the Franciscans temporarily claimed purview over the Indians and lands around the first buildings to the point where that territory overlapped the claims of a neighboring mission. In the case of San Gabriel Mission, this claim originally included all of the modern Los Angeles metropolitan area and beyond. Over time the civil authorities cut away large chunks of the original, vaguely defined mission claim. Usually, Spain rewarded retired soldiers with use of such partitioned lands. However, the first area removed from the mission was the grant made to the pueblo of Los Angeles, four square leagues or about 17,000 square miles. This square-shaped land grant would eventually include downtown Los Angeles and such Eastside communities as Boyle Heights and Lincoln Heights. Much of the modern Eastside and unincorporated East LA remained grazing land outside the pueblo and part of the mission throughout the Spanish colonial era.[8]

The Mexican Period

In 1821 Mexico gained its independence from Spain and retained California as part of its national territory. Despite this, the new nation continued many of the colonial policies of its predecessor in developing the far northern frontier. Indeed, Mexico thus instituted its own form of colonialism, internally. During the Mexican era, the government built on Spanish precedent by granting land to settlers who offered to improve the property. Ultimately, local and national authorities in the 1830s issued the orders secularizing the missions in California, freeing the Indians and virtually all their lands from the control of the missionaries. Unfortunately, the Indians thereby lost their lands as the authorities, following colonial practice, granted most of the mission property to settlers, contrary to the ideals of secularization. In 1831 Juan Ballesteros received Rancho Rosa de Castilla, a vast tract of the former Mission San Gabriel that would later include El Sereno and sections of adjacent communities, including unincorporated East LA. This vast grant became a bone of contention after the United States conquered California in the Mexican War of 1846–48.[9]

The United States Marines landed at the harbor of San Pedro in August 1846. They advanced the ten miles to Los Angeles and after a skirmish occupied the pueblo. Further resistance from the Mexican population arose a month later partly because of a perceived threat to property. The rebellion, led by the Mexican officer Juan María Flores, spread throughout southern California, driving the American troops from the region and delaying the final conquest for four months. However, U.S. military and naval reinforcements, from occupied northern California and San Diego, subsequently defeated the Mexican troops, leading to their surrender at Cahuenga Pass on January 13, 1847. On February 2, 1848, near Mexico City, the signing of the Treaty of Guadalupe Hidalgo confirmed the conquest of California.[10]

The American Colonial Cycle

This conquest launched a new cycle of colonialism in California. In the aftermath of the Treaty of Guadalupe Hidalgo that transferred far northern Mexico to the United States, Mexican owners lost land throughout what had become the Southwest. The complex process of dispossession resulted from the introduction of a new legal and socioeconomic system that benefited newcomers from the East who understood all its subtleties. In southern California the new economic system proved a greater problem than the legal system. Many ranchers lost land in forced sales brought about by insufficient experience with the new market economy of the United States. Initially prospering in the boom resulting from the demand for beef in the gold fields, ranchers by the early 1860s faced a drastic drop in prices and high taxes, in addition to drought, flood, and diseased cattle. Finding it necessary to cover their losses, Mexican landowners lacking cash turned to Anglo-American investors for loans at exorbitant rates with predictable consequences. In the infamous case of Julio Verdugo, a loan of $3,445 in eight years became a debt of $58,000, causing the rancher to sell out to an Anglo-American, leaving the former destitute. The property was Rancho San Rafael, 36,403 acres now largely occupied by the city of Glendale, just north of the Los Angeles pueblo grant.[11]

While Mexican problems with the new legal system occurred more frequently in northern California, such problems also affected the south. At the request of Anglo-American squatters, the United States Congress passed the Land Law of 1851 compelling all land grantees in the state to validate their titles, placing the burden of proof on the owners. This created costly problems, such as the retention of lawyers, the surveying of lands, or even the forced sale of unconfirmed property.[12] On the Eastside the case of Rancho Rosa de Castilla revealed the legal mechanics of internal colonialism in detail.

The Rosa de Castilla grant, including much of present East LA and nearby communities, failed to receive confirmation. First, the Board of Land Commissioners rejected the claim because of its unclear boundaries. Second, the commissioners held that the original grantee, Juan Ballesteros, and his family had not occupied the land continuously as required. María Figueroa de Ballesteros, the grantee's widow, testified that she had been forced to leave the rancho after her eldest son died in battle against the United States.

Subsequently, U.S. troops had camped on the vacant property and left it in ruins. Despite the widow's testimony, the commissioners rejected the claim, leaving Rosa de Castilla public land. Thereafter, newcomers with outside sources of capital purchased the grant in sections, leading to further subdivision in the early twentieth century.[13]

The erosion of the land base undermined Mexican culture throughout the Southwest, California, and the Los Angeles area. The U.S. conquest of the region had taken military control from Mexicans. The Gold Rush, the influx of foreigners into California, transformed Mexicans from a majority into a minority no longer in control of its political destiny. Their economic interests immediately suffered as passage of the Land Law of 1851 attested. As the Mexican elite lost property, it lost social prestige as well. Increasingly, Mexican culture was confined to the lower classes as the whole ethnic group experienced downward mobility. Even those who had been poor before 1846 experienced greater difficulties as their employers and governors now belonged to a different cultural group. Generally by the end of the nineteenth century, Mexicans in California had become a small landless group of often transient laborers, rarely identified with the "Spanish" history of the state they had earlier settled. When immigration from Mexico surged at the beginning of the twentieth century, the newcomers would inherit the colonized status imposed on their compatriots in the previous century.[14]

These macrocosmic events naturally affected the development of Mexican-American Los Angeles. In the 1850s within the city, Anglo-American merchants, lawyers, and speculators with outside sources of capital quickly bought up land at low prices. Interestingly, recent arrivals from Mexico also purchased land to the extent that by 1880 some recovery of landholding by Mexicans occurred. Nevertheless, according to Richard Griswold del Castillo, "In terms of the total Spanish-speaking population, fewer and fewer individuals were able to enter the landowning class and stay there." Mexicans remained in the old deteriorating sections of town near the plaza, where Los Angeles began, while Anglo-Americans grad-

The Chicano Movement on the Eastside   53

ually developed the surrounding land and populated it with their own.[15]

Significant change to the landscape of southern California did not occur until the coming of the railroads in the 1870s. Then a population and real estate boom transformed the landscape from cow pastures to budding Anglo-American towns surrounded by orchards. Even then urbanization on the Eastside did not come all at once. Development proceeded from the plaza to Boyle Heights on the eastern side of the Los Angeles River. Boyle Heights, today clearly within the Eastside, initially developed as a relatively wealthy suburb established in the 1870s within the original pueblo grant. By the turn of the century the area had declined and become more affordable for the growing number of immigrants of various nationalities who by then lived in the county.[16]

Mexican-American Demographic Recovery

Mexican Americans continued beyond the city limits of Los Angeles into unincorporated East LA after 1910. Joining them were increasing numbers of newcomers from Mexico drawn largely by the industrialization of the city. At first the Spanish-speaking made up a minority among the various European groups that initially occupied the area's housing. However, by the 1920s when East Los Angeles had largely developed its present physical layout, the Spanish-speaking population had rapidly grown, and it would become the majority by the 1930s. By then, at least in terms of numbers, people of Mexican descent had retaken a large portion of Rancho Rosa de Castilla. However, the Eastside had become increasingly blighted, and it continued to deteriorate through the 1960s.[17]

Though Mexican Americans gradually became the majority on the Eastside, they did not control the area in any meaningful way. By 1960 control of the Eastside's government, business, education, and even religion continued in the hands of outsiders; Mexican Americans remained a laboring class, though some by then owned the homes they occupied. In this sense then the situation of Chicanos on the Eastside was analogous to that of peoples in the Third World. People of Mexican descent were native to the area through their Indian and Spanish predecessors who once controlled this former part of Mexico. Once Anglo-Americans occupied the land, Mexicans had declined and reached a low point in 1885, when they comprised only 21 percent of the population of Los Angeles. With renewed immigration, however, the possibility of their recovery evolved. As the population of Chicanos increased, demands for correction of historical wrongs would rise.[18] This process became evident in the 1960s, and TELACU evolved in this process.

The history of the Eastside sustains the image of the area as an internal colony if we perceive the residents as groups rather than as individuals, if we consider the history of Mexican Americans as a people rather than as individuals. In tracing the genealogies of local families, we find most are second- or third-generation residents of the United States, but in tracing the history of their culture in the region, their heritage gains great depth. Moreover, in studying their political and socioeconomic condition, we find it directly attributable to the conquest of their Mexican predecessors and to the colonization of the region by Anglo-Americans.[19] The turmoil that East Los Angeles faced in the 1960s had its roots in the 1840s; recognition of this fact would give TELACU its full historical significance.

Chicano Resistance on the Eastside

A major reaction to the decades of second-class citizenship experienced by Mexican Americans began in September 1965 when César Chávez and the farm workers struck against the grape growers in California's Central Valley. The ethnic appeals made by the farm workers' union roused Mexican nationalism throughout the Southwest, in urban as well as rural areas. This resurgence led to an increasing interest in Mexican-American history and to a revision of the simplistic depiction of Mexican-origin people as immigrants in the region. Before long, irredentist sentiments developed in what came to be called the Chicano movement; the view of Chicanos as native to the Southwest gained currency. Chicano activists called the region Aztlán, in reference to the ancient Aztec homeland said to be in the pre-Columbian Southwest. This myth, though inaccurate in detail, served to highlight the fact that Chicanos did have

Indian ancestry, Aztec or other—ancestry that tied them to the region. The myth encouraged historians to examine the real ties of Chicanos to the land they claimed, a search that publicized the fact that people of Mexican origin were predominantly Indian and had intermingled with native Indians throughout the Southwest.[20]

By the founding of TELACU in 1968, these ideas had circulated in seminal form through leaders such as Rodolfo Gonzales of Colorado and Reies López Tijerina of New Mexico. In addition, rising black nationalism with its emphasis on internal colonialism and black power encouraged Chicano militants to view their own communities from the new perspective. Activists increasingly spoke of self-determination, of regaining control of minority communities for their residents. The question of tactics arose, with many new groups favoring confrontation; many considered demonstrations, boycotts, and even violence in hopes of bringing about change. Interestingly, despite having the country's largest concentration of Mexican Americans, Eastside residents commenced their front of the Chicano movement relatively late. The front opened in East LA in full force only in March of 1968, just as TELACU began operations.[21]

TELACU's Context—Changing Visions and New Organizations

The high school walkouts of March 1968 were the first major event of the Chicano movement on the Eastside. The process leading to the dramatic walkouts parallels the changing ideology of the Mexican-American leadership at that time and helps explain TELACU's ideological position in the community. During the year or so preceding the East LA "blowouts," a number of organizations came into being that would provide the context for much of TELACU's early activities. Among these groups were the Brown Berets, the United Mexican-American Students, and the Congress of Mexican-American Unity. These groups all advocated the betterment of the Mexican-American community though they differed in tactics and rhetoric, from radical to left-of-center. Those differences seemed unimportant in 1966–67 when the groups first formed.[22]

While the original issue concerning all these organizations was the poor education of Mexican-American youth, behind that issue lay the question of historical identity. This question eventually led students from several East LA high schools to found what later became the Brown Berets. In April 1966 these students had attended a summer camp sponsored by several liberal Jewish organizations and the Los Angeles County Commission on Human Relations, but run by Mexican-American adults. The camp had focused on the issue of Mexican-American identity and naturally dealt with questions of culture and history. Subsequently, students who had attended the camp formed Young Citizens for Community Action, a moderate civic-minded group that initially surveyed student needs, met with school officials, and became involved in the Los Angeles school board race. In the fall of 1967, however, the group rapidly evolved into a radical organization; its activities went from discussions of Chicano culture and history to public confrontations with the police. This evolution echoed in its changing name—first to Young Chicanos for Community Action, then to the Brown Berets. In imitation of the Black Panthers, the radical Brown Berets now described Chicanos as a colonized people and justified violence in defense of the community.[23]

A parallel development was the establishment of the United Mexican-American Students (UMAS). As some of the original members of the Young Citizens for Community Action went on to college, they left the latter group to youth in the barrio and sought to develop their ideas on campus. Again the students initially had narrow educational goals and non-confrontational tactics, but as with the Brown Berets, this changed rapidly. In May 1967 at a conference at Loyola University in West Los Angeles, students laid the groundwork for UMAS chapters throughout the metropolitan area. By September 1967 the central body had begun operations as had the two most influential chapters, one at the University of California, Los Angeles, the other at California State College, Los Angeles. These chapters at first sought to raise scholarship money and to provide mutual social support for Mexican-American students.[24]

However, a series of catalytic events radicalized UMAS. First, Governor Ronald Reagan threatened to charge tuition, which encouraged the group to demonstrate. Secondly, a conference at the

The Chicano Movement on the Eastside 57

University of Southern California exposed the local members to the ideas of the New Left through contact with students from northern California. Finally, at a conference at UCLA, UMAS members heard radical leaders Tijerina of New Mexico and Gonzales of Colorado espouse nationalism and call for Chicano self-determination in the Southwest. Though avoiding the self-defense tactics advocated by the Brown Berets, UMAS entered the arena of radical protest politics.[25]

Another influential group, the Congress of Mexican-American Unity, directly tied to TELACU, began and remained in the mainstream because of its broad base in the community. This organization initially gathered representatives of thirty smaller groups to nominate a consensus candidate for the Board of Education of the Los Angeles Unified School District. The representatives first met on January 15, 1967, as the Council of Mexican-American Organizations and nominated Julian Nava as their unity candidate. Significantly, this action led to the election in June of the first Mexican-American member of the board in the twentieth century. Because of this success, the congress in February 1968 held another convention to nominate Mexican-American candidates for other local elections. Members of both the Brown Berets and UMAS became involved in Nava's campaign and also participated in the February convention. TELACU members, especially Esteban Torres, took leading roles in the congress. The latter two groups would share more conciliatory tactics and goals than those advanced by the youth in the Brown Berets or UMAS. Nevertheless, the cooperation with regard to electoral politics indicated that all the groups within the congress sought political self-determination.[26]

The High School Walkouts

Since the Brown Berets, UMAS, and the congress had all started with educational concerns, naturally the first dramatic event of the Chicano movement on the Eastside involved the schools. On March 1, 1968, thousands of students at Roosevelt, Lincoln, Garfield, and Wilson high schools walked out of the classrooms to protest problems ranging from poor cafeteria food to the absence of Mexican-American history in the curriculum. Before the actual walkout, a few parents, teachers, UMAS members, and high school students had planned to present a list of proposals to the board of education with the threat of walkouts if the board did not cooperate. Apparently in preparation, *La raza*, a newly established underground newspaper, began publishing articles on general and specific educational problems in the local area. Before formal demands reached the board, however, Wilson students walked out because their principal banned a play due to objections to its language. While the trigger had little to do with the major issues, explosions followed on other campuses.[27]

The walkouts took place the first week of March 1968, involved thousands of students, and drew the attention of the entire metropolitan area. Officials called in the police as the students marched around the schools, under the protection of the Brown Berets and UMAS members. A number of bottle-throwing incidents and some arrests occurred, but on the whole the demonstrations remained peaceful. The school board immediately called a meeting at Lincoln High School to deal with the students' demands, over thirty in all. Many of the demands dealt with mundane matters of school policy, but several went to the heart of the conflict between the dominant society and the Mexican-American minority.[28]

The students demanded more Mexican-American teachers and bilingual-bicultural education. In advancing these demands the students rejected the assimilationist ideology dominant in the schools and insisted on appreciation of their ethnicity. Obviously, the students had stepped toward the separatist ideology increasingly advocated in black communities. The discussions that went on at the board meetings, in the newspapers, at local conferences, both during and immediately following the walkouts indicated a move away from the integrationist ideology of the early sixties. About this time *Chicano* as a label for Mexican Americans gained currency because, among other things, the term connoted native as opposed to immigrant origins.[29]

During the weeks preceding and following the walkouts, Chávez, Tijerina, and Gonzales, the most prominent Chicano activists, continued speaking at various rallies and conferences on local college campuses. These activists set the present oppression of Chicanos in the rural and urban Southwest against the historical background of Anglo-American conquest. Local activists argued that this key historical event needed elaboration in the school curricula. Indeed, in the midst of the controversy, a supportive Anglo teacher wrote in the faculty bulletin that because Anglos had imposed their culture on Mexicans through conquest, the schools needed to counteract that imposition. With this historical background emphasized, the colonial analogy soon gained support among activists.[30]

Understandably, after the walkouts ended, the educational controversy persisted. The board of education continued to have well-attended and often bitter meetings to discuss the various demands. Major issues to be settled involved the participants in the walkouts. While the board had absolved students, it had suspended Sal Castro, the leading teacher in support of the movement; the community demanded his reinstatement. In addition, the police had arrested twelve off-campus individuals for disrupting the schools. Though the courts had to decide this issue, it directly influenced discussion before the board. These matters kept the community in turmoil throughout the first year of TELACU's existence.[31]

Through most of 1968 and 1969, TELACU as an organization kept a low profile. On the other hand, members of the community union became deeply involved in the tumultuous events on the Eastside, especially TELACU personnel who joined the Congress of Mexican-American Unity. In the congress labor formed a powerful bloc, particularly the representatives of the United Auto Workers, TELACU's union parent. This bloc of labor votes would eventually catapult Esteban Torres to the presidency of the congress in 1970, the critical year when mass violence broke out on the Eastside. Until then, however, TELACU remained in the background, establishing its operations.[32]

Esteban Torres's Constructive Vision

In keeping with his pragmatic approach to community issues, Esteban Torres busily set up TELACU in the midst of the turmoil surrounding the East LA blowouts. Nominated by Paul Schrade's labor advisory committee and appointed executive director by the community union's board, Torres proceeded to staff the new organization. To assist him the UAW, through the Citizens' Crusade Against Poverty, sent out Walter Reuther's own nephew, Eric V. Reuther. Holding a master's degree in Latin American studies, the younger Reuther had acquired three years' seniority with the UAW in Fremont, California. He had been in Venezuela with the Peace Corps and had worked for Interstate Research Associates, a Mexican-American consulting firm in Washington, D.C. In addition to a social consciousness, he had the technical expertise Torres needed to develop the economy of East Los Angeles. Reuther would train the staff and handle communications while Torres temporarily filled the office of comptroller in addition to his role as executive director.[33]

TELACU's Holistic Approach and Complex Structure

Behind Torres and Reuther stood the four directors of the five original divisions of TELACU. These divisions and their names would change repeatedly over time in response to new circumstances, but their original labels revealed the scope of the organization's activities throughout its history. From most to least important, the divisions were Economic Development, Housing–Physical Development, Manpower–Job Development, Community Issues Action, and Youth–Education Affairs. Though based on economic development, the divisions revealed a holistic approach to the problems of the community. This approach would eventually embrace a combination of for-profit enterprises and social services, the former designed eventually to support the latter.[34]

Joseph Avila, Economic Development

In early November 1968 Torres named Joseph S. Avila director of the most important division, Economic Development. Avila had solid qualifications for the job. A graduate of Garfield High, East Los Angeles Junior College, and Los Angeles State College, Avila had recently obtained a law degree from Southwestern University Law School (future LA Mayor Tom Bradley's alma mater). Avila, a self-employed businessman for eight years, had worked for the Office of Economic Opportunity and subsequently for the Department of Labor managing federal employment and small business projects. He had the technical expertise Torres sought to develop East LA economically.[35]

Reporting on the hiring of Avila, the *East Los Angeles Gazette* described Torres's hopes for East LA: "the projected goal will be community development *through entreperenurial [sic] self-determination* [emphasis added] from within the community." In speaking of self-determination at this early stage in the building of TELACU, Torres doubtless had radical colonial theory in mind. He believed that the community suffered from economic dependence on the surrounding metropolis. However, the use of *entrepreneurial* as a modifier clearly indicated he sought independence through accommodation with the capitalist system and the larger society. He sought practical business solutions to community problems even if these resulted from macrocosmic events, such as a historic conquest. Though Torres envisioned economic self-sufficiency for his Chicano community, he did not call for the extreme separatism or socialism advocated in some quarters.[36]

The *Gazette* also quoted Avila regarding his division's more specific plans: "initial efforts will be towards the development of a viable program to strengthen and expand existing concerns located within the community." Avila went on to discuss the community union's role in attracting loans and investment capital to help develop larger business concerns. In this endeavor technical assistance would come from local businessmen, educational institutions, and labor unions (ironically, labor unions would help set up businesses).[37] Supporting businesses in the community certainly did not seem a radical, let alone socialist plan of action, but such support could help East LA gain economic independence. Indeed, economic development would remain TELACU's major contribution to the self-determination of East LA and the general Mexican-American community.

Carlos J. García, Housing-Physical Development

The Economic Development Division, aimed at long-term self-sufficiency for the community, would take a while to get its business projects under way. On the other hand, the Housing-Physical

Development Division by August 1968 had already embarked on its first low-cost housing project for East LA. In charge of this division, Torres placed Carlos J. García, a man who would stay with TELACU for many years. Born and raised in East LA, García had received degrees from East Los Angeles College, the University of Southern California, and the University of San Fernando Valley Law School. He joined the community union after holding a number of positions involving social work with the county of Los Angeles and the state of California. As an attorney, he specialized in housing and consequently real estate.[38] The connection between housing and real estate in the long run would be important. For though housing formed a non-profit branch of the community union's operations, the division would eventually provide experience in real estate development. This experience would benefit TELACU's profit-making arms—to the point where real estate would become the most significant economic development activity.

García embarked on an $80,000 project when the Housing Division took over an effort launched three years earlier by residents of Hubbard Street in East LA. Despite the support of several other local organizations, the project had not received the approval of the Federal Housing Administration when the community union entered the picture. Though the pilot project comprised only six units, the FHA had stalled the effort because of its experimental nature. The units, condominiums, were to be purchased at low interest rates with low monthly payments by the families that resided in them. Furthermore, the buyers themselves would do the unskilled work on the project, thus cutting their mortgage payments through "sweat equity." García's division had to design the project, secure funding through the FHA, and hire the builder. In addition the division had to guarantee employees and subcontractors would be representative of the community.[39] Thus, García and Torres hoped to make the residents independent homeowners while providing business and jobs to help make the overall community more self-sufficient. Paradoxically, the federal government had to invest the capital for this experiment in self-sufficiency, a paradox that would haunt TELACU's operations.

According to Torres, the Hubbard Street project marked the inception of a combined assault by labor and the community on blight in the cities. This complex undertaking required the technical expertise Torres expected of the community union. Though the nonprofit project taxed the community union's resources to the limit, the experience gained in real estate development and urban renewal proved invaluable. Henceforth, TELACU impacted the landscape of East LA dramatically. By the end of 1969, TELACU was considering involvement in three other low-income housing projects: the Monterey Hills, Cleland House, and El Hoyo projects.[40] Though TELACU ultimately limited its participation in these, a pattern of housing development had formed, a pattern that would eventually lead to for-profit real estate ventures. Gradually, TELACU would pursue economic self-sufficiency for the community, primarily through real estate development.

Roy Escarcega, Manpower-Job Development

From its inception TELACU aimed to provide jobs for the community. Torres charged Roy Escarcega with this task as head of the Manpower–Job Development Division. A native of East LA, Escarcega had graduated from California State College, Los Angeles, with a degree in industrial education. After teaching for nine years, most recently at the East Los Angeles Skills Center, he joined the new communiy union. As manpower director, he arranged an on-the-job training program in cooperation with the United Auto Workers, "placing 123 local workers (100% of all those completing the training) in good steady jobs." Later his division would also arrange job training for local residents in connection with the Department of Labor. In addition to the community union itself, the Kaiser Foundation, Arrow Truck Body Company, Hollytex Carpet Mills, and McDonnell-Douglas were potential employers.[41] The community could only claim self-sufficiency if its residents had good jobs.

Luana Eppert, Community Issues and Education Affairs

Torres hired Luana Eppert to direct the divisions of Community Issues Action and Youth–Education Affairs. Another graduate of Cal State, Los Angeles, Eppert had majored in drama and English; prior to joining Torres's staff, she had worked as an office manager and teacher. In general she applied her skills to "youth employment, tutoring, adult education, individual casework, and community organizing." A specific social service she established for East LA was a branch of the national Reading Is Fun-damental Program. This program allowed children to acquire books they liked without cost, in hopes that personal ownership would stimulate reading.[42] While Glenn O'Loane had launched the community union with social services, Torres quickly deemphasized them. Such projects smacked too much of dependency. While they remained necessary and eventually became beneficiaries of TELACU's for-profit enterprises, social services alone could not gain independence for the community.

Despite this, TELACU could never quite escape its image as a social service agency. The complex structure of the comunity union made it difficult to define; consequently, the public often misconstrued the organization's mission. Through their publicity Torres and his staff continually attempted to explain:

> what it all leads to is not just greater affluence, but greater ability to influence the political and social institutions that control the community. It leads, in other words, to union among free and independent people . . . a community union . . . a true Community Union for the East Los Angeles barrio.[43]

Throughout, TELACU's founders had designed the complex structure of the organization to end internal colonialism in the barrios through social and economic development, with emphasis on the latter.

Pragmatic Action to End Colonialism

Influential in TELACU's initial structure and program of action was UCLA's Institute of Industrial Relations. Affiliated with labor, this academic institute had already cooperated with the UAW in founding the new community union. In the fall of 1968, it assisted Esteban Torres's efforts by funding a nine-week training seminar "addressing itself to an examination of the major social, educational, economic, and political issues currently confronting the predominantly Mexican-American community of East Los Angeles."

Twenty-two leaders of organizations in the area received invitations to participate. "Resource personnel" discussed the following topics: "a. the status and future of education; b. housing and ELA; c. the zoning and incorporation issues and their impact upon ELA; d. rural technology and its urban impact; e. politics and the Barrio, and economic development in ELA."[44] Except for rural technology, the other topics reflected the community union's very structure; they had already been analyzed within the organization. Torres now hoped to disseminate information regarding these matters to other key figures in the community. To carry out its program, TELACU needed to communicate its vision, something it would not always succeed in doing.

In 1969 Carlos J. García's Housing Division received a unique opportunity to build TELACU's reputation in the community. The city of Los Angeles threatened to demolish unused boating facilities at a lake in Lincoln Park, a popular Eastside recreation area. A coalition of citizens' groups gathered to oppose unilateral demolition of the site by the city's parks department. Because TELACU in its first year of existence had already gained a reputation for technical expertise in development, the citizens' groups called on it for assistance. They asked Torres to develop plans to convert the unused buildings along the lake into a cultural center. Torres and García enthusiastically embarked on this project, which came to be known as Plaza de la Raza. Although the city funded the entire project, García successfully converted the citizens' wishes into a plan acceptable to the municipal authorities. The buildings of the renovated complex reflected the area's Mexican heritage as would its collections. Eventually, exhibitions of such prominent artists as Frida Kahlo would appear in the new facility.[45] This project established Plaza de la Raza as one of the major arts centers on the Eastside. As such, the project demonstrated Torres's holistic approach to community development. Through its growing expertise in real estate development, TELACU had contributed to the cultural self-determination of the Eastside.

In addition to participating in Plaza de la Raza, Torres and his staff rapidly became involved in other projects requiring expertise in real estate development. Carlos J. García became a representative and a consultant to the federal Model Cities redevelopment program on the Eastside. His Housing Division administered the Community Advisory Committee to the H.O.M.E. Program, designed to assure building code enforcement. The Congress of Mexican-American Unity asked García to head its housing committee. Moreover, Joseph Avila's Economic Development Division was instrumental in setting up the Greater Eastside Builders Association, a nonprofit corporation designed to help Mexican-American building contractors compete more effectively for jobs.[46] Clearly, real estate development early became the community union's forte.

Despite this, Esteban Torres wished to promote manufacturing through the Economic Development Division. The community union's first foray into manufacturing, and its first for-profit subsidiary, was the TELACU Mattress Company. The company in order of priority would provide: (1) profits for the community union as a whole, (2) employment for East LA residents, (3) training for Mexican Americans in industrial management, (4) a model of successful enterprise, and (5) quality bedding at good prices for local residents. The company opened on May 2, 1969, only days before the Mexican celebration of Cinco de Mayo. At the opening Esteban Torres informed the press that the new company represented "the first cooperative business enterprise owned by a non-profit corporation in the entire East Los Angeles area."[47] Nonetheless, the paradox of a nonprofit corporation making profits contributed to the enigmatic image of TELACU.

Unfortunately, the new enterprise failed within three years basically because the company could not absorb the high cost of the mattresses' fine materials. In addition the area's generally low-income customers often fell in arrears on their payments. The enterprise employed only two people, who turned out a high-quality product, but the lack of custodians left the premises a poor showplace. A companion firm TELACU Headboard Company produced Spanish-style furnishings and headboards, obviously designed for their cultural appeal. These products sold well in the showroom shared by the companies, but the slow sale of the relatively expensive mattresses doomed both businesses.[48] It became evident to

Torres that manufacturing would be a hard road to self-sufficiency for the community.

Despite the failure of the Mattress Company, in 1968–69 TELACU attempted activities that no other organization in East Los Angeles had dared on such a broad front. In addition to the bedding companies, Torres and his staff in the first few years also planned a printing company, a demolition firm, and a maintenance and home repair company. The last ultimately succeeded due to its close relationship to real estate. Besides setting up companies, TELACU's staff also helped many other local businesses obtain loans from various public and private sources.[49] Indeed, despite their mistakes, Torres and his officers had become the technocracy of the Eastside. Clearly, to gain self-determination, the community needed a group of such trained leaders.

Insurrection in East Los Angeles

However, TELACU's efforts, successful or not, were overshadowed by increasingly ominous political events in East Los Angeles. The tensions resulting from the high school walkouts of March 1968 continued in East Los Angeles at least through mid-1970 when a state appellate court finally dropped the charges of conspiracy against Sal Castro and twelve other activists. During the early part of this period, the Educational Issues Coordinating Committee, formed as a result of the walkouts, served as a broad-based organization unifying the community in its dealings with the school board. The core of this organization included members of the United Mexican-American Students, parents from advisory committees to the local schools, and professionals, many of whom had worked for Julian Nava's election. The Brown Berets and several underground newspapers also sent representatives. The loosely structured coordinating committee stressed participation, rather than formal membership. Thus informally, various individuals linked to TELACU became involved in the school conflict by virtue of their personal interest.[50]

Increasing Tensions

In 1968 the tensions escalated. Prior to the walkouts and his presidential campaign, Robert Kennedy had quietly discussed community issues with student activists on the Eastside; in May he visited again only two weeks before his disillusioning death. Meanwhile, the coordinating committee organized numerous demonstrations usually concerning education but also became involved in other community issues, such as police brutality, the grape boycott, and welfare rights. On June 3 committee members picketed the administration building of the Los Angeles Police Department; they then marched to the plaza, the cornerstone of the city, for a rally protesting the indictments of the thirteen activists involved in the walkouts. In September the situation became more heated. After repeated picketing at Lincoln High School, the coordinating committee staged a sit-in at the board of education in an attempt to get Sal Castro reinstated to his classroom. The police then arrested about thirty-five student members who refused to leave the board room. The committee provided bail even though few of its own members were among those detained. This action demonstrated that the insurrection against the school system had support across various sectors of the community.[51]

The sit-in finally convinced the Los Angeles school board to reinstate Castro by October 1968; consequently, tensions over educational issues lessened somewhat. Indeed, by June of 1969, the school board agreed to accept what amounted to the transformation of the Educational Issues Coordinating Committee into an official advisory body, the Mexican-American Education Commission. The new commission would do research and recommend programs to alleviate the drop-out problem and send more Chicanos to college. Vahac Mardirosian, chairman of the old committee, became chairman of the new commission. Thus, the coordinating committee and the school board began to move from confrontation to accommodation.[52]

One prominent individual from TELACU involved in the educational controversy was Gordon Moreno. On TELACU's board of directors, Moreno joined the Mexican-American Education Commission after serving on the old coordinating committee. Politically conservative relative to TELACU and the community as a whole, to the extent that he carried a weapon for fear of radical reprisals, Moreno exemplified the broad base of the early Chicano movement on the Eastside.[53] While the students in UMAS and the barrio youth in the Brown Berets gave the movement an increasingly radical perspective, parents and community people such as Moreno anchored the movement in practical concerns. Though influenced by radical ideas, people connected with TELACU generally sought rapprochement, rather than conflict with the larger society.

Just after the Los Angeles school board agreed to reform education in the colonia, the Chicano movement challenged the hierarchy of the Roman Catholic Church. In late 1969 Católicos por la Raza, composed of activist priests, nuns, and lay people, formed to pressure the archdiocese of Los Angeles to assist the Chicano community. The hierarchy, led by James Francis Cardinal McIntyre, was extremely conservative even by the standards of the American church at the time. Católicos argued that the archdiocese ignored the spiritual, cultural, and economic needs of its rapidly increasing Mexican-American parishioners. The complaints initially involved the closing, for alleged lack of funds, of Our Lady Queen of Angels, a predominantly Mexican-American girls' high school. When Católicos sought a meeting with the cardinal regarding this matter, he rebuffed them. Beyond the educational issue, Católicos sought general assistance for Chicanos, especially for housing.[54]

The issue of housing evolved from the fact that the archdiocese had just completed St. Basil's Cathedral, a huge edifice on Wilshire Boulevard, LA's major thoroughfare on the wealthy Westside. Católicos argued that if the church could afford such a rich building, it could certainly provide funding to house the poor on the Eastside. The cardinal's refusal to discuss the issue led to a dramatic protest at St. Basil's on Christmas Eve 1969. Católicos picketed in front of the church in an orderly fashion. However, when Mass began and demonstrators attempted to enter the church, armed policemen acting as ushers expelled them. Once outside, additional police met the demonstrators and arrested about twenty. Of those who stood trial for disrupting a religious gathering, only the leader was finally convicted of a misdemeanor in 1972.[55] Needless to say, in the interim the publicity surrounding the case aggravated tensions and caused some divisiveness in East Los Angeles.

Despite the housing issue, neither TELACU nor its members became directly involved in the church demonstrations. Given the overwhelmingly Catholic Mexican-American community, the protest at St. Basil's led to much controversy on the Eastside. Nevertheless, organized community support for Católicos was almost as strong as support for the East LA walkouts had been. On February 14, 1970, the Congress of Mexican-American Unity unanimously passed a resolution in support of Católicos. Obviously, Torres and the other TELACU personnel in the congress voted for the resolution. All groups in East LA had found it increasingly difficult to distance themselves from controversial positions as social unrest broke out repeatedly in the colonia during 1970.[56]

The East LA Riots

Violence flared immediately on January 1, 1970, as about five thousand New Year's revelers stormed along Whittier Boulevard in East LA, breaking windows and looting a few stores. It took police about two hours to quell the disturbance. While the immediate causes of this disturbance seemed apolitical at the time, the pattern of tension preceding and following this event indicated that it resulted from more than an excess of New Year's spirits.[57] The colonial analogy suggested that rebellion was imminent.

Early in 1970 TELACU stepped directly into the turmoil through the participation of its personnel in the Congress of Mexican-American Unity. Supported by the large contingent of TELACU and union members in the congress, Esteban Torres was elected president of the organization on March 12, 1970. During his presidency, the congress included over three hundred organizations of various types from throughout the Los Angeles area, but especially the Eastside. It represented groups as radical as the Brown Berets and as conservative as the Eastmont Parent-Teacher Association.[58] As president of the single most representative organization on the Eastside, Esteban Torres would be a key community leader in that turbulent year.

The Chicano Movement on the Eastside 71

That same March hundreds of Mexican Americans from throughout the United States met in Denver for the Second Annual Chicano Youth Liberation Conference. The first conference the previous year had promulgated "The Spiritual Plan of Aztlán," uniting the Chicano movement under one historic vision—the desire to recover the conquered Southwest. The second conference stressed specific approaches to current issues, especially the Vietnam War. From December 1967 to March 1969, Mexican Americans numbered 19 percent of all casualties from the Southwest while comprising only 12 percent of the region's population. Because Chicanos suffered such disproportionate casualties, the war had become an ethnic as well as a national issue. Activists began to argue that Chicanos were fighting for imperialism abroad, even as colonialism victimized them at home. Consequently, the delegates at the second conference planned hundreds of local antiwar demonstrations for communities throughout the Southwest and elsewhere. At the planning sessions in Denver, the Brown Berets most vociferously promoted the nationwide demonstrations. Unsurprisingly, the delegates set the climactic protest for August 29, 1970, in East Los Angeles.[59]

Even before the second Denver conference, the Brown Berets had formed the National Chicano Moratorium Committee and had held their first antiwar protest on December 20, 1969. Over two thousand people participated. At this point Rosalio Muñoz, a former UCLA student-body president who resisted the draft, became co-chair of the moratorium committee. On February 28, 1970, again prior to the second Denver conference, the new committee staged another march, this time involving over six thousand participants who showed the intensity of their commitment by marching in the pouring rain.[60] All of this naturally created greater tension with the police, who resented such "subversive" activities.

In addition to the tension created by the war, the police themselves frayed nerves on the Eastside. Increasingly, activists saw the police as part of the same imperialistic system that waged war in Vietnam and oppressed Chicanos at home. Police brutality became a major concern in the community. For example, on July 4, 1970, residents demonstrated against the Los Angeles County Sheriff's

Department. They protested the deaths of six Mexican-American inmates over the previous five months at the East LA substation. Only the night before twenty-two people had been arrested, and one youth injured, in a spontaneous protest over the same issue on Whittier Boulevard. In this outbreak the street suffered more broken windows as 250 sheriff's deputies and California Highway Patrol officers tried to quell the disturbance.[61] Seemingly, the police contributed to the spread of insurrection.

Given the pressures building in the community throughout 1970, the planned August 29 demonstration seemed sure to turn violent. To avoid this, the Chicano Moratorium Committee led by Rosalio Muñoz sought and received wide support in the community for a peaceful march and rally. When asked for assistance, Torres and the Congress of Mexican-American Unity agreed to cooperate. The congress applied for the parade permit in July, and Torres offered the offices of TELACU on Atlantic Boulevard as a meeting place for marchers. As part of the congress, a contingent of TELACU staff would march in the parade.[62]

The moratorium committee arranged for its own monitors to watch the march and requested that sheriff's deputies keep a low profile to avoid provoking the crowd. On the morning of August 29, from Belvedere Park the march proceeded east on Third and Beverly, then south on Atlantic Boulevard near the TELACU offices, and turned west onto Whittier Boulevard. Along the way, a number of minor incidents occurred that might have led to rioting had not cooperation between police and monitors held. Monitors quickly restrained a marcher who threw a bottle at a police car. Apparent opponents of the march threw bottles onto the participants from the Long Beach Freeway overpass, but trouble subsided despite a few cuts. A potentially serious problem developed when marchers took over both sides of the boulevard. Although the permit only allowed use of half the street, the police wisely refrained from insisting on the letter of the law.[63] Calm persisted until the end of the march at Laguna Park, about a block east of Indiana Street—the boundary of the old pueblo land grant.

At Laguna Park the marchers seated themselves on the grass in front of a stage set for musicians and speakers. The crowd included not only youths, but whole families; children played on the grass as their parents enjoyed picnics and listened to those on stage. However, about 3 P.M. a disturbance outside the park triggered a wider outbreak of violence. Apparently, teenagers in a crowded liquor store had pilfered some soft drinks. Police later claimed the owner called for their assistance, a claim denied by the owner. On the arrival of numerous squad cars, bottles flew at the police. Rather than isolating the problem on the street, the police decided to break up the entire demonstration at the park. Ignoring the pleas of the monitors, the police advanced into the park and met increasing resistance. They began firing tear gas into the crowd though many demonstrators heard no order to disperse and were unaware of the danger. Panic ensued when most of the crowd tried to escape through narrow exits away from the police advance. On the other hand, angered youths counterattacked with whatever weapons they could find. Rather than successfully breaking up the demonstration, the police action led to more open violence. The disturbance spread from the park down Whittier Boulevard. Stores were looted, buildings set afire, and police cars attacked.[64] Insurrection reached its peak in the colonia.

The violence continued for several hours during which three Chicanos died, including the most prominent Mexican-American journalist in Los Angeles. Ruben Salazar, a reporter for the *Los Angeles Times* as well as Spanish-language KMEX-TV, was killed by a tear-gas projectile fired indiscriminately into the Silver Dollar bar where he sat. The circumstances surrounding his death created controversy for weeks thereafter. The county coroner's office held an inquest into the death, a proceeding monitored by the Congress of Mexican-American Unity, including Esteban Torres and other prominent community leaders. Televised for days throughout the metropolitan area, the inquest became a forum for debate concerning the events of August 29. Though the hearing officer favored the authorities, enough information surfaced, especially on film, to lay significant blame on the police.[65]

Tensions in East Los Angeles and wherever Chicanos resided in southern California continued for months. Immediately following the August 29 riot, disturbances occurred in the barrios of Wil-

3. The Bell Plastics Building. Workers in front of burned ruin in East LA after riot of August 29, 1970. Courtesy of *Los Angeles Times* Photographic Archive, Department of Special Collections, University Research Library, UCLA.

mington and Riverside. Another broke out in East LA on September 16 after a Mexican Independence Day parade. To avoid a street confrontation, Esteban Torres had asked for a permit to celebrate the sixteenth at a local stadium, but the authorities denied the request.[66] Subsequently, police harassment of community groups, especially the Chicano Moratorium Committee, intensified.

In response the Congress of Mexican-American Unity issued an open letter in the *Eastside Sun* "urgently appealing to the Anglo community throughout Southern California to come to the assistance of the Chicano people." In the letter Esteban Torres, Rosalio Muñoz, and other prominent local leaders charged "that the police department is deliberately attempting to foment rebellion as an excuse to enter the community on a 'shoot-out basis.'" Shockingly, this radical interpretation of events came from a broadly based community group. The letter clearly revealed the colonia's desperate feelings of persecution at the hands of authorities and isolation from the surrounding metropolis. On the other hand, the appeal to the Anglo majority's sense of fairness expressed the Mexican-American community's desire for reconciliation. Further alienation could only lead to more repression and more civil disorder.[67]

The period of insurrection ended in 1971 with two final outbreaks on January 9 and 31, again on Whittier Boulevard. The last of these fit the description of purposeful rebellion predicted by some observers because the rioters struck intentionally at police, rather than at private property. Prior to the latter incident, Rosalio Muñoz representing the Chicano Moratorium Committee had published another open letter, this one in the *Los Angeles Times*. In this letter he argued that the contemporary conflict between the police and Chicanos had "its roots in the mid 1800's when another police government body—the U.S. Army—forcibly took the land away from the Mexicans in this area."[68] Muñoz had interpreted current events historically, according to internal colonialism and "The Spiritual Plan of Aztlán." The current violence was not the aimless criminality of immigrant neighborhoods, but the purposeful revolt of a native people.

TELACU, Recovery, and Reconciliation

But revolt could not lead to independence in the way such conflicts had secured freedom from empire for formal colonies. An internal colony, such as the Eastside, existed in a larger society from which it was neither possible nor desirable to secede. As Chicano columnist Tony Castro once commented, an accommodation had to be reached.[69] TELACU's seemingly contradictory position, as an advocate of self-determination as well as reconciliation, mirrored the situation of the community itself. The Chicano community sought to control its own political and socioeconomic destiny; it sought recovery of the place its culture had once enjoyed in California; but it sought these goals as an integral part of the United States. TELACU had the potential to deal with these paradoxical goals and to offer solutions once the violence had ended. Eventually, the East Los Angeles Community Union would leave its imprint on the recovering community, through economic and especially real estate development.

THREE

Nueva Maravilla and East LA Self-Government

Recovery Through Political Participation

Days after the major riot of August 29, 1970, the colonial analogy never seemed more appropriate as hundreds of police officers in helmets patrolled the barrios of East Los Angeles in a show of force resembling an occupying army. Windows and doors shattered in the outbreak were boarded up along Whittier Boulevard. Iron grates proliferated on storefronts all along the commercial strip. Several lots contained only rubble and ashes, evidence of the fires that had destroyed several buildings. Anglo commuters passed quickly through the neighborhood fearful that they might become the targets of further violence. The distance between the colonia and the surrounding metropolis rarely seemed greater.[1]

After the East LA riots of 1970, both government and the colonia desperately needed leadership that could end the violence and reconstruct social relations. That leadership would need to maneuver delicately between the conservative establishment, radical activists, and the general public caught between them. Key participation in recent events, especially through the Congress of Mexican-American Unity, placed the East Los Angeles Community Union in a position to serve as the intermediary for all sides at this critical juncture. Beyond political credibility, the community union had the technical expertise to act as broker for the community. As in Watts, the riots in East Los Angeles led government at various levels to place increased attention on the troubled area, and TELACU more than any other local organization could focus that attention.[2] For above all, TELACU could offer solutions from an ideological position that mirrored the needs of the community.

During the period of the riots, Esteban Torres, as head of the Congress of Mexican-American Unity, had followed a policy strongly in defense of community militants and critical of local authorities, especially the police. On the other hand, as TELACU's executive director, Torres had mapped out a course of community development in the mainstream, one that sought improvements through the system. The latter made him and TELACU more acceptable to government officials, more acceptable than militant groups, such as La Raza Unida Party soon to become a force on the Eastside.[3] Despite Torres's accommodating tactics, the radical ideology based on the internal colonial thesis continued to influence the actions of TELACU. After the violence of 1970, more than ever before, it seemed necessary for "self-determination" to move beyond mere rhetoric toward reality. Consequently, the struggle for political self-determination remained central to TELACU's operations and central to the life of East Los Angeles.

From early 1971 through 1974, the community's drive for political self-determination would transform the structure of the East Los Angeles Community Union, focus its economic activities increasingly in real estate, involve its members in a campaign to incorporate East LA as a city, and further complicate its public image. Over these four years TELACU would become a federally funded community development corporation, thereby securing its survival and expanding its power. It would also undertake its first major real estate development, the successful renewal of the Maravilla housing project. And though the campaign to incorporate East LA would fail, the result would make TELACU the provider of many of the community services otherwise absent for lack of a municipal government. The experience gained in electoral politics would also draw TELACU, especially Torres, into the concentric circles of political power.[4] This was of course an integrative process, for as Mexican Americans sought self-determination for East Los Angeles, they also sought greater power within the social system of the region and the nation. Though not always successful in its endeavors, TELACU would come to represent socioeconomic recovery through sophisticated participation in democratic politics.

Failed Experiments in Free Enterprise

The first half of 1971 began inauspiciously for both East LA and TELACU. Riots broke out again on January 9 and 31, as if auguring another year of violence for the community. The general disorder seemed to affect the operation of TELACU itself as its internal affairs became disorganized. The community union in attempting a comprehensive approach to East LA's critical problems found itself overextended and ill-focused. A sign of this was a loss of funds that the Ford Foundation had provided earlier for a home repair program. Another sign was the poor performance of the mattress manufacturing firm begun in early 1969. Moreover, a gasoline station launched as a retailing venture in December 1970 showed little promise almost from its inception. These small, long-term projects seemed futile given the crisis in the community.[5] Although economic development remained TELACU's hope for the future of East LA, political involvement offered more solutions to the most immediate problems. As a result, TELACU would seek for several years to achieve both its short- and long-term goals through government and politics in general.

The TELACU Mobil Service Center exemplified the difficulties Torres and his staff experienced with their privately financed long-term projects. The "mission" of the gasoline station located on Telegraph Boulevard in Commerce, followed the guidelines set for TELACU's Economic Development Division in general. The mission included providing revenue for TELACU and its limited partner the Mexican-American Community Programs Foundation, later called the Euclid Foundation. Providing East LA residents with employment, management training, and an example of a successful enterprise were other goals of the venture. The Euclid Foundation had invested $4,000 in the gasoline station while TELACU had invested $5,000 borrowed from Pan American Bank, a local Mexican-

American lender.⁶ The project involved neither government funds nor government contracts as TELACU had yet to develop its later extensive political network.

By mid-September 1971 the service station closed. In its first seven months the station had lost over $8,000 and owed over $8,000. Torres and his staff closed and sold the property to minimize their losses by reclaiming the equity. The conditions that had made the station initially promising had deteriorated, making further investment unwise. Across the street a large motel planned by another company never came about; instead, two competing stations appeared. Newer and more accessible to traffic, these cut into TELACU Service Center's receipts dramatically. Management and employees became demoralized, and consequently maintained the premises poorly. Clearly, the staff had not achieved the goals of the venture. Given that Mobil Oil Corporation and subsequent owners had failed to turn a profit at that location prior to TELACU's involvement, profitable investment at the location had hinged on the proposed motel. The discontinuation of that development doomed TELACU's retail venture. This experience, together with that of the failed mattress company, had its lessons. Thenceforth, Torres and his staff would steer away from privately financed mom-and-pop ventures in retailing and manufacturing.⁷

The movement in the direction of real estate development seemed more promising in 1971. By then Carlos J. García's Housing Division had already participated in the Hubbard Street, Plaza de la Raza, and several other land development projects generally linked to government. In addition Joseph Avila's Economic Development Division had established relations with Mexican-American building contractors and launched a small building-maintenance firm with another loan from the Pan American Bank. In 1970 Torres and his officers had scored a major coup when they won grants of $323,000 from the Ford Foundation and the Southwest Council of La Raza for housing rehabilitation. To administer the funds, they founded TELACU Home Repair Corporation in August of that year as a subsidiary of the community union. This corporation also processed the sale of prefabricated houses and handled promotions in connection with home repairs. Another subsidiary, TELACU Construction Development Corporation, carried out the actual home improvements and repairs. After these activities had got under way, however, the Ford Foundation withdrew its funding because of a disagreement over ultimate goals. Short of capital, the community union, established to promote self-sufficiency, ironically found itself dependent on philanthropic sources. And TELACU's officers discovered that private financing even from nonprofit foundations could be unreliable.[8]

Though blaming the Ford Foundation for some of the misunderstanding over goals, Esteban Torres, his staff, and TELACU's board of directors reexamined their own management and concluded that it needed improvement. Turning to government, they won a small grant from the federal Economic Development Administration, a grant Torres used to secure the services of Llewelyn-Davies Associates to reorganize his operations. Llewelyn-Davies was a New York community planning organization recommended by the Center for Community Change (the latter, headed by Jack Conway, had merged with the Citizens' Crusade Against Poverty). A planning team formed, including top TELACU staff, representatives of Llewelyn-Davies and the center, and other associates of Torres in East LA. Pleased with TELACU's willingness to undertake self-criticism, the Ford Foundation in 1972 provided $25,000 for the "Barrio Housing Plan." This document, resulting from three months of self-criticism, ultimately oriented TELACU's future activities toward real estate development.[9] Torres and his officers had successfully combined government and private funding sources in this new endeavor, a success that suggested the staff's increasing sophistication.

Maravilla and Participatory Democracy

The planning team urged that the community union complete its present housing projects, but that it soon target a single area in East Los Angeles with a comprehensive approach to the environment. The team recommended Maravilla "on the grounds that it was within the 'hard-core' area with one of the highest proportions of Mexican-American population, a high percentage of deteriorated and dilapidated housing, few proposals for the area and high visibility to the Chicano community." At the heart of Maravilla stood an old project partly built during the thirties as housing for the poor and partly during the forties as temporary housing for World War II veterans. The substandard project, owned and managed by the county, included sixty acres occupied by 480 families. "Abandoned buildings, houses beyond repair, and housing requiring either major rehabilitation or assistance" surrounded the project.[10] Of course, the physical environment reflected the area's social problems, problems poorly addressed by government and the private sector for decades.

Poverty and powerlessness had left Maravilla's inhabitants suspicious of change. Urban renewal programs of the recent past had removed whole barrios in the name of progress. The most notorious example had been the bulldozing of Chavez Ravine to make way for Dodger Stadium in the late fifties. A major part of the Maravilla effort would involve winning over the residents by organizing them for meaningful participation. TELACU's first job would be to "identify or build a neighborhood organization . . . able to enlist the support of the diverse elements in the community, to begin to establish and achieve specific goals, and eventually build its capacity as a powerful force for attracting and controlling the substantial public and private investment necessary for major redevelopment." Torres understood the negative history of urban renewal. It had simply reconstucted physical areas without regard for the needs of residents, who often found themselves unable to afford the higher rents charged for new or reconstructed housing. Since the Nueva Maravilla redevelopment would involve clearance and replacement of old housing, resistance would certainly arise from the current residents unless they participated in the process.[11] TELACU thus faced a problem requiring an essentially political solution.

To overcome the apprehensions of the barrio, Torres and his officers essentially planned a political campaign to win over the residents of Maravilla. They laid out a comprehensive approach to the area, in keeping with their holistic philosophy toward community recovery. In the "Barrio Housing Plan" the planning team recommended an inventory and analysis of all Maravilla's existing organizations and their leadership. The political backing of such prominent groups as Cleland House, a Presbyterian settlement house serving the community for over fifty years, would be critical for success. After soliciting the support of these groups, a preliminary effort to organize these groups into a coalition would follow. This effort would involve identifying more leaders, community concerns, issues, and attractive projects. The preliminary effort would also determine the need for staff, its training, support, and supervision.[12] All of this involved organizing skills that Torres's officers were fast developing, skills useful in the later acquisition of formal political power.

With the political spadework complete, the next step would be to focus the coalition's activity on housing, economic development, and job training to attract even greater support. The final step would be steering that support toward TELACU's goals of "Beautification, rehabilitation, and new construction in the three block action area." The "Barrio Housing Plan" indicated that while Torres and his officers sought input from the neighborhood democratically, they expected to set the agenda and direct the barrio toward redevelopment.[13] In doing so, TELACU would experience a recurring political problem faced by all community organizations: How to bring the goals of the organization and the wishes of the community together. By taking a comprehensive approach and doing their political spadework, TELACU's officers increased their chances for success in this endeavor.

TELACU in President Nixon's New Federalism

While the planning team formulated the "Barrio Housing Plan," TELACU's major endeavor involving government was coming to fruition. In 1969 Torres's staff had applied to the Office of Economic Opportunity (OEO) for a planning grant to transform the community union into a federally funded community development corporation. Curiously, the Special Impact Program had survived Robert Kennedy's death partly because Richard M. Nixon favored the idea of community development corporations. Perceiving them as capitalist vehicles for the revival of poor areas, Nixon liked their emphasis on self-sufficiency. During his 1968 presidential campaign, he had actually supported the unsuccessful Community Self-Determination Act sponsored by the Congress of Racial Equality. Consequently, the Nixon adminstration, after some bureaucratic infighting, permitted CDCs to increase by allotting them most of the Special Impact Program's funds. Though Nixon did not support CDCs as strongly as Kennedy had, they survived the change to a Republican administration with the aid of administrators linked to liberal Republican Senator Jacob Javits, co-founder of the program. As an organization with ties to the labor movement and the Democratic party, TELACU needed such political connections to win full funding from a Republican administration.[14]

Fortunately for TELACU, the Nixon administration saw the Special Impact Program and CDCs as ideologically acceptable means of appealing to minorities. Hoping to make inroads into a traditionally Democratic constituency, Nixon had placed several Mexican Americans in his administration. In October 1969 one of his appointees, Martin Castillo, chairman of the cabinet-level Inter-Agency Commission on Mexican-American Affairs, visited TELACU's offices in East LA on a trip to review local self-help organizations. In discussions with Castillo, Esteban Torres pointed out that when he requested federal assistance, agencies usually responded, "Don't call us; we'll call you." Despite Torres's animosity, Castillo replied, "with greater local support we can help you get what you need out of Washington. We've got to work together and try to overlook our areas of disagreement." Castillo's visit encouraged Torres to apply for a planning grant under the Special Impact Program.[15]

Despite Castillo's assurances, funding shortages at OEO left the application in the air for over a year. The Special Impact Program had become involved in complex bureaucratic changes in Washington as the Nixon administration rearranged the programs of Lyndon B. Johnson's Great Society. National concern over the war in Vietnam also made it difficult for the domestic agenda to gain a proper hearing in Congress. Finally, solid support for CDCs, including research by the Senate staffs of Javits and Edward Kennedy and a personal appearance at the hearings by Ethel Kennedy, won continued funding, further secured in legislation during 1972. Fortunately, in June 1971 at the close of the fiscal year, the OEO found enough extra dollars to fund Torres's planning proposal for $123,825, just in time for the community union to benefit from the recent legislative advances for CDCs in general. By late 1971 the OEO planning grant and the "Barrio Housing Plan" were providing Torres and his officers with the much-needed reevaluation that would help them overcome many of the problems they faced early that year.[16] Significantly, as TELACU made stronger political connections, its reliance on government increased, leaving the community union with the recurrent question of how to maintain its independence.

Self-Determination for Nueva Maravilla

By late 1971 Esteban Torres was ready to put the "Barrio Housing Plan" into effect. During his term as president of the Congress of Mexican-American Unity, Torres had developed the contacts with local organizations and leaders necessary to gain political support for the redevelopment now called Nueva Maravilla. For example, his connections with David Lizarraga, head of Casa Maravilla, helped resolve one of the critical problems the project faced—the area's youth gangs. Torres's staff held many contentious meetings with gang members and the various social service agencies that worked with them. Above all, Torres wanted the gangs to refrain from violence in the renovated housing project. In addition, because of TELACU's concern with image the gangs had to refrain from vandalism and graffiti. Of course, Lizarraga and the social service agencies agreed with this, but they and the gangs themselves wanted to know how youth might benefit directly from the redevelopment.[17]

Ultimately, Torres and Lizarraga agreed to find jobs for the youth in various phases of the demolition and construction of the Maravilla project. With the details worked out, the development gained the full support of the gangs and agencies. Indeed, as a result of the meetings, the local gangs formed the Federation of Barrios Unidos de Maravilla to maintain peace among themselves. By mid-1972, in a letter to Torres, the gangs showed how strong their appreciation for the development had become:

> As vatos de los barrios de La Rock, La Lomita, and La Arizona, we feel that the new homes we will be living in will do alot to bring dignity and beauty back to our barrio. . . . It is hard to be proud of housing that is deteriorating. It is hard not to 'plaquiar' and deface something that you cannot be proud of. . . . We sincerely hope that this new Pueblo de Maravilla may help to build pride . . . to stop the fighting . . . to pull together our people for the benefit of all La Raza.[18]

Significantly, the land development and its buildings began taking on some of the identification that the gangs felt for their "turfs." Because of TELACU's political negotiations, Nueva Maravilla would remain generally free of the graffiti covering the landscape of East LA.

In late 1971 with the gang negotiations under way, TELACU also organized the residents of the old project into the Tenants Advisory Board. This group through a series of meetings conducted by TELACU had input into both the planning and decision making. The residents had become interested in every detail that affected them personally, from the design of the bathrooms to management of the completed project. TELACU advised the residents on the technical aspects, from consulting architects to seeking funding. But the community union's most important role was encouraging the residents' democratic participation in their immediate community. Indeed, grass-roots leaders such as Pilar Hernández came out of this effort; a monolingual Spanish-speaking homemaker, she became a vocal community representative who later sat on TELACU's board. Clearly, the community union had some success in promoting the political self-determination of Maravilla.[19]

By January of 1972 TELACU had stimulated formation of the consortium of government agencies and private companies necessary to redevelop Maravilla. The major financial sponsor of the project would naturally be the Los Angeles County Housing Authority, the owner and manager of the old housing project; the U.S. Department of Housing and Urban Development (HUD) would also contribute funds. Lacking capital, not to mention engineering and architectural resources of its own, TELACU nevertheless served as the catalyst in the redevelopment of Maravilla. In

1971 TELACU had pressured the housing authority and HUD to consider the redevelopment. As we have seen, TELACU had also won over the residents and organized their direct participation in the project. Interestingly, the Magnolia Land Company, a business with connections to President Nixon, became the developer. Magnolia soon negotiated a contract directly with Esteban Torres offering TELACU about $30,000 for six months of assistance in the planning phase of the project, especially to maintain the political support of the residents.[20]

Magnolia, as the land developer, assigned various parts of the Maravilla project to subcontractors. For example, VTN Los Angeles, an engineering and architectural firm, would draw up the plans for the site. Leon Glucksman A.I.A., Architect and Associates, would design the buildings. Ultimately, TELACU's job fit along the lines of social service. First of all, the community union helped "achieve maximum feasible minority participation" in the construction of the project and in the relocation of the residents. Second, TELACU recruited and trained minority construction workers and subcontractors. Third, it monitored construction bids to insure "entrepreneurial and employment opportunites for local residents." Fourth, it encouraged building trade unions to follow affirmative action. Fifth, the community union assisted minority contractors in meeting financial qualifications for participation. Sixth, TELACU developed grant proposals to meet the costs of the affirmative action program. Seventh, it coordinated relations with tenants and the community to meet their needs, as well as "minimize opposition." And finally, TELACU provided employees to assure fulfillment of its own mission.[21] Clearly, these services consisted of the human rather than the material sort. With regard to Nueva Maravilla, the community union would continue to function as a catalyst, politically influential despite its minimal financial weight.

TELACU, Community Development Corporation

The rest of 1972 as regards Nueva Maravilla involved planning, with demolition of the old housing project not beginning until January of the following year. However, the internal reevaluation in 1971, which led to TELACU's catalytic role in the redevelopment of Maravilla, continued and eventually led to structural changes within the organization that assured its survival and growth before the end of 1972. Critical to this continuing internal reevaluation was OEO, the government agency that provided the planning grant for TELACU's restructuring. The principles behind the "Barrio Housing Plan" that had so successfully focused TELACU's activities on real estate also served as a foundation for the organization's successful bid to become a federally funded community development corporation.[22] Of course, the government regulations of OEO came along with the funding.

OEO's planning grant led TELACU to sharpen its mission and restructure itself to meet the guidelines for major funding from the federal government. That mission, as finally stated in TELACU's proposal for funding through the Special Impact Program, was "the maximum possible improvement of the quality of life, as defined by income level, living conditions and self-image, for the Mexican-American community of East Los Angeles." Several other goals supported this general mission. TELACU would evolve into "the organization with which all public and private institutions must deal when making decisions affecting the future of East Los Angeles." TELACU would create, strengthen, or manage businesses contributing to at least two of what follows: the community's "physical improvement," acquisition of resources or skills, the supplying of necessities and services, and the creation of employment. Finally, the CDC would naturally do all this for the benefit of the Eastside.[23]

Municipal Image

Of course, these principles lay behind the "Barrio Housing Plan" and the Maravilla redevelopment, but several points now stood out more clearly for the community union as a whole. As part of its mission, TELACU made the community's "self-image" a matter of high priority. To Torres and his staff it mattered what things and people "looked like" and what impression they left both inside and outside the community. Physical appearance could symbolize prosperity or decline and affect attitudes toward the landscape and people of East LA. Such attitudes could affect investment and employment decisions. As we have seen, TELACU's concern with the "physical improvement" of East LA manifested itself in the community union's involvement in housing redevelopments, such as Nueva Maravilla. But even more significant in the mission statement was TELACU's goal of becoming the central institution in East LA. Indeed, that goal amounted to claiming powers usually reserved for a municipal government, which of course East LA lacked.[24] Clearly, TELACU aimed to become the chief vehicle for achieving the political self-determination of East Los Angeles.

Nevertheless, one of the ironies of this drive for self-determination was the need to appeal to Washington for funding. Such funding naturally came with strings attached, a situation obviously not in keeping with the ideal of self-determination. The strings became tighter as TELACU struggled to restructure under the guidelines of the OEO planning grant. The major change required involved the board of directors. Up to that point seven union representatives, most holding seats from the beginning of the community union, had comprised the board. OEO demanded that TELACU expand the board by at least eight seats and give control to new members representing other organizations in the community. Naturally, TELACU resisted this move, arguing that the union members as community residents already represented East LA. However, OEO apparently believed the unions, rather than the local community, would dominate the organization if the board remained as originally established. Government funding promised TELACU prosperity, but clearly threatened the community union's independence.[25]

The disagreement was resolved, but not without a great deal of reflection on TELACU's part. TELACU's roots ran deep in the union movement, as its very name indicated. TELACU naturally feared that major government funding would undermine that special relationship. More importantly, if that relationship deteriorated and government funding disappeared, TELACU might lose its life. Up to this point, the community union had undertaken its projects with grants from labor, private foundations, and some government agencies. Loans from banks had also been secured for business enterprises. However, the United Auto Workers, TELACU's parent organization, had subsidized the daily operating budget. OEO offered to provide a much fuller operating budget in exchange for TELACU's restructuring. The OEO's Special Impact Program would allow TELACU to engage in much fuller activities, subject to review every two years on application for renewal. OEO could renew the grant indefinitely as long as the CDC showed progress toward eventual financial independence. The opportunity to invest government funds directly in private enterprises seemed a major advantage because it offered the CDC self-sufficiency. Finally, the community union decided that the promise of eventual self-determination outweighed the burden of immediate dependency. TELACU accepted the federal government's stipulations.[26]

The government's requirement that TELACU restructure turned out well. Since the seven union delegates still remained at-large members of the board of directors, labor retained a voice, a significant one at that. Moreover, the new members came from community groups already closely associated with TELACU. The new membership, now the majority, would vary in number over time, but would consistently represent the following or similar community groups: Plaza de la Raza, Casa Maravilla, Federation of Barrios Unidos, Arizona Mothers Association, El Hoyo Association, Maravilla Tenants Association, Maravilla Service Center, Cleland House, Senior Citizens, and the Lote Association. These groups in turn represented artists, gang members, settlement houses, parents, renters, specific neighborhoods, social workers, and senior citizens. As we can see, the Maravilla barrio had a strong contingent on the new board. Despite restricting TELACU's independence, the federal government had forced the community union to become somewhat more democratic though the CDC never carried out its original plan to include rank-and-file members or stockholders.[27]

Corporate Image

Finally, on November 14, 1972, the Office of Economic Opportunity designated the East Los Angeles Community Union a federally funded community development corporation. In practical terms this meant TELACU would receive $1 million over two years from October 1, 1972, to September 30, 1974. This funding came from appropriations arising from important amendments to the Economic Opportunity Act in 1972. Congress had placed the Special Impact Program and its funds under Title VII, labeled "Community Economic Development." Title VII stipulated that OEO support the fullest possible economic programs of the local organizations known as "community development corporations." Under Title I-D of earlier versions of the Economic Opportunity Act, community development corporations had only appeared as experimental entities. Under the amendments of 1972, CDCs became regular parts of the federal budget, consequently gaining a measure of longevity. (Despite this, with funding resting on periodic appropriations, CDCs needed to become independent quickly.) Title VII clearly outlined the activities of CDCs as economic; these activities marked CDCs unequivocally as business corporations, though cooperative in nature. In fact, the federal government had granted public funds for TELACU to set up businesses in the private sector.[28]

According to Title VII of the Economic Opportunity Act, the key purpose of CDCs was to establish or assist businesses. These businesses in turn should engage in housing development to increase employment and entrepreneurial opportunities for local residents. In addition to direct OEO grants, Title VII allowed CDCs to apply for funds from other government agencies under different programs. Various provisions of the 1972 title coordinated this process. Curiously, while Title VII allowed TELACU to become more business oriented than ever, obviously government funding and government contracts would pave the way to success.[29]

The complexity of community development corporations, not to mention their government funding, would not permit their simplistic classification as business corporations. Despite orienting itself more toward business, the East Los Angeles Community Union continued to claim powers usually reserved for local governments. Actually, the history of American business corporations provides many precedents for such claims. As early as 1629, a joint-stock company chartered for commercial purposes became the de facto government of Massachusetts Bay when the board and stockholders agreed to move their meetings from Britain to New England. By 1631 the board had extended the franchise to at least 40 percent of the colony's adult males, thus expanding the democratic nature of the enterprise. In terms of providing government services, the history of the United States is replete with corporations that established company towns providing every service imaginable, especially the housing and boarding of workers.[30] Thus, TELACU's claims to governmental powers paradoxically rested on a certain business tradition.

Limited Representation

Most of TELACU's founders had hoped to create an organization similar to a democratic labor union with the residents of the community forming a mass membership that would elect the board of directors. Esteban Torres, however, opposed the idea on the grounds of voter apathy and the danger of factionalism. In the mid-sixties OEO's community action programs, attempting to operate on a mass basis, had experienced turnouts of less than 5 percent in elections. In these groups factionalism, often fomented by militants wielding disproportionate power due to voter apathy, had rendered many organizations ineffective. Torres had consequently pushed for limited representation of the community, with board members appointed on the basis of residency by the officers of broadly based labor unions. As we have seen, OEO had made TELACU more democratic by insisting on greater representation of various community groups on the board, groups that themselves had broad memberships. Though close allies ultimately filled the board, the CDC nevertheless represented East LA to a good degree. TELACU deserved consideration as the central institution of the area, an institution steadily acquiring government functions.[31]

Self-Government for East Los Angeles

Despite this, TELACU in late 1972 did not have the strength to take on all the functions of municipal government. Aware of this, TELACU's leaders took a more traditional route toward political self-determination for East Los Angeles. Esteban Torres launched a major campaign to incorporate the area as a city. Significantly, in this drive he would argue that the long-established community's lack of municipal government clearly illustrated East LA's colonial status.[32]

History of Municipal Incorporation Efforts

Considering that surrounding communities—Alhambra, Monterey Park, and Montebello—had become cities in 1915, 1916, and 1920 respectively, the failure to incorporate East LA seemed especially unjust. That failure had not come for lack of effort. Indeed, the first attempts had arisen as far back as 1925–26 when "sentiment against the fragmenting of the 'Great Eastside'" unfortunately carried the day. In 1931 the Los Angeles County Board of Supervisors squelched two efforts with the argument that taxes would be too high. In 1933 industrial firms that preferred the lower taxes of unincorporated territory succeeded in defeating a proposal taken to the voters—8,439 to 462. That resounding defeat for incorporation left the issue dead for the next thirty years.[33] East LA remained a colony of county government as community after community in the metropolitan area gained home rule.

In the 1960s the issue of incorporation rose again in various forms. A serious blow to East LA's chances for cityhood occurred in 1960 with the establishment of the city of Commerce. This case remains one of the most notorious in southern California history because of the way the incorporation served business interests. The southern, heavily industrialized section of the unincorporated Eastside became a municipality despite the fact that it had virtually no residential areas. Large companies pushed through the incorporation to forestall inclusion of their firms in any new East LA city embracing the poor, heavily populated areas just to the north. Creation of Commerce meant that the new city had an enormous tax base and vitually no residents to supply with local services. In this way Commerce businesses avoided much higher assessments. As it happened, Commerce became an enclave controlled by business with little input from residents, an undemocratic situation that eventually led to municipal corruption. Henceforth, the remainder of the unincorporated area, stripped of an enormous tax base, had to struggle with the charge that East LA could not support municipal government.[34]

To avoid further erosion of the tax base, the Citizens' Committee to Incorporate East Los Angeles once more brought the issue to the ballot on April 25, 1961. Despite support from the area's county supervisor, the fire department, and a prominent local clergymen, this effort also failed. Arrayed against the citizens' committee composed largely of Mexican Americans were the Property Owners Association and the Whittier Boulevard Businessmen backed by the *Eastside Sun*, a coalition largely representative of Anglo absentee owners. The citizens' committee did not have the resources to combat the property owners, who narrowly won by again raising the specter of higher taxes. This confrontation would give credibility to the colonial analogy. In 1965 what remained of the committee could not even return the issue to the ballot.[35]

Incorporation would not revive as a campaign issue for another five or six years. Of course, Chicano activists during the late sixties heatedly discussed the issue, especially at the meetings of the Congress of Mexican-American Unity. With the rhetoric of self-determination filling the air, East LA's lack of political autonomy naturally became a topic of debate. The riots of 1970 and the subsequent doubts concerning county government, especially the sheriff's department, resurrected incorporation as a campaign issue. In November of 1970, the Congress of Mexican-American Unity under Esteban Torres formed an ad hoc committee to examine the possibilities of East LA becoming a city.[36]

What finally pushed the issue beyond the talking stage, however, was Monterey Park's attempt to annex the northeastern corner of East Los Angeles. This section included significant numbers of middle-class Anglo- and Asian-Americans who felt more comfortable in middle-class, multiethnic Monterey Park than in lower-class, Mexican-American East LA. Indeed, residents of the northeastern section itself had petitioned to join Monterey Park. Annexation would of course deprive any future East LA municipality of revenue; more significantly, annexation would move the campus of East Los Angeles College to Monterey Park. Such a move would clearly be a blow to the prestige of Mexican-American East LA. A major reason for placing the attractive, modern, two-year college on the Eastside had been to serve the Mexican-American community. Indeed, though Chicanos suffered underrepresentation even at this institution, it remained one of the few colleges in California with numerous students of this ethnic background. The loss of the campus would deprive East LA of one of its most important architectural symbols. It would also deprive East LA of one of its most attractive landscapes, further damaging the community's image.[37]

The Ad Hoc Committee to Incorporate East Los Angeles

To avert Monterey Park's annexation attempt, the leaders of the East Los Angeles Community Union started a new incorporation drive. In late 1972 Esteban Torres formally established the Ad Hoc Committee to Incorporate East Los Angeles (ACTIELA) as an entity separate from the Congress of Mexican-American Unity. Though officially independent, ACTIELA was clearly a satellite of TELACU, which provided virtually all the leadership, staff, and offices for the new organization. Once again TELACU took on the role of catalyst. Though the CDC as an institution lacked the power and legitimacy to govern East LA, it could nevertheless instigate the process leading to self-government for the area. Torres and his staff saw immense opportunities for the rebuilding of East LA if TELACU and the new municipality could form a partnership. The former could provide the advantages of the private sector while the latter provided public services. A strong municipal government could relieve TELACU of some its social services so it could push ahead with economic development.[38]

Esteban Torres and the Colonial Analogy

Interestingly, TELACU's leadership perceived these practical considerations in the context of the colonial analogy. In an interview concerning the philosophical underpinnings of the latest incorporation campaign, Esteban Torres clearly manifested the influence of such Third World thinkers as Albert Memmi and Frantz Fanon. In the interview Torres responded in the following way to a question suggesting that perhaps county government was adequate for East LA:

> I would say analogous to that [county government] is a form of colonialism. It's a form of French power over some desert or African state whereby, really, the French run it to their pleasure or whatever with little interest in the well-being and welfare of that community. But use the "colony," so to speak, as a source of manpower, revenue, as a source of control over people without really allowing those people the ability for self-determination. So I think that's one of the moving forces why I feel incorporation is necessary.

Memmi and Fanon had interpreted colonialism from their experiences in the French empire, especially in North Africa; Torres, obviously familiar with their works, interpreted the situation of East LA in a similar light. The residents of East LA provided labor and taxes to the rest of the county, but lacked an equal voice in governance. Consequently, county government paid little attention and provided few resources to these residents; in short, that government treated the area like a colony. The solution, to extend the analogy, was independence or incorporation of East LA as a separate city.[39]

Partially due to the colonial analogy, Torres's opponents charged that radicals were driving the cityhood movement. Torres responded that communities regularly incorporated throughout the United States, and East LA deserved to do the same. But given the colonial analogy he had just used, his response seemed disingenuous. When asked whether incorporation actually resembled a drive toward "separation," Torres answered:

> separatism exists now. It is now that E.L.A. is a segregated "city.". . . Again it is a colony whereby surrounding jurisdictions draw from it in terms of a labor pool; in terms of selling to those people. . . . As an independent force—what really would happen by incorporation is that those barriers would be knocked down. E.L.A. . . . would be able to integrate into . . . the mainstream . . . in terms of dealing with its own economy; dealing with its own governmental process. . . .

Torres thus reconciled the principle of self-determination with the need for accommodation with the larger society, the seemingly contradictory stance taken by TELACU from its inception. Basically, Torres argued that incorporation would allow East LA to make laws, regulations, and policies putting it on an equal political and economic footing with surrounding cities. East LA could not negotiate such matters if it remained a mere dependency of large, distant, and impersonal county government. In effect, rather than a colony gaining national independence, East LA winning incorporation would be similar to a territory entering the Union.[40]

However, incorporation of East LA was a cultural as well as a political issue, and in that sense differed from the situation of most territories admitted to the United States. Given the violence associated with the Chicano movement, opponents feared a politically militant Chicano municipality would arise on the Eastside, "with all the [cultural] trappings of Mexico." Because of their overwhelming majority, clearly Mexican Americans would control the new city though Torres expected some Asian- and Anglo-American representation on the city council. Despite this, if we compare East LA to a territory, New Mexico and Puerto Rico best illustrate the role of culture in attempts at integration with the larger society. In effect colonial possessions of the United States, both territories were predominantly Hispanic, a situation that delayed their admission to the Union. New Mexico finally achieved statehood when its population became sufficiently Anglo to satisfy Congress. Puerto Rico remains a Spanish-speaking commonwealth, neither independent nor politically integrated into the United States. While other factors affected these cases, clearly the dominant society would not readily integrate politically with communities that threatened to remain culturally distinct.[41] Needless to say, East LA remained such a community.

Commenting more frankly on the cultural issue in an article for *La Luz*, Torres admitted that the desire for incorporation of East LA involved the desire to reassert the place of Mexican-American culture in public life:

> Finally, incorporation will give an added dignity to an area already rich in cultural and historical heritage. The dream of standing in the great cultural and business center of East Los Angeles, the Zocalo, is worth translating such community objectives as social advancement, planned economic development, equitable taxation, improved land use, and responsive education into visible *realities*.

Even as Torres argued for incorporation, he visualized this political goal in concrete cultural terms, clearly revealing TELACU's concern with imagery. Even as ACTIELA campaigned for incorporation, TELACU officials dreamed of a revived downtown. They imagined a cultural, commercial, and civic center reflecting the heritage of Mexican-American East LA in the way Mexico City's great plaza reflected the heritage of the Mexican nation. At this point TELACU's zócalo remained a conversation piece, but before long it would actually move to the drawing board.[42] In any event incorporation for East LA obviously meant much more than simply self-government.

In February of 1973, ACTIELA prepared to submit the application for East LA incorporation to the Local Agency Formation Commission (LAFCO). A unit of county government established by the state, LAFCO had the responsiblity of assuring that the area could survive as a city. The proposed city needed some homogeneity, an adequate economic base, and sufficient community support. By April Esteban Torres and ACTIELA, which had already commissioned an economic feasibility study, received the results and submitted the formal application for cityhood to LAFCO. This agency's technical staff reviewed the application over the next few months; finding the application sound, the staff sent it to the commission's board for public hearings. On August 8, after hearing arguments for and against the proposed city, LAFCO permitted the process to proceed.[43]

By this time the issue had moved from the political back rooms to the public forum. LAFCO's public hearings had, of course, warned potential opponents of the new incorporation movement. Art Montoya, president of the E.L.A., Maravilla, and Belvedere Park Property Owners Association, led the opposition. As a columnist for the *Eastside Sun* and a large property owner, Montoya had helped defeat the incorporation attempts of the 1960s; again he galvanized the opposition with the old charge that East LA could not support city government without higher taxes. Though the opposition had failed to convince LAFCO of this, the argument moved to the people. In October 1973 ACTIELA began the process of circulating petitions. Within the next few months supporters of incorporation had to obtain the signatures of 25 percent of the area's registered voters to put the issue on the ballot. This naturally meant the larger community, both individuals and organizations, had to become involved. ACTIELA, at that point still comprised basically of TELACU and its affiliates, had to reach out to the rest of East Los Angeles. This political effort would consume much of TELACU's energy over the next year.[44]

TELACU's Constructive Operations

Meanwhile, Nueva Maravilla had moved off the drawing board toward reality. In January of 1973 Shapell Government Housing and Goldrich & Kest commenced demolition of the old units. "High visibility" of minorities was maintained as the job got under way since TELACU had earlier stressed employment opportunities in convincing the locals to support the project. To keep that promise some featherbedding occurred during demolition, but once actual construction began in February, the practice stopped to keep the project within budget. Nevertheless, local residents and "Spanish-American" subcontractors found work. Once construction began minority subcontractors carried out a number of operations: on-site engineering by Kemmerer, painting by A&A Camacho, metal work by Service Sheet Metal, landscaping by Reliable Landscaping, rough carpentry by Albert A. Hernández, ceramic tile by Dan Tiscareno, and plastering by Rafael Corral. Though Anglo firms still received most of the major contracts, this resulted from the general shortage of Mexican-American construction firms large enough to handle projects of this scale. Construction of the first section of Nueva Maravilla took the rest of 1973, with the remaining sections scheduled for completion in 1974. As the buildings went up, TELACU's reputation rose as well, for though government financed the project, the community recognized the CDC's role as catalyst.[45]

As Nueva Maravilla moved ahead, TELACU's managers embarked on ventures more closely tied to government contracts, ventures more likely to succeed on a large scale than the earlier mom-and-pop operations. Food Stamp Outreach was one such venture, designed around better distribution centers than private banks. An-

4. Nueva Maravilla. Low-income housing redevelopment over twenty years after completion. Photograph by author, 1997.

other venture, Community Planning and Development Corporation, evolved from housing rehabilitation under government contracts toward pure development research. This subsidiary would eventually become one of TELACU's most creative companies. Another economic development strategy also gained ground in TELACU as a result of the Maravilla project. Having experienced the advantages of a catalytic role, TELACU's managers increasingly looked to "leveraging" in both business and social service. They had learned they could greatly influence activities even with minimal investments of TELACU's resources. TELACU's experience in making government more responsive in Maravilla had proven that. Beyond these larger strategies and ventures, day-to-day through 1973 the CDC "continued to promote and administer its programs in business loan packaging, contract procurement for minority businesses, housing, and on-going social programs in job training and for senior citizens."[46]

David Lizarraga, Interim Director

After two successful years of expansion and consolidation, a number of important developments occurred during 1974 that would strengthen the East Los Angeles Community Union in the long run. This period nevertheless evinced all the characteristics of a year of transition. By January, with the first phase complete, Nueva Maravilla rapidly moved ahead. However, with this first major success securing TELACU, Esteban Torres increasingly turned his eyes toward a political career. In early 1974 he resigned as executive director of the CDC to run for Congress. Expecting his return if he lost the election, TELACU operated under interim director David Lizarraga. Not until the fall, when Torres declined to return, did the board make Lizarraga's appointment permanent. During the interlude of uncertainty, TELACU at mid-year successfully applied for a two-year renewal of its OEO operational grant, thus assuring the CDC financial stability through September of 1976. Despite this, the exact role of TELACU in the future of East Los Angeles remained unclear as long as incorporation seemed possible. Since cooperation with the new city would be critical for any new projects, TELACU awaited the outcome of the election before proceeding with any more major efforts. Given that TELACU's own managers were running ACTIELA, the incorporation campaign of 1974 consumed much of the CDC's energy anyway.[47]

Independence Denied

By early 1974 the incorporation campaign had become more complex as other East LA groups became involved:

> This broadening of the base of support was necessary because ACTIELA was for all practical purposes the political arm of The East Los Angeles Community Union. . . . This umbrella organization was seen by many to be a warmed over, smaller scale version of the old Congress of Mexican American Unity [indeed, ACTIELA not only derived from, but essentially replaced the congress].

To counter this perception, ACTIELA sought the support of the United Farm Workers, an ally of TELACU since its founding. The UFW gave its endorsement to the effort, a valuable contribution because of the labor union's visibility in the community. However, because the issue did not affect farm workers directly, the UFW never became very active in the campaign. More significant was the participation of La Raza Unida Party, a new political force on the Eastside.[48]

La Raza Unida Party

Launched successfully in Crystal City, Texas, La Raza Unida Party had shortly thereafter organized in California. La Raza Unida followed the "The Spiritual Plan of Aztlán" proclaimed in Denver at the first Chicano Youth Liberation Conference of 1969. The plan promoted an image of the Southwest as the Chicano homeland, framed the image within the ancient Aztec myth of Aztlán, and set the goals of the Chicano movement within that concept. Because of its ethnic nationalism and socialistic tendencies, the party had a radical reputation that opponents of incorporation used to frighten voters. However, La Raza Unida had enjoyed success, especially in Texas, by appealing to ethnic pride. Given the overwhelmingly Mexican-American population of East LA, that appeal gained a hearing. In any case, La Raza Unida's involvement in the campaign meant that the issue of self-determination was advanced in rhetoric more radical than that generally used by TELACU, a circumstance that made the latter seem increasingly accommodating toward the larger society.[49]

While ACTIELA had sought the support of La Raza Unida, the two organizations remained separate backers of incorporation. Even before Esteban Torres had requested La Raza Unida's participation, the party had begun circulating petitions to put incorporation on the ballot. Indeed, the party eventually put forward its own slate of candidates for city council (the seats were included on the ballot in case incorporation should pass). La Raza Unida derived its supporters primarily from college campuses, a circumstance that gave it access to many students willing to campaign door-to-door. Raúl Ruiz, a professor of Chicano studies at California State University, Northridge, led the party's effort and its slate of candidates. Richard Santillán, chair of the Department of Chicano Studies at California State University, Los Angeles, served as an important publicist for the party.[50]

By contrast with La Raza Unida, ACTIELA acquired a reputation as the less radical component of the incorporation coalition. This organization, reflecting TELACU's image consciousness, promoted itself as a group of professionals volunteering their time for a worthy political goal. During the petition phase of the campaign, Torres projected this accommodating image by appointing prominent activists over age fifty as captains of the drive. These "elder statesmen" each directed the effort in one of the areas into which Torres had divided East LA. In April 1974 this phase of the campaign succeeded when the county certified that the required number of registered East LA voters had signed the petition. The issue then went to the Los Angeles County Board of Supervisors.[51]

Opposition, Torres's Departure, and Factionalism

For the next two months, the incorporation of East LA awaited the board of supervisors, which held hearings regarding the exact boundaries of the proposed city. Opponents of incorporation had followed a strategy of circulating counter-petitions in areas on the fringes of East LA, petitions to exclude those areas from the new city. Since such areas might expect eventual annexation to surrounding suburbs, opponents hoped to encourage their withdrawal from the proposed city, a move that would deprive it of more valuable taxable property. However, the counter-petitions failed, and on June 13 the board decided to set the boundaries as originally requested and to set the election for November 5, 1974. Thus began the five final months of intensive political campaigning.[52]

Unfortunately, the campaign encountered insurmountable obstacles. Esteban Torres's decision to run for Congress created a major problem. Since his campaign overlapped the incorporation effort until June, his performance as head of ACTIELA suffered. Although he had resigned as executive director of TELACU in early 1974, his energies were still divided. Because Mexican Americans in California had only one representative in Congress, Torres hoped to increase that number through his own candidacy. Running against an incumbent, however, doomed his effort to failure; he was eliminated from the contest during the June primary election. Though TELACU had expected his return, he chose his former job with the United Auto Workers in Washington, D.C. Unfortunately, before the incorporation campaign ended, he left his position with ACTIELA as well.[53]

Before Torres's departure, however, serious problems had surfaced for the proponents of incorporation. ACTIELA and La Raza Unida began to position themselves for control of the proposed city council. Since about forty candidates had filed for city council, La Raza Unida advanced a slate of five for special support. Fearing that the party would control the new city, Torres and ACTIELA put together their own slate of five. Needless to say, cooperation between the two organizations foundered. Moreover, ACTIELA had gathered less than a quarter of the $40,000 believed necessary to wage an effective campaign. ACTIELA's failure in this regard left the closing battle to La Raza Unida, which brought in 250 volunteers to get out the vote just before the November 5 election.[54]

Despite the high turnout triggered by a gubernatorial election, the measure lost. Although 66 percent of the registered voters went to the polls, 29.2 percent voted against incorporation, 21.33 voted for it, and 16.12 failed to vote on the proposition. The core of East LA, the Belvedere precincts, voted solidly for the measure, but the more affluent, less Mexican-American areas on the borders with surrounding cities voted against the new city. Ultimately, opponents of incorporation succeeded in convincing the electorate that higher taxes would result from the proposition. More significantly, the opponents apparently convinced the voters that ACTIELA and La Raza Unida were simply making emotional appeals to Mexican pride. Proponents had failed to convince voters of the concrete advantages of cityhood. Thus, East Los Angeles remained the most populous community in the inner county dependent on the board of supervisors. East LA's colonial status seemed confirmed.[55]

Recovery and Integration Delayed

The defeat of incorporation forced TELACU once again to reevaluate its goals. Since East LA would not have a municipal government after all, the partnership envisioned between the CDC and the new city disappeared. The task of setting the new agenda fell to David Lizarraga, an unlikely candidate in some ways. A product of the colonia himself, he had worked primarily with gangs through Casa Maravilla; thus, he came to TELACU with a background mainly in social service. The question remained whether he could successfully lead TELACU in economic development, the CDC's primary mission. Since the political course taken in 1974 had caused TELACU to founder, the institution's officers looked ahead uncertainly as the year ended.[56]

Despite this, in only six years Esteban Torres had made the East Los Angeles Community Union the leading intermediary between the colonia and government, between the community and the larger society. While the failure of incorporation had shown that TELACU had neither completely won over the community nor mastered the political system, the success of Nueva Maravilla demonstrated the institution's increasing technical skill in dealing with government, as well as business. While TELACU had failed to win political self-determination for East Los Angeles, the institution had shown ways to make government more responsive to the community's socioeconomic needs. As a federally funded community development corporation, TELACU had become somewhat more democratic and more capable of functioning successfully in the capitalist system. Although dependence on federal funding had further clouded TELACU's image as a symbol of self-determination, TELACU had suggested ways Mexican Americans could recover their autonomy as well as their place in society by skillfully accommodating the system.[57]

FOUR

The Master Plan and TELACU Industrial Park

Recovery Through Economic Development

On December 4, 1974, public ceremonies, held at the site itself, marked completion of the Nueva Maravilla redevelopment. The 504-unit complex was comprised of modern two-story buildings laid out among landscaped areas, giving the redevelopment the appearance of a middle-class condominium complex, rather than a low-income housing project. The adobe-yellow plaster walls and plain reddish roofs subtly reflected the ethnicity of the buildings' occupants. Here and there vigas and murals highlighted the Hispanic presence. At the ceremonies Los Angeles County Supervisor Ernest E. Debs commented that "The community had a strong voice in the design decisions, and this is one reason why Maravilla is considered the finest housing development of its kind in the United States," a statement supported by the U.S. Department of Housing and Urban Development. He then added, "It is a place where persons of modest means can live in comfort and dignity, and with pride in their heritage." Since TELACU's surveys and meetings had amplified the voice of the people, the East Los Angeles Community Union could justifiably claim a good deal of responsibility for recovery of the Maravilla barrio and the rekindling of its ethnic pride.[1]

Nueva Maravilla was concrete evidence that by the end of 1974, TELACU had become a major force for empowerment of the Eastside. On the other hand, TELACU had clearly experienced political defeat with East LA's failed incorporation effort in November. Also, the goal of Chicano self-determination seemed as distant as ever given Esteban Torres's unsuccessful campaign for Congress earlier that year. As a result, despite the shining image of Nueva Maravilla, TELACU found its future cloudy as 1975 began. Its political ambitions temporarily contained, the institution reemphasized its economic activities. Over the next five years, TELACU would seek to implement a master plan of economic development—the most successful financial component of which would be Community Thrift & Loan, an institution explicitly designed to help East LA recover from colonial dependency on the larger economy. However, even more significant than the thrift would be the community development corporation's major real estate venture—TELACU Industrial Park.[2]

Constructive Leadership

As interim executive director, then as permanent president, David C. Lizarraga had guided TELACU for over six months by 1975. In time his title would lengthen with the addition of "chief executive officer." This addition would be more than cosmetic; indeed, it would signal that under Lizarraga's management TELACU would more than ever resemble a business corporation rather than a labor union or social service agency. Although Lizarraga had previously directed TELACU's Social Services Division, he decided to follow the path of business even farther than had his predecessor, a leader more inclined toward government and politics. A business orientation was naturally more accommodating to the larger capitalist society and consequently more integrative on the whole, though such an orientation could lead to a controversial image in a working-class community.[3]

David Lizarraga, President

The new architect of TELACU's fortunes, David Lizarraga was born and raised in East LA. Like many of the community's other leaders, he attended East Los Angeles College and California State University, Los Angeles. In 1963 Lizarraga had started out as the youth program director for Cleland House, a settlement house later affiliated with TELACU. "We came from a very activist and militant period in the late 60s and early 70s," he recalled in a later interview. "We did a lot of arguing over the many problems facing our society"; finally, "We began to see that we needed to deal with solutions to the problems and not just argue the fact that there was a problem." In 1969 he sought to alleviate East LA's gang problem by founding Casa Maravilla, the social service center subsequently involved in the construction of Nueva Maravilla. He then moved to TELACU's Social Services Division. Though none of this background involved business, Lizarraga's association with TELACU's managers brought out his latent business aptitude. Though he recalled that Torres's staff organized "around political and economic issues," Lizarraga found himself more inclined to the latter than the former.[4]

Fortunately, Lizarraga inherited an experienced board of directors and a seasoned corps of executives. George Solís, one of TELACU's founders, became chair of the board in 1975; such veterans as Glenn O'Loane and Gordon Moreno continued on the board, as did Esteban Torres, despite his self-imposed exile in Washington. Now legal counsel, Carlos J. García, another charter member of TELACU, headed the list of highly qualified managers. Among the more experienced of the other ten or so executives was Magdalena Aparicio. Like most other corporations, TELACU had a predominantly male board and management. And as in many other corporations, women comprised the majority of TELACU's personnel because clerical positions made up most of the jobs directly with the CDC.[5] Although TELACU had had female representation on the board from its inception, Maggie Aparicio's presence in management led the CDC to become more conscious of the value of women to the organization and the community. Moreover, her experience and leadership proved critical to TELACU's renewed drive into business.

Magdalena Aparicio, Business Executive

Aparicio was easily the most powerful woman in TELACU as Torres's era gave way to Lizarraga's. Prior to joining TELACU in

1971 Aparicio had spent seventeen years in banking. According to the *Belvedere Citizen*, she had "gained a knowledge of business economics by working her way up through a banking system that was not always encouraging to women." She started out in personnel, where she eventually trained staff for various banking positions; from there she climbed rung by rung "to supervisor of credit and collection, operations officer and loan interviewer, and assistant manager of a bank branch." At TELACU Aparicio became a business finance specialist; in that capacity she assisted minority business people in starting or expanding enterprises. With Aparicio's technical expertise TELACU put together about $5 million in loan packages for this purpose. Her success in this endeavor led to her promotion to director of TELACU's Business Development and Assistance Division. In that capacity, she supervised six people who provided technical assistance, loan packages, and contract procurement services to entrepreneurs. By the end of 1974, Aparicio's business division had "surpassed its projected goals" significantly.[6]

A Master Plan to End a Colonial Economy

The success of Aparicio's division encouraged Lizarraga and his experienced team to set a more expansive economic agenda in 1975. They incorporated that agenda into TELACU's master plan for financial, business, real estate, and overall economic development. Overall community economic development could only proceed if financing became available, and TELACU proposed establishing financial institutions that could meet the need. This required complex institutions because East LA lacked financing of all sorts. Entrepreneurs needed seed capital to start businesses, equity capital to expand them, and long-term loans for construction. Consumers needed loans. In addition to financial services, business people required administrative, technical, and professional assistance.[7] Because Aparicio's division already successfully provided some of these services, TELACU devised an even more ambitious plan to fill the overwhelming economic needs of the community.

Surprisingly, radical colonial theory underlay this capitalist master plan. Lizarraga and his planners reasoned that East LA, like a

The Master Plan and TELACU Industrial Park   111

colony, had experienced "a net outflow of capital, or disinvestment." Traditional savings-and-loan associations, as well as banks, had taken deposits from the inner city and invested them in the suburbs to earn higher returns. The colonia had thus lost money required for its own improvement. Lizarraga and his staff hoped to reverse this pattern, to keep resources in the colony and bring investment from the metropolis. Only thus could economic development and possibly political self-determination be achieved. As if directing the economy of a small dependent country struggling to raise its Gross National Product, TELACU's executives spoke of raising the "Gross Community Product" in hopes of gaining self-sufficiency and independence. Their strategy relied on venture capital, ironically provided largely by government, to establish financial institutions that would lend or invest money to create employment for the residents of East LA. Of course, employment was the benefit the colonia would appreciate most from TELACU's economic planning, and its managers fully expected that benefit to reach ordinary residents.[8] TELACU did not expect to end the colonial status of the community without promoting self-determination of the individual.

Colonial theory thus supplied the underpinnings of TELACU's master plan—the strategy of building financial institutions to free East LA from economic dependency. However, TELACU's managers had to develop the tactics to implement their full strategy. With the new financial institutions in place, management had to develop a practical approach to investing to gain the most benefit from the capital of the new institutions. Since most of TELACU's limited funds initially came from the federal Special Impact Program, management had to "leverage" these funds to achieve as much influence as possible for the CDC. By lending money and buying stock in firms throughout the area, TELACU's managers could gain influence if not control over a good deal of the local economy. For example, they could fund labor-intensive manufacturing concerns to promote employment. However, rather than seeking to capture control of existing businesses, which could be costly and alienating, TELACU's officers preferred to create new enterprises that would increase permanent employment more surely in the long run, if not in the short. The CDC could retain control of these subsidiaries by owning decisive amounts of equity in them and by placing TELACU directors on the boards of the new companies. These varied leveraging tactics might permit the CDC to guide the overall development of East LA.[9] Such tactics might permit TELACU to achieve its goal of economic self-sufficiency for East LA.

Building Financial Institutions

Four institutions would form the key financial components of TELACU's master plan to develop the economy of East LA: The Business Development Office (Aparicio's office renamed), TELACU Investment Company, Community Thrift & Loan, and the Bank of East Los Angeles. TELACU's Economic Development Division would carry out the master plan through TELACU Industries, a for-profit corporation established solely "to hold the stock of its subsidiaries and investments." Additional subsidiaries as needed would be linked by function to the key components.[10] As we can see, TELACU was moving toward banking, one of the most basic capitalist activities. Despite the CDC's cooperative goals, radical theoretical base, and government funding, socialism hardly permeated the corporation. Indeed, the CDC sought to draw East LA into the capitalist system of the United States on an equitable basis.

Of the financial components of TELACU's economic plan, only Aparicio's office existed in January 1975. As we have seen, business loan packaging, contract procurement, and technical assistance were the three main functions of Aparicio's Business Development Office, which received $150,000 annually for administrative costs from the Office of Minority Business Enterprise, an agency of the U.S. Department of Commerce. As part of the master plan, the Business Development Office would collect data on the many local businesses that Aparicio had helped to obtain seed capital. This data could then go to the proposed TELACU Investment Company to help it decide whether a particular business merited an investment. Through such teamwork among its own subsidiaries, TELACU could make investments safely and wisely.[11] As the first financial component of the economic plan actually in operation, Aparicio's office set the path for the new institutions to follow.

David Lizarraga hoped to establish TELACU Investment Company as the second financial component of the master plan. This institution would be a licensed Minority Enterprise Small Business Investment Company, known in community-development circles as a MESBIC. Congress instituted MESBICs to funnel money into the hands of small entrepreneurs in minority areas not well served by private investors. A MESBIC, compared with TELACU's Business Development Office, had the power to provide long-term or permanent capital to established companies; Aparicio's office, on the other hand, could usually only assist entrepreneurs starting businesses, generally with funds from the Small Business Administration. By offering long-term investment the CDC also expected TELACU Investment Company to lure proven businesses to relocate in East Los Angeles. Since a MESBIC's capital initially came entirely in federal dollars, licensees effectively had the privilege of investing public funds in the private sector. In setting up TELACU Investment Company, Lizarraga and his executives again demonstrated technical expertise in bridging the public and private sectors to improve the economy of East LA.[12]

The third and ultimately most important financial component of the master plan was the Community Credit Corporation, especially its subsidiary Community Thrift & Loan. The thrift would handle accounts receivable and provide financing for equipment and inventory for seasoned businesses recommended by the Business Development Office. Unlike the typical savings-and-loan association that specialized in long-term home mortgages, Community Thrift & Loan would provide short-term real estate, business, personal, and collateral loans of no more than $25,000. These medium-sized loans would be at competitive rates for three years, turnover being desirable to reach more needy borrowers, large and small. Unlike federally chartered savings-and-loan companies, TELACU's state-chartered thrift could pay higher interest rates on savings, making this institution more attractive to depositors. The thrift would temporarily house several other operations and agents of the Community

Credit Corporation. Among these were a personal property broker, an insurance agency, an underwriter of credit life insurance, an escrow service, and a mortgage banker.[13] The complexity of these business activities and the ultimate success of Community Thrift & Loan attested to the growing sophistication of Lizarraga and TELACU's other executives.

The CDC's management planned the variously titled East Los Angeles Bank or Community Bank of California as the final financial component of the master plan. TELACU's managers believed they had already invested enough in the Banco de San José (apparently located in San Jose, California) to have a branch opened in East LA. A bank would be beneficial because it could offer the widest range of services, including checking, to a larger group of residents, businesses, and institutions. At that time East LA had only one bank owned by Mexican Americans; tellingly, Pan American Bank alone provided full bilingual services. At other banks potential borrowers in East LA encountered redlining; bankers often refused loans to customers based on their place of residence, rather than on their individual credit rating. TELACU's proposed bank would be a neighborhood operation that would share with residents the risks of location in the inner city. To establish the bank, as well as implement the complete master plan, TELACU required the approval of the Community Services Administration, the successor to the Office of Economic Opportunity. In fact, TELACU launched the first phase of what later became the master plan with OEO's grant for 1974–76; the plan itself appeared as part of TELACU's refunding proposal for 1976–78. Despite the goal of economic self-sufficiency, TELACU was becoming more dependent than ever on federal funding.[14]

Framing a Corporate Image

As we have seen, Maggie Aparicio's excellent performance as director of the Business Development and Assistance Division motivated TELACU to develop other financial institutions. During the key years of 1974 and 1975, 75 percent of loan packages submitted by Aparicio's division, mostly to the Small Business Administration, received approval. Over $7 million in loans went to over a hundred businesses. Through her efforts local businesses also received thirty-two contracts for a total of nearly $3 million. On the whole during the two years, over a thousand businesses secured aid through the Business Development and Assistance Division.[15] This track record left a strong impression on southern California businesses as well as national funding agencies. Ultimately, TELACU won approval from the Community Services Administration for most features of the master plan, in no small part due to the successful performance of Aparicio's division.

The Business Development and Assistance Division not only succeeded in its basic operations, but also succeeded in promoting the pro-business image of TELACU. That impression partially resulted from a long publicity campaign waged by Maggie Aparicio. In the early 1970s Aparicio inaugurated an award for best local business person of the month. With files that included many of the Eastside's business people, of various ethnic groups, her office had enough information regarding their activities to judge their merits well. As a result, local businesses—such as the Pasta House restaurant and Synterra, Inc., a chemical firm—received positive press coverage when their owners won the award. By boosting business people on a monthly basis, Aparicio also promoted TELACU's entrepreneurial image in local newspapers for several years. Of course, this image did not particularly appeal to all elements in the blue-collar community.[16]

By 1975 the fact that several women had received TELACU's monthly business prize inspired Aparicio to sponsor an annual women's achievement award, also in the CDC's name. She herself had won similar awards in August 1974 at a dinner sponsored in her honor at the Montebello Country Club by the West Coast Businesswomen's Association. For her general work assisting women and minorities, she was commended by Congressman Edward Roybal, state Senator Al Song, Assemblyman Richard Alatorre, and Los Angeles Councilman John Ferraro, to name the most notable political dignitaries present. In addition, she received recognition for her activism in the West Coast and Southwest regional conferences of the Businesswomen's Association. Beginning in October of 1975, Aparicio and TELACU honored thirty women of various ethnicities and occupations for general achievements, with emphasis on those who had gone unheralded. Nonetheless, prominent women also received accolades; for example, in 1977 the achievement award went to Romana Bañuelos, owner of Romana's Foods, trustee of the Pan American Bank, and former Treasurer of the United States.[17] Based more on community service than business, the women's achievement award served to enhance the public-spirited image of TELACU, as well as everyone else involved.

Maravilla, Expanding Redevelopment

Although preoccupied with economic planning in 1975, the East Los Angeles Community Union remained influential in local political affairs. Although the CDC had withdrawn from the thinly veiled activism of the East LA incorporation campaign, members of TELACU continued to participate in a variety of organizations that insured the CDC's political influence throughout the area. In 1975 two key community issues reverberated from the Nueva Maravilla project and the East LA incorporation drive—redevelopment and annexation. As both involved the larger principle of self-determination, it should be no surprise that TELACU remained at least marginally involved.

Plans for Nueva Maravilla had been under way for two years when the Los Angeles County Board of Supervisors decided to expand the redevelopment area to the west of TELACU's project. Extending west of Mednick Avenue to Ford Boulevard, between Floral on the north and Third on the south, were 218 deteriorating acres of central East LA targeted for improvement. Adopted on January 30, 1973, the redevelopment plan resulted from over seventy neighborhood and fifteen town hall meetings open to the general public. At these well-attended gatherings, residents voiced their concerns and participated in decisions about the project. Indeed, the Maravilla Neighborhood Development Project had been initiated by residents themselves inspired by TELACU's earlier grass-roots gatherings for the development of Nueva Maravilla.[18] TELACU had taught the residents to organize politically in their own socioeconomic self-interest, and they had learned well.

The Master Plan and TELACU Industrial Park 117

TELACU did not become directly involved in this project as the county's Community Redevelopment Agency stayed in charge. However, key TELACU people joined the Maravilla Project Area Committee, a democratic advisory group established to monitor, as well as work with the redevelopment agency. The committee consisted of 23 members: 14 elected from owners or tenants in the community, 3 appointed by local business people, 3 selected by absentee landowners, and 3 chosen from social service agencies. All 23 also sat on the board of directors of the Community Redevelopment Agency, which meant they had real decision-making power. Significantly, the advisory committee included Roy Escarcega, George Murillo, and Joe Elizondo, the first a manager and the latter two board members of TELACU. Since Elizondo chaired the committee, the CDC clearly exerted considerable influence over the new redevelopment.[19] However, TELACU did so through leveraging—though lacking majority control of the committee, the CDC placed knowledgeable individuals in positions to encourage decisions in keeping with its views. Thus, though preoccupied with its economic master plan, TELACU retained some local political power.

By 1975 the Neighborhood Development Project was moving along. Unlike most urban renewal programs, this project eliminated only those homes that the redevelopment agency could not rehabilitate economically. Restored structures hauled in from other locations replaced the irreparable houses. The agency then offered the restored houses for sale to local residents or owners only; in accordance with rules established by local owners, no one outside the area could purchase property in the redevelopment. Various governments cooperated in rebuilding the area: the California state government donated some move-on housing, the Los Angeles Unified School District agreed to construct a new elementary school, and the state and county agreed to undertake necessary road work. Relocation services appeared for all residents required to move from deteriorated housing; fortunately, the redevelopment agency found it unnecessary to evict anyone or condemn any property. By early 1975 over 141 families had successfully relocated to renovated housing that met their needs. Local youth had also been employed, during the previous summer, repairing structures that needed minimal work. Clearly, the Neighborhood Development Project followed TELACU's successful experiments in resident participation pioneered in the Nueva Maravilla housing project.[20] The CDC's earlier efforts had obviously instigated the renewal of surrounding property, both public and private. By exercising influence over the Neighborhood Development Project, TELACU continued its critical role in the revival of East LA.

East LA's Territorial Losses

Though TELACU had thus successfully influenced the course of redevelopment in East Los Angeles, the CDC's hopes for political self-determination of the area declined after the failure of incorporation. As incorporation proponents had predicted, neighboring Monterey Park in June 1975 began annexation proceedings for East LA's Bella Vista neighborhood, its residents having circulated a petition for that purpose. Initially, Monterey Park did not include East LA College in the Bella Vista boundaries sought from the Local Agency Formation Commission. Annexation quickly drew opposition, including Assemblyman Art Torres and his administrative assistant Gloria Molina, a former TELACU employee and later prominent politician. Interestingly, Art Montoya of the property owners who had helped defeat incorporation joined his former adversaries in opposing annexation. To forestall such piecemeal annexations, Los Angeles Deputy Mayor Manuel Aragón and Councilman Art Snyder suggested East LA simply merge with the city, a suggestion that proved economically unfeasible because of incompatible energy suppliers.[21]

For those wishing to preserve the integrity of East Los Angeles, the political situation only worsened. In August, following Bella Vista's lead, East LA's Montebello Park petitioned for annexation to a neighboring city, in this case naturally Montebello. To make matters even worse, in October the Local Agency Formation Commission encouraged Monterey Park to include East LA College in its Bella Vista annexation and by December had approved the proposal. That virtually guaranteed victory for the city. Despite a brief suit against the commission, in June 1976 residents of Bella Vista voted 394–260 for annexation to Monterey Park. The courts confirmed East LA's loss of the area and the college campus when they ruled in favor of annexation the following month. East Los Angeles nevertheless succeeded in retaining Montebello Park. Although TELACU kept a low profile throughout this struggle, Pilar Hernández, homemaker turned board member, joined the thick of the fight as one of the plaintiffs in the suit.[22] Through her presence the CDC exerted its political influence even though annexation lacked the priority incorporation once received.

Implementation of the Master Plan

Stress on the master plan for economic development had drawn TELACU away from such explicitly political issues as annexation. Though fully aware of the importance of politics, Lizarraga believed that the future of the CDC and East LA hinged more on economics. He sought to implement the master plan immediately to establish a track record of success in time for the Community Services Administration's review of TELACU's refunding proposal for 1976–78. While the Business Development Office had existed for several years, Lizarraga's staff had to build the other financial components of the plan from scratch. The second basic component, TELACU Investment Company, received its license in October 1975. As a subsidiary completely owned by TELACU Industries, the MESBIC was initially capitalized with $500,000 of the 1974–76 grant from the Community Services Administration and a $200,000 loan from Commonwealth Bank, a commercial lender. In 1976 the Small Business Administration invested $700,000 in preferred stock, adding $2,100,000 thereafter. This large infusion of federal funds gave TELACU Investment Company the opportunity to have a significant impact on the economy of East LA; unfortunately, mismanagement of the company would later seriously damage the CDC's reputation.[23]

Interestingly, although founded to bolster East LA's economy, the new company invested in many other parts of the United States. Understandably, TELACU Investment Company put

$160,000 into Atlas Aquarium Engineering Company, a firm that planned to move into East LA in 1977 with the expectation of creating seventy-five new jobs in the area. Since Atlas Aquarium had registered $2.5 million in sales already, it promised to bring dividends to TELACU and employment to East LA. But investments made in distant regions of the country would cause controversy. In Montana TELACU bought stock in the Blackfeet Indian Writing Company, an American Indian manufacturer of markers, pens, and pencils. In New York City TELACU invested in a slick new Latino magazine called *Nuestro*. In the Midwest funds went to the black Illinois Neighborhood Development Corporation, the holding company of South Shore National Bank of Chicago. As the pattern suggests, the investment strategy was to provide promising minority enterprises in other parts of the country with capital that would return long-term dividends to East Los Angeles. Since greater opportunities for profit often existed beyond the Eastside, TELACU believed its portfolio would suffer if it strictly confined investment to the local area. Eventually, critics would berate TELACU for investing any of its funds outside the local area.[24]

Community Thrift & Loan

Unlike TELACU Investment Company, Community Thrift & Loan, basically the third financial component of the master plan, worked as expected. In mid-1975 TELACU began planning the thrift, receiving its state charter in June 1976. The enterprise was capitalized at $1,250,000 through a public offering of stock within the state. TELACU Industries initially purchased 80 percent of the stock with a $750,000 grant from the Community Services Administration and a $250,000 loan from a local commercial bank. Individuals, including TELACU executives, invested most of the remaining $250,000. As such, this enterprise had more individual stockholders than most of TELACU's other companies ever would. To assure complete control of this critical subsidiary, members of TELACU's own board and management filled all the seats of the thrift's board of directors. Through the services of Edward Carpenter and Associates, a banking consultant, TELACU found an experienced Mexican-American executive willing to serve as president of the promising new local institution.[25]

Emil Avellar, Manager

Emil S. Avellar successfully launched Community Thrift & Loan and soon it became one of TELACU's most profitable enterprises. Holding a degree in business administration from Pasadena City College, Avellar had worked in the thrift industry since 1959, first at Beneficial Finance, then at Amfac Thrift and Loan, a national company, where he had become a regional vice president in 1970. In that capacity he supervised nine branches with a total of fifty employees who monthly generated a loan volume of $850,000. In 1968 he had been named "Manager of the Year" in his division by that company. Avellar had the kind of technical qualifications and leadership skills that TELACU sought to promote.[26] Since political and economic development of the community could not occur without leadership, one of TELACU's major achievements was providing training and opportunity for Mexican-American leaders in business and politics.

Community Thrift & Loan enjoyed immediate success because of high local demand for relatively small auto and furniture loans. This success showed that East LA borrowers could be reliable, contrary to the beliefs of an industry that had long redlined the area. The thrift's first office, with only a staff of five, opened in middle-class Monterey Park, just outside of East Los Angeles. The branch could thus draw deposits from nearby middle-class residents and still make loans to local East LA borrowers. This reflected colonial theory in that deposits were taken from the surrounding more affluent metropolis and invested in East Los Angeles, thus reversing the traditional flow of capital. Unlike TELACU Investment Company, the thrift had a better chance of keeping dividends and investments on the Eastside. Within five years branch offices opened in Carlsbad, Costa Mesa, Woodland Hills, and the Simi Valley—all affluent southern California communities whose deposits flowed toward development of East LA. Between 1978 and 1980 deposits more than tripled, and loan volume per month averaged $1.5 million by 1980. In that year Community Thrift & Loan posted "the second highest earnings in the industry."[27] The success of the thrift made the last financial component of the economic plan, a full-service bank, unnecessary, and the latter never appeared.

Urban Planning and Other Activities

As TELACU set up the financial institutions of its master plan in 1975, the Economic Development Division successfully operated other subsidiaries. For example, the former food stamp company founded in October 1971 expanded its operations and changed its name to TELACU Currency Exchange (partly to avoid the stigma attached to food stamps). TELACU had originally established the company because recipients had found distribution of food stamps through banks inadequate, especially the long lines and condescending monolingual service. Statistics revealed the success of this company. By the end of 1975 customers had jumped from 76 to 25,000 per month, and offices had sprung up in Montebello, La Puente, El Monte, and Santa Fe Springs, in addition to East LA. During the same year the Currency Exchange had earned over $264,000 in fees from $30 million worth of food-stamp transactions; it had also taken in an additional $23,000 from new check-cashing services. Besides offering a convenient service to residents, the Currency Exchange employed thirty-two people in its offices, all from East LA. By the end of 1975 TELACU Currency Exchange had become the largest company of its type in California and obviously contributed to the local economy.[28]

In January 1976 the Economic Development Division launched the Eastland Leasing Company to take advantage of the vehicle needs of TELACU and its subsidiaries. Rather than TELACU purchasing or leasing cars from an outside dealer, the new subsidiary acquired them directly from manufacturers and financed the leases of the other TELACU companies. By placing the new company in the role of middleman, TELACU kept the profits generated by the needs of its own affiliates. Eastland Leasing began with $30,000 from a local commercial bank and would remain an in-house operation until large enough to compete for outside business. The possibilities were good since TELACU's other companies could refer customers to Eastland through daily business contacts. While auto leasing had potential as a profit-making venture, Eastland remained marginal to the overall economic development plans of the CDC. Rather, in keeping with TELACU's philosophy, Eastland Leasing exemplified the entrepreneurial attitude of taking advantage of the opportunities presented by circumstances. In 1976 other ventures spun off from the key components of the economic plan; for example, the minor firms TELACU Ven Cap and First Southwest Capital derived from TELACU Investment Company.[29]

A company not directly part of the master plan, yet intimately involved with it, Community Planning and Development Corporation evolved into a highly creative urban planning think tank. CPDC incorporated in 1973 and by 1976 had received $400,000 from the Community Services Administration. Initially, CPDC purchased repossessed houses from the Department of Housing and Urban Development for renovation and removal to sites such as those of the Maravilla Neighborhood Development Project. When HUD withdrew from this activity, however, CPDC lost $250,000 in attempting to continue the purchases on its own. This disaster discouraged CPDC's further direct involvement in construction. Although CPDC, with Majestic Realty, continued construction on a Community Thrift & Loan building, emphasis shifted to urban planning.[30]

CPDC's urban planning division emerged as a consultant on designing and implementing development projects with community participation. As such, the division grew directly from TELACU's involvement in Nueva Maravilla. From 1974 through 1979, CPDC undertook a number of major studies for local governments that significantly affected East Los Angeles because of the empirical data provided, data that helped anchor future development in the reality of local residents. Among the studies undertaken were a housing study, the already-mentioned Zócalo project, a transit needs study, and most importantly "The Unincorporated East Los Angeles Environmental Assessment Program." To carry out these plans TELACU assembled a staff of technocrats—engineers, urban planners, and architects led by Dr. Xavier Mendoza—professionals who would repeatedly win awards for their designs and surveys.[31] CPDC's activities significantly contributed to the real estate focus of TELACU's thinking about the economy.

CPDC's plans led to some real changes in East LA. The transit needs study, for example, empirically demonstrated that residents of East LA depended on public transportation more than did other county residents. In the LA area this meant dependency on a slow and inefficient bus system, curiously named the Southern California Rapid Transit District. Especially vulnerable were senior citizens. In addition to encouraging more bus routes, the study allowed TELACU to establish a nonprofit dial-a-ride service for seniors in the local area. Though the state financed the study, the county funded the service finally initiated and operated by TELACU.[32] Because the county, East LA's only local government, found CPDC's work impressive, the board of supervisors funded several studies and implemented all of them in one form or another.

For example, the housing study and the Zócalo project gave CPDC the credibility necessary to win the county's contract for the major "Unincorporated East Los Angeles Environmental Assessment Program." In 1973 the Southern California Association of Governments awarded $95,000 to CPDC to survey East LA residents regarding their housing preferences. Interestingly, in the study completed in July 1974, most of those contacted expressed a positive attitude toward East LA and a desire to remain in the area if they could find desirable housing. Despite its poverty, the area's culture appealed to the residents. In September 1974 the National Endowment for the Arts awarded CPDC nearly $50,000 to study the possibilities of a renewed central business district for East LA, a district CPDC named after Mexico City's great plaza. The award-winning Zócalo study led to over $100,000 for further research on ways to implement the plan. These successes brought CPDC to the attention of the county's Regional Planning Commission and to a collaborative effort in assessing the overall socioeconomic standing of East LA.[33]

In October 1975 the Regional Planning Commission and CPDC began "The Unincorporated East Los Angeles Environmental Program." Over the next few years four volumes of data on various facets of life in the area were produced. These volumes quantified and charted the area's demographics, its traffic flow, its industrial base, its commercial potential, its residential zones, and more in the most comprehensive land use study of the area ever undertaken. Moreover, CPDC assured community participation through block and town hall meetings, in the tradition of the Nueva Maravilla project. When the final report came out, it received widespread praise in the community although incorporation opponent Art Montoya of the *Eastside Sun* criticized the assessment as an omen of impending urban renewal.[34]

The East LA assessment had a definite impact because the county of Los Angeles considered the study's findings when authorizing later development in the area. Since CPDC completed the last three volumes without the Regional Planning Commission, TELACU's ideas greatly affected future development. Through CPDC, TELACU exercised influence normally reserved for community redevelopment agencies. Since East LA lacked the municipal government to establish such an agency, the county had designated CPDC for the job. TELACU had acquired significant influence because redevelopment agencies often amount to "economic government" in that they can direct entire local economies. The power delegated to CPDC was only for planning, rather than funding or actual development, but TELACU could readily position itself to bid for the latter powers.[35] Despite its current emphasis on business, TELACU, through CPDC and other subsidiaries, continued to use government to promote economic development.

TELACU also used CPDC in the private sector to influence economic development by leveraging the subsidiary's planning skills and technical know-how. Through its contacts with local businesses, TELACU encouraged and assisted the formation of local development corporations for business associations on the Eastside. Local businesses themselves then undertook revitalization projects with plans drawn up in consultation with CPDC and its successor, the Community Research Group. Out of the Zócalo project and the East LA assessment, concluded in late 1977, grew one very important local development corporation. Comprised of the merchants on East LA's major commercial strip, this group together with TELACU began the Whittier Boulevard Commercial Revitalization Project in 1978. As a result, by the late eighties after years of delay, East LA's major thoroughfare was widened and improved with attractive new facades. The life of the shopping area revived and the entire community got a facelift. The North Broadway Commercial Revitalization Project in Lincoln Heights, begun at the same time and in the same manner, had similar success.[36] Given the importance of retail sales, these projects did much to improve the economy as well as the landscape of the Eastside.

Curiously, after David Lizarraga assumed the leadership of TELACU in 1974, he deemphasized the Social Services Division and increasingly integrated its activities with projects in other parts of the CDC. Of the original social service groups, TELACU Senior Citizens remained autonomous under Glenn O'Loane, having established a food cooperative for its members. However, the old job-training activities of the Social Services Division were subsumed under new programs, funded by the federal Comprehensive Employment and Training Act (CETA) of 1973, that operated throughout the CDC. (From 1968 through 1975, more than 3,500 people received jobs through the various programs of the Social Services Division.) Under CETA TELACU contracted with the city and county of Los Angeles to employ and train individuals in regular jobs in the various offices of the CDC. Plans for a health center, the major new proposal in social services, remained on the back burner until the late 1970s. Social services generally received support through specific grants from foundations or government with very little coming from the Special Impact Program, the basic CDC funding source, or profits from TELACU's businesses.[37] Lizarraga preferred this arrangement since he hoped to reinvest as much money as possible in areas that would provide a profit. Social services generally did not. Lizarraga and TELACU operated in the belief that economic development would do more for the community than any project traditionally considered charity.

Nevertheless, with TELACU's reemphasis on economics in mind, the Social Services Division undertook several new creative activities. One new program, part of the California Employment

Development Project sponsored by CETA, involved renovation and beautification activities. In 1975 Roy Escarcega, director of the Social Services Division, contracted with the state to have teenagers from eighteen high schools on the Greater Eastside paint murals, generally on Chicano themes, at locations frequently covered with graffiti. As part of the program, youths also converted an old jail in Lincoln Heights into a gymnasium for their own use. In economic terms the youth and the community benefited from the employment and renovation; moreover, in cultural terms they obviously gained from the product. Carried out in conjunction with GOEZ, an art studio affiliated with TELACU, the program's themes demonstrated the CDC's interest in the imagery of self-determination.[38] The program encouraged the youths to display their heritage in public places, allowing Mexican Americans to recover that space for their culture. That youth carried out these activities encouraged future economic self-sufficiency and cultural self-determination for the Mexican-American community.

A Landmark Industrial Park

In 1975 and 1976 while TELACU set up financial institutions under its master plan for economic development, David Lizarraga also sought the industrial and commercial opportunities that would most profit the CDC and the community. TELACU's small manufacturing companies having failed in the past, Lizarraga sought more sizable and stable undertakings. With the vision of a community developer, he saw the perfect opportunity hidden in a local economic disaster. In early 1975 B. F. Goodrich was closing its local tire manufacturing plant, part of a pattern that ultimately led to the demise of southern California's automobile industry. Approximately 2,000 jobs would disappear when the plant finally closed its doors in the summer of 1976. Because of TELACU's connections with the United Auto Workers, Lizarraga clearly understood the critical situation. In August 1975 he wrote to Congressman Edward Roybal to inquire about the availability of federal funds to help TELACU purchase and develop the forty-acre site in an effort to miti-

5. TELACU Industrial Park. A later addition to the Eastside complex revealing Spanish Colonial architectural influence. Photograph by author, 1997.

The Master Plan and TELACU Industrial Park 129

gate the loss of the tire plant.[39] Obviously, TELACU's reemphasis on business did not preclude the CDC from using its connections in government and labor.

On the Goodrich site Lizarraga and the CDC envisioned TELACU Industrial Park, a complex that would lease office and industrial space to light manufacturing companies, warehouses, and similar operations. Lizarraga obviously expected to attract tenants to the park and jobs to the local area. While these jobs would not easily replace the high-paying positions lost at Goodrich, employment opportunities would reappear. The asking price was unofficially $8 million—a price, as bidding later revealed, much higher than the market value of about $4 million. As justice would have it, the Ford Foundation, a philanthropic organization established by the auto industry, became the lead lender for the purchase. Negotiating from February until the closing on August 31, 1977, TELACU secured a $5 million loan from Ford and Crocker National Bank to purchase the site at a price substantially below that originally asked, but also substantially above three other bids by private developers.[40] The lenders apparently believed TELACU's project would best serve the community. Having secured financing for the purchase, Lizarraga and the CDC still needed funds to cover demolition of the old plant and the construction of new buildings.

Political and government contacts paid off when TELACU assembled the financing for demolition and construction. Shortly after TELACU's purchase of the tire plant, the Economic Development Administration granted $3.7 million for demolition of the old buildings and for site improvement. The Community Services Administration granted $1.2 million in working capital for construction. With federal funds committed, Lloyds Bank and a local commercial lender offered up to $18 million of additional funds to build on the site. Financing went so well that by July 1978 TELACU repaid $993,000 of the land loan with additional funds received in grants. The resulting equity in the park strengthened TELACU's overall financial position.[41] TELACU Industrial Park was indeed shaping up as the CDC's most successful enterprise.

In August of 1978, only one year after TELACU acquired the Goodrich property, the first tenant moved into the industrial park.

That tenant was Aaron Brothers, a retailer of art supplies and a subsidiary of the Chromallay Company. Aaron Brothers moved into a 179,000-square-foot building and immediately issued a hiring call in cooperation with TELACU's Social Services Division. Aaron Brothers and subsequent tenants would eventually fill 1,000,000 square feet of industrial space and 100,000 square feet of office space, the total construction costing nearly $25 million. TELACU leased its new buildings almost as quickly as it put them up. In subsequent years other major tenants followed Aaron Brothers—Stationers Corporation, Winkler-Flexible Corporation, and the Federated Group—all of whom required more space than the initial tenant. TELACU also constructed multitenant buildings for smaller companies requiring less room. TELACU's own subsidiaries, such as Aquapet Inc., occupied some of these smaller units along with affiliates, such as GOEZ Studios. Eventually, over fifty businesses employing over two thousand people settled in the park.[42] To a good extent, TELACU Industrial Park replaced the old Goodrich plant in the local economy.

Imagery and Cultural Preservation

Nevertheless, the figures on space and employment did not measure the full impact of the industrial park. The new complex also gave the Eastside a landscape designed to instill greater pride in the community, for TELACU had envisioned the park as a monument to the Hispanic heritage. The architecture, an updated, utilitarian imitation of Spanish Colonial Revival, hardly merited critical acclaim. Given the anticolonial ideology on which TELACU rested, Spanish Colonial Revival did not carry the appropriate symbolism. Just the same, the buildings' off-white stucco walls and red tile roofs did somewhat reflect the identity of the local population. The mission-inspired architecture, easily built in California, was commonly recognized as Hispanic—if not distinctively Mexican. Furthermore, the wrought-iron gates and manicured lawns of the park demonstrated TELACU's concern that its corporate image be one of Hispanic efficiency. Interestingly, the crowning edifice of the park, TELACU Resource Center, would incorporate a more contemporary style. Scheduled for completion in 1983, this office building would display *The Pride of Our Heritage*, the three-story mural depicting Mexican-American history. As the headquarters of the CDC, this building would become a landmark of the community.[43]

TELACU's interest in preserving and promoting the heritage of Mexican Americans found expression in entertainment programs as well as in architecture and murals. One of the most popular of these programs, "Domingos Alegres," consisted of a live series of performances presented in East LA's Belvedere Park in conjunction with the Los Angeles County Parks and Recreation Department. Beginning in April 1976 twenty variety shows per year featuring mariachis, *ballet folklórico*, magicians, and comedians—including both local and international talent—were presented free for the community. Crowds averaged ten thousand per event and filled the small amphitheater to capacity. The performances achieved such success that eventually TELACU formed the Inter-American Entertainment Company to expand such programming into radio, television, and film.[44] As part of the southern California economy, East LA could tap into the entertainment industry.

Overextension

In 1977 David Lizarraga and TELACU were still implementing their master plan for economic development drawn up in 1975. However, the Community Services Administration requested, as part of the refunding proposal for 1978–80, a new five-year overall development plan for the CDC, running to the fall of 1983.[45] The new plan, drawn up in the midst of rapid expansion, would propose more projects, but in a less coherent fashion than in the master plan of 1975. As plans for the future overlapped, chaos seemed to engulf the CDC and would threaten its survival in the early eighties.

Repeated Restructuring

The 1977 plan called for TELACU to reorganize its structure even more along the lines of a business corporation. TELACU Industries Division moved up the organization chart to replace the old Economic Development Division in a change designed to eliminate an unnecessary administrative layer. The former Social Services Division was renamed the Urban Development Division, a change in nomenclature that further deemphasized TELACU's social service dimension. The new plan created the Community Development Division, a unit primarily including departments involved in planning and development; the new division grew out of the old CPDC, whose functions scattered among a number of new departments and subsidiaries. The Communications Division became a department directly attached to TELACU's administrative office because the former's limited functions did not warrant division status. The Finance Division, with TELACU's controller, also shifted to central administration. Although TELACU's rapid expansion, especially in economic development, necessitated periodic restructuring, the frequency with which these confusing changes occurred suggested an underlying instability that would later become evident.[46]

The most important organizational change under TELACU Industries Division was the creation of TELACU Development Corporation from the old CPDC. Significantly, the new corporation would develop and manage real estate. In partnership with Majestic Realty, another local firm, TELACU Development would complete the construction of Community Thrift & Loan's first building in Monterey Park. Especially designed to manage the industrial park, the new corporation would collect a fee based on rentals, eventually a lucrative business. In addition TELACU Development would work with Majestic Realty to build the Eastland Center in Commerce. With a 50 percent interest in the center, TELACU Development hoped to build a four-hundred-room hotel, a ten-story office building, and a ten-thousand-square-foot convention center.[47] Though the Eastland Center later proved impractical, it demonstrated the potential impact of TELACU's new subsidiary on the local economy.

The new Community Development Division engaged in many of the same operations as TELACU Development Corporation, but the latter remained independent. Its management of the industrial park made TELACU Development too large to be subsumed under the new division. The Community Development Division included Maggie Aparicio's old business development office and two new subdivisions derived from the old CPDC: the for-profit Community Research Group and the nonprofit Urban Planning and Research Department. Besides the subdivisions' differences with regard to profits, the former could undertake projects beyond TELACU's special impact area while the latter could not. Otherwise, the subdivisions engaged in similar activities.[48] All of these complex units allowed the local economy access to the expertise of highly trained professionals, professionals who prior to TELACU's existence had rarely found opportunities to invest their technical skills in East Los Angeles.

The Community Research Group, TELACU's new for-profit think tank, initially continued some of CPDC's projects. Among these were the transit study and an assessment of East LA's health needs, both funded by government agencies and thus profitable for CRG. The Eastside especially benefited from the health study because it subsequently led the Department of Health, Education, and Welfare to designate the community a "health manpower shortage area." This designation would allow funding for the TELACU Family Health Center in Highland Park, a project that began to revive TELACU's reputation for social service. CRG would eventually impact areas far beyond the Eastside, a future predicted by its promotion of community development through seminars sponsored by various government agencies. Preparation of a community development manual for nationwide distribution also predicted that the innovative Community Research Group would spread its technical expertise well beyond the local economy.[49]

Real Estate Reemphasized

The new, highly technical Community Development Division included the Urban Planning and Research Department as well as the Community Research Group. The department continued the old CPDC's North Broadway and Whittier Boulevard renewal programs. In addition, this department in conjunction with CRG produced "A Framework for Greater East Los Angeles Industrial Development," a study of the economic possibilities of unincorporated

East LA and the parts of Los Angeles, Commerce, Montebello, and Monterey Park within TELACU's special impact area. The study thus necessitated the cooperation of a committee of local political leaders under the chairmanship of David Lizarraga. Funded by the Economic Development Administration, data collection and planning were carried out with the assistance of UCLA's Graduate School of Management and the county's Department of Regional Planning, in an effort obviously requiring much coordination. Among its conclusions, the study stressed that the area lacked vacant land for firms hoping to open or expand and consequently recommended a land banking system for Greater East Los Angeles. Possibly under TELACU's direction, the system would permit purchase and resale of parcels of land for the collective economic benefit of the area.[50]

The 1977 plan restructured TELACU to reflect its ever increasing interest in real estate. As we have seen, the activities of the old Community Planning and Development Corporation had diversified and expanded to such an extent that several units appeared to replace it. The major new entity was the Community Development Division, primarily concerned with real estate. The CDC's heightened interest in this field of business naturally grew with the construction of TELACU Industrial Park.[51] Since the major financial institutions designed under the master plan of 1975 now existed, new ventures in this direction slowed. Moreover, despite restructuring for a more aggressive advance into real estate, movement in this field would also slow by 1981.

In the short term according to the 1977 plan, Lizarraga and his executives chiefly sought to strengthen Community Thrift & Loan and TELACU Industrial Park, the most successful endeavors to date. In the long term through 1983, TELACU's managers envisioned more promising projects involving land. Most ambitious among these was the already mentioned Eastland Center planned for Commerce. But TELACU also hoped to acquire several blocks on Atlantic Boulevard, left vacant by closed auto dealerships, for development of an entertainment complex including restaurants and theaters. Another long-term possibility for development as a regional shopping center was the architecturally splendid Uniroyal tire plant, which had closed shortly after the Goodrich plant. TELACU saw similar possibilities for Union Station in downtown Los Angeles, a vestige of the railroad era.[52] However, of the long-term possibilities listed in the 1977 plan sent to the Community Services Administration, only expansion of the industrial park and the Family Health Center finally came about. The 1977 plan lacked the practicality of the earlier master plan. The general failure of the 1977 plan and a further reorganization of TELACU in 1981 indicated that its managers had overextended themselves.

A Historic Landmark to Recovery and Integration

David Lizarraga's appointment as executive director of TELACU began the mature phase of the CDC's growth. The political activism of the organization temporarily declined with the defeat of incorporation in November 1974 and the end of the local Chicano movement thereafter. Under Lizarraga TELACU's drive for the self-determination of East Los Angeles inclined toward the economic, rather than the political, as we have seen. Implementation of TELACU's master plan for economic development of 1975 signaled the renewed emphasis. The financial institutions established under the plan, especially Community Thrift & Loan, offered East LA more than a vision of self-determination; they actually reversed the flow of at least some resources from the metropolis to the community. The dynamic TELACU Industrial Park reinforced the eroding economic base of the Eastside, showing the way to recovery. In 1977 Lizarraga described the Eastside as an "underdeveloped nation," suggesting that the colonial analogy still underlay TELACU's efforts. For despite some progress, the area and the CDC remained dependent on the larger society.[53] After all, TELACU's dependence had led to the ill-conceived plan generated in 1977 at the request of the Community Services Administration.

Under David Lizarraga the East Los Angeles Community Union had aggressively followed a business orientation. Finance companies, investment firms, and real estate ventures were the stuff of capitalism. But in accommodating the system, TELACU had also grasped its tools. By acquiring and using this technical knowledge, the community development corporation was forcing the economic system to open itself to Mexican Americans and integrate them. The CDC had, nevertheless, retained its underlying philosophy—it remained committed to self-determination for the Eastside, its people, and their culture. Although TELACU had become a complex business organization, it remained a cooperative institution, dedicated to the social recovery of the community. Despite the inappropriate colonial architecture, the rising structures of TELACU Industrial Park served as a landmark to the historic recovery of Mexican Americans.

FIVE

Regional, National, and International Networks

Recovering Latino Communities

Despite revitalization plans, Whittier Boulevard, the central commercial strip of East Los Angeles, remained run-down in 1977. Although the boulevard continued to be popular among local residents, its stores, restaurants, and other small businesses barred their doors and windows in the evening, a visual reminder of the violence at the beginning of the decade. Despite the riots of 1970 and the electoral revolt of 1974, the colonia remained politically and economically subordinate to the surrounding metropolis. On the other hand, East LA had made some visible progress toward independence by 1977, especially in Maravilla. And as we have seen, the East Los Angeles Community Union planned more visible improvements—TELACU Industrial Park in particular.[1]

Although TELACU provided multifaceted services for the community, planning stood out among these. The community development corporation had perforce taken on urban planning and many of the other functions of municipal government because East LA had failed to become a city. In spite of TELACU's renewed business orientation under David Lizarraga, the CDC exercised so many municipal functions that it sometimes seemed a government agency itself. However, lacking the taxing power of municipal government, TELACU had built its strength on grants from private and especially from public sources. This activity had made the institution's staff expert at writing proposals and at planning in general. Eventually, this expertise became the forte of the Community Research Group (CRG), an arm of TELACU that would design plans having an impact far beyond East Los Angeles.[2]

As we have seen, CRG was a successor to the planning division of the old Community Planning and Development Corporation, founded in 1973 and reorganized in 1977. As a result of this reorganization, CRG became TELACU's for-profit think tank, shedding direct responsibilities for development. In this capacity the Community Research Group became the subsidiary that generated some of the most creative ideas for the entire conglomerate. In doing so, CRG led TELACU to see the Eastside more clearly in regional, national, and even international contexts. In this expanded vision, the colonialism that affected the Eastside appeared more clearly as part of an international phenomenon that affected Latinos almost everywhere. This vision led TELACU to begin an ambitious program to spread its ideas regarding economic development well beyond its immediate community. The major vehicle for this program would be the CRG's Hispanic American Coalition for Economic Revitalization (HACER), one of the most visionary endeavors ever undertaken by the community development corporation.[3]

However, the broadening of TELACU's vision resulted from changes in Washington, D.C. The inauguration of President Jimmy Carter began a heady period for the East Los Angeles Community Union. From 1977 to 1981 the possibilities of community development corporations seemed limitless and TELACU's evolution seemed to support that impression. As we have seen, TELACU was stabilizing its new financial institutions and laying the foundations for its industrial park when it precipitously launched a new plan in 1977. Lizarraga and his staff took this step partly because they believed proposals for increased funding had a greater chance of success under the new Democratic adminstration. Although the new plan created confusion and controversy by overextending TELACU, the plan's most innovative offspring—CRG and HACER—illustrated the intriguing possibilities of a regional or national Mexican-American CDC network.[4] The dream of a network of self-sufficient Mexican-American, or even Latino, communities guided by institutions like TELACU seemed possible. With initial federal funding and strong mutual support, these institutions could inspire the self-determination of their communities and gradually guide them to socioeconomic recovery and integration into the nation on a equitable basis.

Influence in the Nation's Capital

TELACU's most important connection in the Democratic administration would be none other than Esteban Torres, the CDC's first executive director and a continuing member of its board of directors. After the defeat of his congressional campaign and of East LA incorporation in 1974, Torres had returned to Washington to serve as assistant director of the International Affairs Department of the United Auto Workers.[5] Continuing in that position for the next two years, he became involved through labor in the Carter campaign for president in 1976. During these two years, he remained in close touch with TELACU and East LA since he realized that a local base would be important to his own political ambitions. Finally, with Carter's victory in November 1976, Torres, TELACU, and East LA looked to gain substantially from the new administration.

President Carter's Appointments

With Carter's election Mexican Americans hoped to increase their numbers in appointive positions since the Democratic candidate had, as usual, received the overwhelming vote of the Spanish-speaking. Among those seeking appointment, Esteban Torres hoped to become assistant secretary of state for inter-American affairs. Given his many years of experience in Latin America with the UAW, he had impressive qualifications. Over two months Cyrus Vance, in charge of foreign affairs appointments for the Carter-Mondale transition team, received strong letters of support for Torres's candidacy from a distinguished array of Los Angeles's Spanish-surnamed leaders. Among these were Assemblymen Joseph B. Montoya and Art Torres, state Senator Alex P. García, Congressman Edward R. Roybal, and Catholic Auxiliary Bishop Juan Arzube. Los Angeles's Mayor Tom Bradley also sent his support.[6]

Despite Torres's impressive letters of recommendation, Terence Todman, a career diplomat, received the post. This choice severely disappointed, not only Torres's Los Angeles supporters, but others as well. Sociologist Leonard Birns, director of the Council of Inter-American Affairs, considered the failure to appoint Torres a blow to the cause of human rights in Latin America. The council, a think tank of prominent scholars, congressmen, and former policymakers, had officially supported Torres's nomination. In an interview with *El sol de México*, Birns argued that career diplomats had opposed Torres because as an outsider he might drastically alter earlier policies. In Birns's opinion these policies had allowed repressive dictatorships to remain in power over the previous eight years. For Mexican Americans even more troubling was Birns's claim that "reliable sources within the State Department affirmed that part of the campaign to eliminate Torres from the running involved convincing . . . [the Department] that Latin American countries would not negotiate with a descendant of Hispanic Americans, considering him socially inferior."[7] While some Latin Americans had such biases, Torres's supporters complained that he should have gotten the opportunity to refute the stereotype by showing competence on the job.

Carter's initial failure to appoint Torres or a significant number of other Mexican Americans to his administration led to both public and private criticism from important Spanish-speaking Democrats. Ed Roybal, California's lone Mexican-American congressman, rebuked the president concerning this matter only a week after the failure to appoint Torres. In the *Eastside Journal* Roybal reminded the administration of the traditional Mexican-American complaint that the Democratic party only acknowledged the barrios at election time. In a private letter to Andrew Young of the transition team, David Lizarraga, whose political credentials were improving, expressed the same general sentiments.[8] Gradually, the Carter administration succumbed to the pressure and made more Mexican-American appointments as openings occurred.

Lou Moret, Gloria Molina, Esteban Torres—Appointees

When the administration finally mended its ways, TELACU gained substantial influence in Washington. After extensive lobbying by David Lizarraga and George Pla of TELACU, Lou Moret, an administrative assistant to Assemblyman Richard Alatorre, was named deputy director of the Office of Minority Business Enterprise in the summer of 1977. According to *TELACU Today*, the company newsletter, the CDC had achieved a major coup in placing one of its "closest friends" in such a pivotal position. The following November, former TELACU employee Gloria Molina, aide to Assemblyman Art Torres since 1974, became assistant director of personnel at the White House itself. As a committee member of Voter Organization through Education (VOTE), TELACU's political arm during the 1976 presidential campaign, Molina had the connections to serve the community well in her new post. But in September President Carter had already made the most prestigious appointment, from TELACU's point of view, when he finally tapped Esteban Torres. The president selected Torres to represent the United States in the United Nations Educational, Scientific, and Cultural Organization (UNESCO). Torres thus received one of the highest ranking federal appointments held by a Mexican American. In making the appointment, Carter also raised the position to ambassadorial rank, clearly a concession to his Spanish-speaking political supporters, but also in recognition of Torres's qualifications.[9]

In an editorial for *TELACU Today*, David Lizarraga made an interesting comparison while commenting on the Torres's appointment:

> In many respects UNESCO and TELACU ... share many common goals and objectives. Just as UNESCO represents the underdeveloped nations and third world peoples of the globe, we, too, represent our own underdeveloped community and its third world people in our part of the globe. We've seen what vast resources can be leveraged to help assist underprivileged people of the world through organizations like UNESCO, and that, for us, is a viable model for implementing local action here at home.[10]

Although in this case Lizarraga likened TELACU to an international body, rather than a government, his merging of the peoples of East LA and the Third World once again suggested TELACU's continuing acceptance of the colonial analogy. Since virtually the entire underdeveloped world had experienced colonialism, East LA's underdevelopment resulted from the same historical process, a process that institutions like TELACU and UNESCO hoped to reverse.

Lizarraga extended the comparison of the institutions while describing the goals of UNESCO and the job Torres had just accepted there. UNESCO and TELACU both leveraged resources to funnel them to communities in need. The organizations similarly established training programs to help people help themselves and encouraged peace through programs of intercultural exchange. In general both organizations sought to raise "the educational, economic and social levels of underdeveloped nations and third world people at home and abroad" (the reference to underdevelopment at home again evoked the image of East LA as an internal colony). Finally, both sought the cause of human rights to build a "lasting worldwide community of man."[11] Torres's appointment expanded TELACU's vision globally, and his new position in the Democratic administration would actually permit the CDC to act on that vision.

No sooner had the administration appointed Torres than it called Carlos J. García, a vice president and general counsel for TELACU, to Washington for a briefing on the ramifications of a new Panama Canal treaty. Realizing that Carter had offended Spanish-speaking leaders in the United States during the appointment process, the administration sought to molify them by keeping them informed of policy decisions regarding Latin America. The briefing of about fifty such leaders was carried out by Vice President Walter Mondale and members of the State Department's team of negotiators. Interestingly, García came away from the meeting with the following sentiment: "I am convinced, after listening to the complete history of the canal from the experts, that the treaty is not a giveaway of land. . . ." After hearing a summary of Theodore Roosevelt's machinations in acquiring the Canal Zone, García came to believe the zone had never belonged to the United States.[12] The administration obviously recognized the colonial relationship between the United States and Latin America and even seemed willing to compensate

Panama. To Spanish-speaking leaders such action in the international arena suggested similar possibilities for their communities in the United States.

David Lizarraga to the National Commission on Neighborhoods

Similar action on the domestic front seemed very likely in December 1977 when President Carter named David Lizarraga to the National Commission on Neighborhoods. Lizarraga qualified for the position especially well since he had served a term as chair of the National Congress for Community Economic Development, the major association of community development corporations. The only Mexican American and the only western representative on the commission, Lizarraga had distinct perspectives to offer. The duties of the commission involved examining neighborhoods throughout the nation and making recommendations to Congress and the president by the end of 1978. Lizarraga and the nineteen other members of the commission had to travel throughout the nation to formulate their report. Participation on the commission gave Lizarraga and TELACU a major opportunity to promote CDCs as models for national urban policy; as Lizarraga noted, "The successes we [at TELACU] have had in revitalizing the residential, business and industrial neighborhoods of our community are viable models to use in planning programs for the rest of the country." Another opportunity to impact urban policy occurred in early 1978 when Carter appointed Roy Escarcega, TELACU's vice president of urban development, to the National Commission for Manpower Policy.[13]

Hispanic Economic Revitalization

Increased contacts in Washington and nationwide during the Carter administration made TELACU one of the leading CDCs in the country and easily the major such Mexican-American institution. Indeed, David Lizarraga's participation in the National Commission on Neighborhoods led directly to an important initiative that extended TELACU's influence throughout the Southwest and beyond. While many of the commission's recommendations were

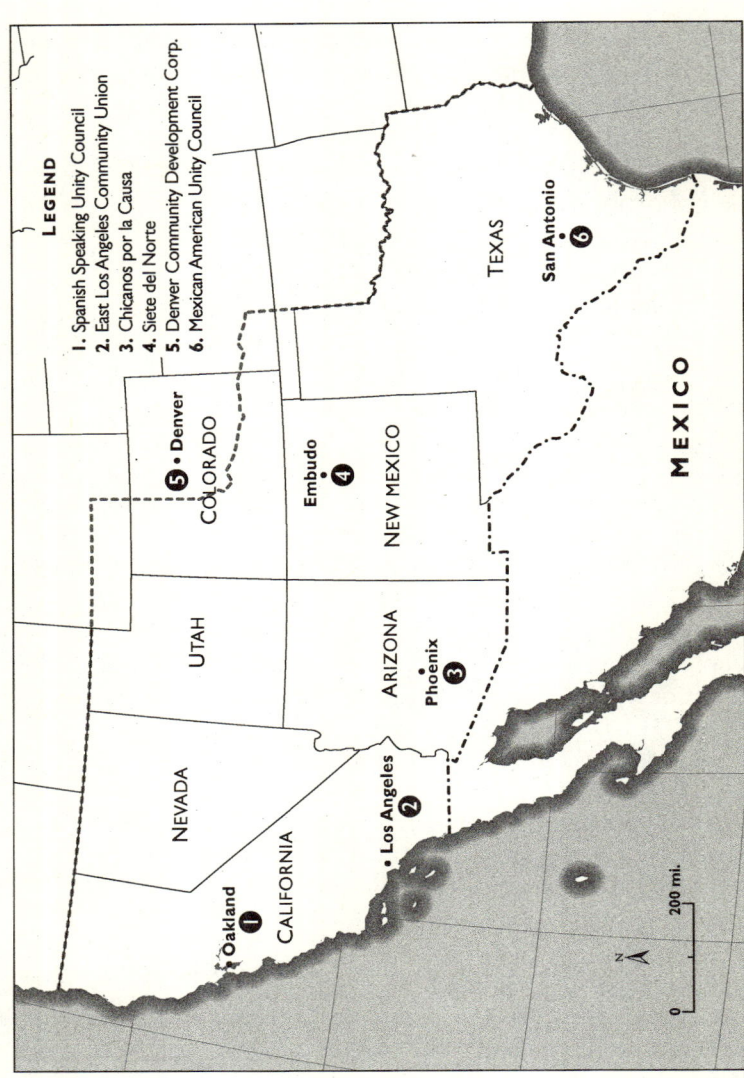

MAP 2. The Chicano Southwest with locations of CDCs joined in the Hispanic American Coalition for Economic Revitalization. Cartography by David Deis.

not enacted or were diluted by Congress, the Economic Development Administration (EDA) received a mandate, flexibility, and resources to try some new solutions to old urban problems. As a result, in 1978 Lizarraga delegated the Community Research Group to draw up a proposal for funding from the EDA for a project that incorporated some of the recommendations of the National Commission on Neighborhoods. Lizarraga's think tank came up with the Hispanic American Coalition for Economic Revitalization (HACER), initially funded for a year beginning May 1979.[14]

An acronym meaning "to accomplish," HACER became a joint effort on the part of the nation's six major Mexican-American community development corporations, most located in the Southwest, the traditional Chicano homeland. In addition to TELACU, these CDCs were: Chicanos por la Causa in Arizona, the Mexican American Unity Council in Texas, Siete del Norte in New Mexico, and the Spanish Speaking Unity Council in northern California. (The sixth organization, the Denver Community Development Corporation, had evolved beyond the traditional Mexican borderlands.) Because of their record of success, these CDCs through HACER would provide technical assistance to other community-based organizations interested in economic development. HACER would supply the latter organizations with some of the services that better banks provided struggling businesses. Although HACER would invest some capital, more importantly it offered the expertise necessary to move new or marginal economic development organizations to stability.[15] In the long run, HACER proponents sought to encourage these organizations to become full-fledged community development corporations. Through HACER, TELACU and its allied CDCs hoped to spread their creed of self-sufficiency throughout the nation, but especially throughout the Southwest, where economic self-sufficiency remained essential to the historic recovery of Mexican Americans.

While TELACU had initiated HACER, it had not of course created the other Mexican-American CDCs in the effort. These had sprouted separately in their own areas; indeed, some predated TELACU, though none could claim as much success. The events that had created TELACU in East LA in the 1960s had also led to the founding of similar organizations in some of the other major colonias in the Southwest. Although these organizations had not initially influenced one another, all learned from CDCs in the black communities. Of course, once funding through the Special Impact Program became more widely available, all came under the Office of Economic Opportunity and its successor the Community Services Administration. In the struggles of the early seventies to insure continued federal funding, all CDCs under the Special Impact Program formed the National Congress for Community Economic Development. This association became a permanent lobbying group that kept its member organizations informed of legislation and other matters impacting on CDC activities. As chairman of this organization in the mid-seventies, Lizarraga established contacts with all CDCs and special ties with the Mexican-American organizations most like TELACU.[16] These contacts formed the network that became HACER.

The Spanish Speaking Unity Council—Northern California

The oldest of the "Mexican-American" community development corporations was the Spanish Speaking Unity Council, founded in 1964. Established in Oakland, California, to serve that city and Alameda County, the council began as a predominantly Mexican-American organization, but following demographic changes in the area, gradually came to serve other minorities as well. Indeed, by the late eighties 39 percent of its constituency would be black, with only 43 percent remaining Hispanic, the last 18 percent consisting of a variety of other ethnic groups. Moreover, the "Hispanics," reflecting the diversity of the Bay Area, would embrace many more Central and South Americans than would be the case in East Los Angeles or other parts of the Southwest.[17] Even at the founding of HACER in 1979, the council's ethnic diversity stood out. Because of this, the council served as a model for organizations in increasingly diverse urban communities, including such areas as South-Central Los Angeles. CDCs had to reflect their specific neighborhoods. The Spanish Speaking Unity Council also served as a model for communication between Latino communities in the United

States, not to mention Latin America. The last would be important in TELACU's later international attempts at economic development.

Although the Oakland CDC did not derive from the labor movement, both the Spanish Speaking Unity Council and TELACU received some of their initial funding from the Ford Foundation. Both organizations also tapped various federal agencies for funds, largely from the War on Poverty. The council began its activities in social service, then increasingly became involved in economic development, a pattern common to other CDCs. By 1976 real estate development had become an important part of the council's overall program. For example, with assistance from the Ford Foundation and the Economic Development Administration, the council constructed the Community Resource Center, a contemporary three-story office building similar in function to the headquarters planned for TELACU Industrial Park. Designed to house a dozen public and private agencies, the Community Resource Center provided a centralized location for the social services required by the residents of Oakland's Fruitvale District. The council attracted the agencies by charging below-market rents for its modern facilities. Furthermore, the attractive new facilities stimulated revitalization of nearby neighborhoods.[18]

As in the case of TELACU, construction for social services became one of the Spanish Speaking Unity Council's key activities. By 1979 the council was building an apartment complex called Posadas de Colores Elderly Housing. Eight stories high with a hundred units, the complex, supported by the Department of Housing and Urban Development, would serve low-income seniors. On the other hand, the council would serve the very young through the Infant Care Center planned for construction in 1981, with funding from the Community Services Administration. Geared to the needs of teenage mothers and their babies, the center would provide parental training and counseling, as well as on-the-job training for a staff drawn from welfare recipients. A subsidiary, Capital Development Group, Inc., also became involved in a variety of real estate ventures, including multifamily housing rehabilitation.[19]

The Spanish Speaking Unity Council had a structure similar to

TELACU's—a nonprofit holding company serving as an umbrella for a variety of for-profit subsidiaries and nonprofit social service agencies, with real estate development serving as a common economic base. The range of the council's social services rivaled that of TELACU, including employment training, alternative education for youth, and health services. In the realm of economic development, the council established the Small Business Clinic to provide technical assistance to local entrepreneurs and the Development Resources Consulting Group to provide similar assistance to private and public organizations.[20] The latter two subsidiaries were clearly equivalent to TELACU's Business Development Office and the Community Research Group. Obviously, the Spanish Speaking Unity Council, like TELACU, had expertise to share through a coalition such as HACER.

The Mexican American Unity Council—Texas

Also older than the East Los Angeles Community Union, the Mexican American Unity Council (MAUC) operated in San Antonio, Texas. Founded in 1967 MAUC, like TELACU, had radical origins, a background the Spanish Speaking Unity Council did not share. MAUC began as a confrontational advocacy group for the Westside of San Antonio; it practiced advocacy along the militant lines of Saul Alinsky's Industrial Areas Foundation (IAF). Indeed, one of MAUC's first directors was Ernesto Cortés, later founder of Communities Organized for Public Service (COPS), also of San Antonio, and the United Neighborhoods Organization (UNO) of Los Angeles, both IAF organizations. (COPS would later lead the effort to enfranchise Mexican Americans in San Antonio and elect Henry Cisneros mayor of the city.) Among the founders of MAUC was Willie Velásquez, one of the original members of La Raza Unida Party and later head of the Southwest Voter Registration Education Project. Juan Patlán, who would direct MAUC for nearly two decades, had also been one of the founders of La Raza Unida. Although Cortés, Velásquez, and Patlán all began their careers in the radical Chicano movement, MAUC like TELACU moved into the mainstream rather early in its existence.[21]

During its first two years MAUC operated "through means

which were available at that time," meaning IAF confrontational tactics. MAUC represented Westside residents in sometimes stormy meetings with government and private agencies, especially regarding educational issues. Despite this political advocacy, MAUC had from its inception sought economic development as the long-term solution to community problems. About mid-1969 the Presbyterian Economic Development Corporation granted MAUC a loan of $100,000 to undertake a housing project on the Westside, a project evidently similar to TELACU's Nueva Maravilla. The following year MAUC committed some of its limited funds to training staff in economic development and then began its first regular business enterprise—a McDonald's franchise. The successful restaurant ranked second in citywide sales, at which point it was sold to a local resident. MAUC thus succeeded in making a profit and more importantly launched a new Mexican-American business. Regarding such experiences, Juan Patlán later commented, "Any investment on the West Side, almost by definition, is highly risky. But if we act in partnership with investors here, we can reduce their risk. That's what our profit-making is all about."[22] Clearly, if MAUC's radical founders had ever advocated socialism, they had never abandoned capitalism.

In 1971 MAUC followed its McDonald's with a string of varied ventures. A building maintenance and janitorial service opened with the help of a minority-business procurement contract from the Small Business Administration. MAUC formed a construction firm and a housing partnership that led to development of single and multifamily units. A second McDonald's was launched. The pace of business increased especially after the Office of Economic Opportunity designated MAUC a federally funded community development corporation in 1972. Once under the Special Impact Program, funds for additional staff, technical training, and advice from consultants rapidly expanded and improved the scope of MAUC's business activities.[23] By this time MAUC and TELACU had become very similar institutions.

Despite its successful business activities, the Mexican American Unity Council, like TELACU, continued to maintain its nonprofit social service agencies. As early as August 1970, MAUC began providing health services to its special impact area, well ahead of similar activities by TELACU. The Northwest Mental Health Program offered a "growth grant" to MAUC for the establishment of a Field Mental Health Program. The program became "a model Mexican American human services delivery system," especially because of the coordination developed with the Bexar County Hospital District and the Community Guidance Center. Also part of this coordinated system was the Child Mental Health Program, initially sponsored in 1971 by a grant from the National Institute for Mental Health. Serving children between three and thirteen years of age, Child Mental Health's Escuelita del Sol became its most notable achievement. This "pre-therapeutic nursery" school for three- to five-year-old children provided "high-risk families" with a comprehensive program to avoid child abuse. Another important social agency founded by MAUC in October 1974 was Casa del Sol Alcoholic Halfway House. Funded by the National Institute on Alcohol Abuse and Alcoholism, Casa del Sol successfully implemented bilingual-bicultural treatment addressing the specific needs of local clients, both individuals and families.[24] Despite their focus on long-term economic development, neither MAUC nor TELACU ignored the immediate social needs of their communities.

Naturally, once MAUC had come under the Special Impact Program, its structure became very similar to that of TELACU and the Spanish Speaking Unity Council—a nonprofit holding company with for-profit subsidiaries and nonprofit social service agencies. Besides this structural similarity, moreover, lay the common emphasis on real estate and landscape. MAUC's early construction of housing would lead this CDC toward the kinds of real estate projects emphasized by TELACU, including an industrial park in the mid-eighties. But, as with TELACU, MAUC acquired real estate and undertook construction with more than utilitarian considerations in mind. Following a holistic approach, both CDCs expected buildings to make cultural statements of value to their communities. For example, the MAUC Center on the Westside at 2300 West Commerce was a renovated Greco-Roman-style public school that had been deteriorating for years. After acquiring the facility, MAUC updated it for its own offices, leaving the lower floors as

6. The MAUC Center. Renovated Greco-Roman-style headquarters of the Mexican American Unity Council in San Antonio, Texas, 1986. Courtesy of the Mexican American Unity Council.

rental space partly occupied by a public library. While the MAUC Center's style did not directly reflect the Mexican heritage of the Westside, the building and its grounds became a model landscape. Both MAUC and TELACU believed that beautiful, well-maintained buildings helped to change the image of entire barrios. Moreover, the impressive center displaying the name of the Mexican American Unity Council marked the organization as a powerful institution belonging to the local community, rather than the larger society. Later buildings entirely constructed by MAUC would more directly reflect Mexican ethnic identity.[25]

Chicanos por la Causa—Arizona

Another key member of the Hispanic American Coalition for Economic Revitalization was Chicanos por la Causa (CPLC), headquartered in Phoenix, Arizona. Founded in 1969 by students from Arizona State University, CPLC like MAUC began as an advocacy group. It received its original funding from the Southwest Council of La Raza (itself supported by the Ford Foundation) and a local Methodist church. In addition to $15,000 in grants from these donors, CPLC received an abandoned church from the Methodists. From this blighted bit of real estate, CPLC created offices and meeting rooms for social services, including outreach.[26] Through this act CPLC began the typical pattern of the community development corporation. To provide social services, the organization found itself revitalizing physical space, an act that almost naturally led to economic and especially real estate development.

As with other CDCs, economic—especially physical—revitalization became the main part of CPLC's agenda quite early. In 1970 the organization began building twenty-two subsidized single-family houses with moneys from the U.S. Department of Housing and Urban Development. A counseling program for homeowners and renters followed. This counseling was naturally directed at low-income Chicano residents of South Phoenix who needed advice regarding purchasing or renting homes, making home improvements, conserving energy, or paying mortgages. As with TELACU and other CDCs, housing showed the way to later, more sophisticated real estate ventures. In 1972 CPLC began construction of an emergency medical clinic in a small town about an hour's drive outside of Phoenix. Constructed with federal funds, the building was clearly a project in health services, but it also suggested that CPLC's future activities lay increasingly in real estate development.[27]

Economic and particularly physical development received a dramatic boost at CPLC in the mid-seventies. By 1972 the Ford Foundation had become the major supporter of the organization, which by then had a staff of twelve full-time employees, evenly divided among housing, health, education, and general community development. But in 1975 CPLC joined TELACU and MAUC under the aegis of the U.S. Community Services Administration. After submitting its application, CPLC received approval of its comprehensive economic development plan as well as official designation as a community development corporation. Since CPLC's special impact area was the entire state of Arizona, the new federally chartered CDC initially acquired greater latitude of operation than even TELACU. Since CPLC's purview included agricultural areas, it could apply for funds covering both rural and urban projects.[28] CPLC's structure of course followed the guidelines set by the Community Services Administration—a nonprofit holding company with for-profit subsidiaries and nonprofit service agencies. Having already functioned in a similar manner, CPLC found the new structure no more burdensome to its operations that had TELACU. Indeed, the new structure would lead to great success.

Pete García, a future president of CPLC, later commented that funding from the Community Services Administration initiated

> a public-private-community partnership. . . . We began to feel that we, as an organization, could become a part of the *solution* to our community's problems. It didn't happen overnight, but you could say that we went from wearing brown berets to dressing in suits and ties.

The changing physical image of the staff reflected the willingness to move from confrontation to participation once the system provided the opportunity. Once government and business recognized their responsibilities to this particular minority community, cooperative problem solving resulted. Even the name of the organization, "Chicanos por la Causa" (Chicanos for the Cause), was later interpreted in mainstream terms by García: "The cause is participation in this country."[29] Though this statement no longer reflected the radical separatist ideals of the 1960s, neither did it acquiesce to permanent dependency, let alone the subordination of the colonial relationship. CPLC, and other CDCs, ultimately sought autonomous participation within the larger economy and society.

As at TELACU and MAUC, the image of the CPLC staff in coats and ties went together with the symbolism of landscaped buildings. In 1979 the organization moved into a new complex, a 7,400-square-foot, three-building facility on Buckeye Road, a major thoroughfare through South Phoenix. According to García, "This gave the group and the community a sense of CPLC's permanence as an enduring neighborhood institution." But the buildings had more than symbolic value for the community; the complex functioned. It made the institution's businesses and social services more accessible to the public. Furthermore, in making the surrounding area more attractive, the landscaped complex had the very real economic effect of raising local land values.[30] Imagery could be profitable as well as socially meaningful.

CPLC's concern with imagery was also evident in a housing rehabilitation program begun in 1979. The city funneled money to the program from a block grant for community development provided by the U.S. Department of Housing and Urban Development. With these funds CPLC renovated houses plagued by hazardous conditions in a five-block area of South Phoenix. The program succeeded so well that another five-block area was subsequently included, with landscaping as a component. The landscaping project involved removing stumps and debris; planting trees, grass, and shrubs; installing driveways; and repairing and painting fences. David Yñiquez, executive vice president of CPLC, reported a positive local response: "When we implemented the landscaping portion of our housing improvement project, it was gratifying to see many of the nearby homeowners start to do their part in upgrading the neighborhood."[31] Like TELACU and MAUC, CPLC realized that skillful landscaping could actually stimulate self-sufficiency, as well as symbolize it. CPLC's housing rehabilitation project inspired homeowners on its periphery to improve their own homes, on their own initiative, once they saw the neighborhood turning around.

While real estate focused CPLC's for-profit activities, economic development took other forms as well. Once the CPLC complex went up, new operations evolved. Critical among these, a federally chartered credit union grew to five hundred members and $750,000 in assets by the mid-eighties. Besides promoting savings, distributing quarterly dividends, and offering loans at reasonable rates, it educated residents about the local economy. The credit union also offered a discount telephone service, an eye-care plan, inexpensive tickets for entertainment, and insurance of various kinds. Another of CPLC's financial operations, the Rural Development Loan Fund, provided revolving credit from federal sources for areas with populations of 25,000 or less. These loans could be used to renovate buildings, or to purchase land, equipment, machinery, inventory, or furnishings. Among the small businesses in Arizona assisted by this program in the late seventies and early eighties were "An electrical wholesaler in Casa Grande, a concrete contractor in Yuma, a pest control business in Lake Havasu, Uncle John's Restaurant in Springerville, [and] an auto parts store in Sunsites. . . ." These loans through the mid-eighties resulted "in hundreds of thousands of square feet of new industrial and commercial space and the creation and retention of hundreds of jobs."[32] Clearly, even through its financial programs, CPLC had an interest in developing real estate, though always with an eye on the employment potential of a particular project.

By the mid-eighties CPLC would achieve state-wide influence. Though headquartered in Phoenix, the institution would come to have fifteen offices around Arizona with a 140 full-time employees. Through its subsidiary TIEMPO, Inc., CPLC would also prepare itself for a much more elaborate expansion in real estate. By the mid-eighties the organization would be a 50-percent partner in developing a shopping center and office complex in downtown Phoenix, called the Mercado. CPLC would undertake the project with financing from a variety of sources, "including a $10-million loan from a consortium of four banks, a $1-million grant from the U.S. Department of Health and Human Services, a $1.3 million grant from the city, plus special tax abatements and land lease arrangements." The ultramodern complex would encourage barrio residents to relocate some of their businesses downtown. In addition, the complex would contain "a Hispanic 'living museum' and cultural center, which . . . [would] feature rotating exhibits of local art and history, theatrical productions and other events."[33] Obviously, in terms of promoting the Mexican-American heritage, CPLC worked as hard as TELACU. Given the similarities with TELACU and MAUC, it should be no surprise that CPLC joined the Hispanic American Coalition for Economic Revitalization in 1979.

Siete del Norte—New Mexico

Of the members of HACER, the most distinct was Siete del Norte, headquartered in Embudo, New Mexico. Incorporated in 1973, later than most of the other Mexican-American CDCs, Siete distinguished itself as the only exclusively rural of these community development corporations. This CDC served "the six northcentral New Mexico counties of Guadalupe, Mora, San Miguel, Santa Fe, Rio Arriba, and Taos." Siete had a typical CDC structure—a nonprofit holding company with a for-profit business branch and a nonprofit social service branch. Philosophically, Siete agreed with the other CDCs in promoting self-determination by fostering, "local ownership and control of resources." Moreover, Siete sought to "preserve and build upon the unique culture, traditions, and physical environment of Northern New Mexico," thus reflecting the concern of CDCs for the preservation of ethnic identity. A significant difference between Siete and the primarily urban CDCs was the natural landscape the rural CDC sought to "preserve and build upon," an example being the 65.5-acre grounds of the former Embudo Presbyterian Hospital purchased in 1983. This parklike facility would come to house Siete's corporate offices, but would primarily function as the Rio Grande Alcoholism Treatment Center, an agency of the CDC exemplifying its strong social service branch.[34] The center's natural setting typified the differences between Siete and the primarily urban CDCs.

Because of its rural surroundings, Siete had a more democratic structure than did the urban CDCs. While TELACU and other

CDC's had boards composed of representatives from other local organizations, low-income residents directly elected the majority of Siete's board of directors. This was possible in rural New Mexico because of the existence of smaller populations in more closely knit communities. As we have seen, in the sixties community action agencies had abandoned mass elections in urban areas because of the low voter turnouts resulting from the anonymity of city life. At Siete, once elected to the board, the twelve local directors forming the majority asked seven professionals to join: four business people and three from other fields. This arrangement assured control by low-income residents even as they acquired necessary technical expertise. The administrative staff remained small, including the president, the vice president, who doubled as controller, and a secretary.[35] In comparison with Siete, TELACU and other CDCs obviously lacked broad-based representation of residents.

Despite its smaller size, between 1973 and 1986 Siete del Norte's activities spread out as much as those of any other CDC. With federal funds, especially from the Community Services Administration, Siete invested nearly $3 million in agricultural cooperatives and other businesses in northern New Mexico. Among these enterprises were Ojo Caliente Craftsmen, a successful sign supplier for the United States Forest Service, and Southwest Cable Corporation. Through the usual federal sources, Siete came up with the start-up capital for Southwest Cable, a television system offering twenty channels, including the Spanish International Network, to over two thousand subscribers in the Española area. Siete maintained 32-percent ownership until the successful venture was sold so that the CDC could reinvest in other businesses.[36] These ventures reflected the cooperative, regional, and cultural characteristics of the New Mexican CDC.

Interestingly, the most important of Siete's subsidiaries was Associated Southwest Investors, a Minority Enterprise Small Business Investment Corporation(MESBIC), similar to the unsuccessful TELACU Investment Company. With authority to operate in Texas, Arizona, Colorado, and California, as well as New Mexico, Associated Southwest nevertheless invested primarily at home, a pattern TELACU Investment Company did not follow. In its six home counties between 1975 and 1985, Associated Southwest invested over $1 million, "resulting in the direct creation of 130 jobs and in the support of 90 additional jobs in other businesses assisted. . . ." Associated Southwest claimed its investment in turn generated $12–15 million in cash flow throughout its home counties. The impact on residents went beyond jobs in that numerous individuals acquired entrepreneurial skills through the operation of successful businesses.[37] Apparently, both the short- and long-term benefits of Associated Southwest Investors remained at home.

In addition to direct investment, Siete supplied grants and loans to nonprofit groups and even small local governments for a variety of "projects such as solar greenhouses, elderly housing, construction of community centers, rural transportation, health clinics, [and] day care services. . . ." In Siete's estimation, the $200,000 thus provided to forty-two projects "leveraged in excess of $3.4 million." Other CDCs obviously shared the leveraging tactic so effectively used by TELACU. Siete also funneled federal funds into low-income housing, into both construction and rehabilitation. Construction and Rehabilitation Enterprises, an independent corporation, was formed with Siete's assistance to carry out much of the housing work that in turn provided training and employment for many low-income youth.[38] As with TELACU and other CDCs, Siete's varied social service projects tended to lead toward real estate development.

Siete had extensive real estate holdings, though of less value than the property of urban CDCs, given the low cost of land in rural areas. On the 65.5 acres of the Embudo property lay the 17,480 square feet of the hospital, the 7,020 of the staff house, the 6,842 of five residences, and the 1,000 of four garages. In Española the CDC owned 1.5 acres of land suitable for industry, including the Siete Building, a prefabricated metal structure of over 32,000 square feet. In the countryside the CDC also held some rather large parcels of land. In San Miguel County, Siete owned the Ribera Ranch, 927.5 acres, of which 160 were irrigated. The facilities included "a ranch house, a commercial size solar greenhouse, an artesian well, and feedlot facilities (mill elevator, scale house, branding house, and corrals)," all used to improve the skills and attitudes of 'high-risk' youth. In addition Siete possessed 18.5 acres of a Luceros property in Rio Arriba County and shares in the 87.6 acres of a Rio del Norte property near Taos, both held for future development.[39] If land ownership symbolized self-determination, Siete had certainly moved toward recovery of the Southwest.

Of course, nowhere else in the Southwest had land remained such a controversial issue as in New Mexico. As in California after the Anglo-American occupation, Hispanos had lost land grants in a variety of legal and illegal ways, but in New Mexico the issue had constantly resurfaced because much of the local population of Mexican descent had remained in place. Northern New Mexico continued to be occupied by the direct descendants of the people who were there centuries before the United States conquered the region. The very name of the CDC, "Siete del Norte," referred to the seven cities of silver that the Spanish had sought in the sixteenth century when they encountered the Pueblo villages. Since that time mestizo New Mexican farmers had eked out a living from the mountainous region, their land base slowly eroding after the U.S. occupation. Repeated outbreaks of violence over this issue had occurred, with that of Reies López Tijerina and the Alianza contributing substantially to the ideology of the Chicano movement that engulfed East Los Angeles in the late 1960s.[40] Nowhere else in the Southwest could activists more cogently argue that internal colonialism continued. Siete del Norte's recovery of land in the heart of the Chicano homeland held great symbolism for Mexican Americans throughout the Southwest.

Promoting Latino Revitalization

In mid-1979 the members of the Hispanic American Coalition for Economic Revitalization met several times to decide on the goals of the new organization. Since HACER had recently received funding from the Economic Development Administration, the members held one key meeting on June 13 at TELACU's headquarters in East Los Angeles. EDA had awarded HACER a contract to provide technical assistance to ten emerging economic development groups anywhere in the nation. The main purpose of the meeting was to exchange information on organizations that might qualify for assistance. In general the EDA required nonprofit corporate status, a board dedicated to economic development, full-time staff, and specific projects capable of implementation within nine months. In late 1979 and early 1980, HACER staff, mainly from TELACU, visited a number of organizations mostly in California, but also as distant as the states of Washington and Florida. Some organizations, primarily oriented toward social service, showed little promise, but others demonstrated viable projects. For example, Economic and Social Opportunities in San Jose had an ongoing greenhouse project that could benefit from HACER's assistance.[41] As the strongest of the Mexican-American CDCs, TELACU moved ahead with HACER in California more deliberately than did its allies in their own areas.

TELACU's activities through HACER received a boost in November 1979 with a grant from California's Department of Economic and Business Development. This year-long grant naturally helped focus HACER's efforts on that state. Among the California organizations assisted were the East Long Beach Neighborhood Center, which sought rehabilitation of a multipurpose building; Santa Barbara's Casa de la Raza, which opened La Cocina Restaurant; the Center for Employment and Training in Salinas, which needed help with an electronics plant; Campesinos Unidos of Brawley, which hoped to build a shopping center; the Small Cities Economic Development Commission, which planned an industrial park in Fresno County; North Coast Opportunities of Ukiah, which sought wool-processing facilities; Siskiyou Opportunity Center, which needed a woodwork shop for the handicapped; Central Coast Counties Development Corporation of Salinas, which hoped to build a strawberry cooler plant; and Proteus Adult Training, which was developing an ethanol project. Though all the organizations and projects differed, HACER staff assessed the feasibility of each project and its fit with the specific organization's overall goals.[42] As the long list of groups, locations, and projects suggests, HACER filled a definite need for an economic development network among Latino communities. The varied list suggests such a network's potential for integrating still autonomous communities into a larger unit capable of exercising greater regional and national power.

The success of HACER's program in technical assistance varied, according to the situations of local groups. For example, after HACER's staff visited Campesinos Unidos twice, the latter decided to drop plans for a shopping center. The meetings with HACER had revealed that the staff of Campesinos Unidos lacked the conceptual maturity to undertake serious economic development. HACER could only serve as an adviser, and Campesinos Unidos seemed overly dependent on the coalition for conceptualization of the project. To its credit, HACER restrained Campesinos Unidos from embarking on a project beyond its current ability. The wool-processing operation of North Coast Opportunities went through initial planning with HACER quite well, but differences with county officials with regard to further local economic growth stalled the operation. On the other hand, HACER succeeded with several other groups. For example, Siskiyou Opportunity Center and Casa de la Raza both developed their projects to the point of winning appropriate funding.[43]

In design the Hispanic American Coalition for Economic Revitalization allowed TELACU the opportunity to spread its ideology and practical knowledge throughout the Southwest and beyond. Ideally, HACER offered to unite Latinos behind organized economic development in a movement to free themselves from the subordination of internal colonialism. In practice, with some aid from the Spanish Speaking Unity Council, TELACU implemented projects where its strength lay—in California. The other Mexican-American CDCs similarly operated in their own subregions. However, this promising effort came to naught before it gained much ground. In 1980 Jimmy Carter's failure to win reelection put a halt to many federally funded social programs. Since HACER's EDA grant was due to expire in mid-1981, TELACU scrambled to replace the funds with grants from philanthropic groups, such as the Whitney Foundation, the Lilly Endowment, and the Hearst Foundation. This effort failed, and HACER folded with the social spending cuts implemented by the new administration of President Ronald Reagan.[44]

Latin American Ventures

But before the seemingly halcyon days of the Carter administration came to an end, TELACU stepped beyond the scope of HACER's regional and even national activities. Because of the CDC's Washington contacts and especially Esteban Torres's position as ambassador to UNESCO, an opportunity arose for TELACU to become involved in international ventures. In August 1980, after two years of preparation, TELACU started up an International Development Department to provide technical assistance to economic development organizations of various types in other countries. As David Lizarraga commented, he and his staff naturally focused on Latin America:

> We have always compared East Los Angeles to the developing countries of Latin America. We share many common problems, such as a lack of capital and resources. And because we share a common bond between our two communities, it was only natural that the principles and techniques that have proven effective here can be applied in other Latin countries as well.

Lizarraga clearly saw East LA as a country in microcosm, one more developing Latin nation. Of course, "developing countries" in colonial theory remained such because outside economic powers drained away the resources.[45] Lizarraga believed TELACU had learned to reverse the flow of capital from the metropolis to East LA. While doing the same for Latin America was obviously beyond any CDC, TELACU could now spread its ideology and tactics in microcosm to a degree never imagined in 1968. In a new, perhaps grandiose Pan-Americanism, including U.S. Hispanics and Latin Americans, Lizarraga hoped to promote both self-sufficiency and international cooperation.

Be that as it may, the U.S. Agency for International Development (AID), the key office for assistance to foreign countries in economic development, encouraged TELACU's new initiative. In June 1980 AID invited staff from several U.S. Hispanic development organizations to a seminar in Washington on program design. Peter Theobold, TELACU's vice president of community development, and Jaime López of the Community Research Group attended. The two were then invited to visit five countries—Ecuador, Peru, Bolivia, Honduras, and Panama—in Latin America over a two-month period. During the tour Theobald and López met with various AID officials and representatives of Latin American agencies as well. The purpose of the trip was to uncover potential projects that could benefit from TELACU's expertise.[46]

The trip ended so successfully that López commented, "Our problem was not a lack of contract opportunities, but rather . . . [of] prioritizing. . . ." The first contract, to begin in August 1980, involved spreading information on community development organizations, essentially a training program in Quito, Ecuador. A second contract for a more specific project, to develop wind power in Bolivia, was scheduled for October, and a third contract was in the works for Panama City. Rather than risk overextending itself, TELACU decided to hold off on further contracts until it had successfully implemented the first three.[47] Of course, no further projects came about, because President Carter lost his bid for reelection in November. TELACU's direct line to Washington snapped.

Jimmy Carter's defeat especially hurt TELACU because the line to the White House had never been tighter. Indeed, by the end of the Carter administration, Esteban Torres had risen to become the most prominent Latino at the White House. During his two years in Paris as ambassador to UNESCO, Torres had served with distinction. In late 1978 the general membership had elected him to UNESCO's "board of trustees by the largest margin in the organization's history." His rapport with Third World countries had gained him the votes needed to join the leadership of UNESCO. Torres's success in Paris subsequently led the administration to appoint him directly to the White House senior staff. On August 10, 1979, at a White House conference of two hundred Latino leaders, President Carter named the highly popular Torres, special assistant on Hispanic matters. In that capacity Torres had direct access to the president on such affairs, including those affecting Mexican-American CDCs.[48] Federal support for HACER and TELACU's International Development Department had followed.

Retreat to the Eastside

The defeat of Carter's reelection bid thus ended many of TELACU's ventures beyond East Los Angeles. Fortunately for the community and the CDC, TELACU had not ignored local issues during its regional, national, and international forays. Indeed, the Community Research Group, the think tank behind HACER and the International Development Department, continued expending energy at home. At home CRG carried out another planning project of cultural as well as economic importance, the Historical Preservation Survey. With funds from the National Endowment for the Arts, CRG catalogued hundreds of architecturally and historically significant buildings on the Eastside by gathering information from community residents themselves.[49] Through this project TELACU committed itself to preserving the historical landscape of the community while redeveloping it. In fact, TELACU would eventually restore some of the very buildings in the survey, while finding new uses for them.

Perhaps the project most beneficial to Eastside residents was the TELACU Family Health Center in Highland Park. This project, opened in early 1981, had resulted from the comprehensive health needs studies concluded by CRG. Because the studies had shown that the medical establishment woefully underserved the Eastside, TELACU had gained funding for the new barrio clinic. Atlantic Richfield, the Johnson and Mott foundations, the county and city of Los Angeles, and the Community Services Administration backed the project. Emphasizing pediatrics and family practice, the clinic offered several distinctive features, including health education, extensive outreach services, and fees based on ability to pay. Hospitalization and specialized care were covered in conjunction with White Memorial Hospital and the University of Southern California School of Medicine. The staff, headed by Gloria A. García, a graduate of UCLA's School of Public Health, spoke both English and Spanish, of course.[50] Unfortunately, TELACU later had to disengage itself from the center when criticism of the CDC threatened to close the clinic.

Lost Opportunity for National Integration

Jimmy Carter's campaign and his election to the presidency in 1976 had drawn TELACU back into the political arena after a few years of withdrawal. This resurgence of interest in politics and government, however, had not eclipsed the business orientation the CDC had set; new federal connections only allowed TELACU to engage in more wide-ranging economic planning and development. During the Carter administration, while TELACU Industrial Park rose on the Eastside, TELACU launched CRG, HACER, and the International Development Department in an attempt to promote the CDC model well beyond the Eastside. As we have seen, HACER briefly linked Mexican-American communities throughout the Southwest in a network of mutual support that promised to lift these colonias from economic dependency to full participation in the society. This would certainly have gone far toward fulfilling the Chicano dream of recovering the Southwest. While TELACU's ventures in Latin America had extended the CDC's vision too far, the forced abandonment of the Hispanic American Coalition for Economic Revitalization destroyed an important opportunity for Mexican-American and Latino integration into the nation.

The advent of the Reagan administration brought apprehension for TELACU and Mexican-American activists in general. In an editorial for *TELACU Today* in early 1981, Lizarraga commented on what the new presidency might mean for Mexico and people of Mexican descent, "As the Carter Administration leaves, the Reagan Administration sets out on what appears to be a new era of cooperation and understanding. Whether that spirit will continue the next four years is a question of keen interest for Mexicans and Mexican Americans alike." Because of its huge recently discovered oil reserves, Mexico in early 1981 had high hopes for rapid development.[51] That nation seemed about to throw off neocolonial dependency and become a full economic partner of the United States. Many Mexican Americans saw their own image reflected in the potential economic independence of Mexico, inasmuch as it could stimulate self-sufficiency within their own southwestern communities. But escaping colonialism would not be so easy.

7. The Roybal Center. East LA's comprehensive health clinic housed in a solid, multicolored structure featuring a horizontal band of Aztec glyphs. Photograph by author, 1997.

SIX

Politics on the Eastside

Democratic Recovery

Because of the momentum gathered from the construction of Nueva Maravilla, the nearby area by the early eighties had substantially improved. For example, in 1981 just south of the housing project, Los Angeles County dedicated a new section of Belvedere Park, Alberto Díaz Plaza, in honor of the publisher of the *Belvedere Citizen*. Since the park already included a public library, a sheriff's station, and a courthouse, this complex formed the "civic center" of unincorporated East Los Angeles. Even though these facilities represented continuing county governance, the added recreational space did much to transform the area's blighted image. More significant culturally and politically was the construction of a medical center in the vicinity. Inspired by pre-Columbian architecture, the new structure included a multicolored frieze depicting Aztec life in a detailed replica of an ancient Mexican codex. The building was suitably named after the area's venerable congressman, Edward R. Roybal, a native New Mexican whose efforts extended the provisions of the 1965 Voting Rights Act to the Spanish-speaking.[1] The Roybal Comprehensive Health Center not only improved the health and physical appearance of the community, but also symbolized its increasing political self-determination. Given the close connection between government and economic betterment on the Eastside, such landmarks held much promise for the Mexican-American community.

Despite the end of the Carter administration in 1981, the Eastside retained and expanded its political strength in subsequent years. The major reason was the rise of the Latino population, which spilled out of the traditional Eastside barrios into the suburbs, especially those in the San Gabriel Valley. Rapidly, much of the valley had become part of a new "Greater Eastside," extending past El Monte, ten miles beyond unincorporated East LA. Reapportionment of many political districts followed the changing demographics. Much redistricting resulted from Roybal's 1975 amendments to the Voting Rights Act, which forbade the dilution of the minority vote through gerrymandering and other maneuvers. In 1982 the power represented by growing numbers would culminate in the election of several new Mexican-American legislators and congressmen, as well as numerous local officeholders.[2]

Despite a brief hiatus after the failure of the incorporation campaign in 1974, the East Los Angeles Community Union (TELACU) became heavily involved in electoral politics from 1976 through 1982. Although politics did not upstage TELACU's economic activities, as had happened during the incorporation drive, the CDC became so involved behind the scenes that its public image became increasingly controversial. Nevertheless, TELACU's politicking benefited the community as several of the Mexican Americans elected to office owed their technical experience and training to the CDC. Most prominent of these politicians was Esteban Torres, elected to Congress in 1982.[3] Indeed, the increased political participation of TELACU and the community signified increasing self-determination and integration into the larger democratic system. To the degree that Mexican Americans in the Los Angeles area won elections, they were recovering their historic place in the government of the region.

Political History of the Eastside

The history of Mexican-American disfranchisement in the Los Angeles area extends into the nineteenth century. After the military occupation of 1846–47, the population remained overwhelmingly of Mexican descent until about 1880 when the railroads brought massive Anglo-American immigration into the region. Until that time Los Angeles City and County had significant numbers of Spanish-speaking officeholders, including Mayors Antonio Coronel, José Mascarel, and Cristóbal Aguilar, and Supervisors F. Palomares and Francisco Machado. However, with the decline in the proportion of Spanish-surnamed voters, their political representation disappeared. By the turn of the century virtually no representative of this group continued in prominent local, let alone state office.[4]

Congressman Edward Roybal

The lack of representation by 1900 made it even more difficult to recover political power once immigration increased the Mexican-American population in the following decades. Then various forms of gerrymandering kept the Spanish-speaking from electing their own once again. While an occasional individual broke through the system to win office—for example, Sheriff Eugene Biscailuz in the 1940s—Mexican Americans could not succeed one another in the same office.[5] No such permanent gain occurred until the election of Ed Roybal to Congress in 1962. He would remain in office for thirty years and be replaced by a Latino at retirement. His election proved the first in a cumulative series of victories that regained permanent representation for the Mexican-American community by the early 1980s.

Still in 1967 Ed Roybal was the only Chicano holding a seat in the various legislative bodies that supposedly represented the Eastside. Though occasionally Mexican Americans sat on the city councils and school boards of the San Gabriel Valley's numerous incorporated suburbs, the Eastside itself remained almost completely unrepresented. Chicanos entirely lacked representation on the Los Angeles County Board of Supervisors, the board of the LA Unified School District, the LA City Council, the California senate and assembly, and the board of the LA Community College District—in other words every major governing body of the Eastside. Needless to say, no Mexican Americans occupied such major local offices as county sheriff or mayor of Los Angeles, let alone statewide offices such as attorney general or lieutenant governor.[6]

Mexican Americans had, of course, long protested this situation and campaigned to overcome it, with some temporary successes. For example, the nonpartisan Mexican-American Political Association in the early 1960s succeeded in placing Philip Soto and John Moreno in the assembly, but these legislators failed to hold their offices and pass them on to other Chicanos. Also, as we have seen, in 1967 the Congress of Mexican-American Unity, with TELACU's support, helped elect Julian Nava to the LA school board. Unfortunately, when he later resigned, he too failed to pass on his office. Not until 1968 with the election of Alex P. García to the assembly did Chicanos add to the permanent gains begun by Roybal six years earlier.[7] García's victory proved a milestone because thenceforth Mexican-American representation from the Eastside in the assembly accumulated.

Alex García and Richard Alatorre, State Legislators

Despite this, progress was not steady. In 1970 García kept his assembly seat, but Democrat Richard Alatorre's attempt to win another in a 1971 special election failed when the Mexican-American vote in his district split. That year La Raza Unida Party, making its debut in a local election, nominated Raúl Ruiz for the same office. Ruiz, also supported by the Congress of Mexican-American Unity, lost the election, but gained enough votes to throw it to Republican Bill Brophy. This of course followed La Raza's strategy—to prevent the complacent Democratic party from taking Chicanos for granted. The strategy worked; the Democrats learned the lesson. In 1972 they once again nominated Alatorre and gave him strong financial backing. Alatorre, also having learned not to take his own community lightly, campaigned especially well along ethnic lines. Since La Raza stayed out of the race this time, Alatorre readily defeated Brophy.[8] Alatorre's election set another Chicano milestone as he eventually became one of the more powerful legislators in Sacramento.

Alatorre and Alex García formed the Eastside contingent in the California assembly between 1972 and 1974, but as junior members of the lower house, the two initially wielded little power. Ideological differences also complicated their relationship. Though both belonged to the Democratic party, García had conservative instincts that contrasted with Alatorre's solid liberalism. Despite this, they cooperated in reaching out to potential candidates in the community so that the Chicano presence could become larger and continuous. When García decided to run for the state senate in 1974, both he and Alatorre supported Art Torres for García's old assembly seat. Thus they set a pattern—whereby an established Mexican American, running for higher office, left his former seat to an aspiring newcomer. The plan succeeded in placing García in the senate and bringing in another Chicano politician who would eventually wield considerable power. The elections of 1974 were successful in this respect, even though they involved the failed measure to incorporate East LA and Esteban Torres's loss of a congressional race in the May primary.[9]

Assemblyman Art Torres

The addition of Art Torres to the assembly proved auspicious because he and Alatorre over the next decade formed what some called the political "machine" of the Eastside. With only Congressman Roybal holding a more prominent position, and García operating individually in the state senate, liberals Alatorre and Art Torres linked themselves to the Democratic power structure in the assembly to gain increasing influence. As their tenure in office lengthened, they climbed the political hierarchy. As they gained prestige, important committee seats, and access to greater political contributions, Torres and Alatorre increased their power on the Eastside. As longtime supporters of these assemblymen, TELACU's members made the CDC seem an integral part of the machine. Since they made political contributions of various sorts, TELACU's requests for government contracts received attention. The simultaneous election of Governor Jerry Brown in 1974 also increased the power of local Chicano Democrats because he replaced conservative Republican Governor Ronald Reagan. Adding to the potential of the machine, four other Mexican Americans joined the legislature from beyond the Eastside. Thus from 1967 to 1974, Chicano legislative representation went from 0 to 6. For the remainder of the decade, the further electoral aspirations of Eastside Mexican Americans remained largely on hold until the 1980 census permitted redistricting based on an expanded Latino population.[10]

Though still severely underrepresented, Chicanos had obviously made strides toward political self-determination by 1980. The movement had nevertheless been slow and tentative. For example, Roybal had held a seat on the LA City Council in the 1950s, but when he left it to run for Congress in 1962, he was not succeeded by another Mexican American on the council until 1985, twenty-three years later. A similar situation occurred with the election of Julian Nava in 1968 to the LA school board. He served for twelve years, but when he retired in 1980, going on to become ambassador to Mexico, another Latino did not win a seat on the board until 1984. Just the same, over the years many groups, including the Mexican-American Political Association, the Congress of Mexican-American Unity, TELACU, ACTIELA, and La Raza, had struggled with increasing success to enfranchise and elect Mexican Americans to office at various levels. Other prominent groups increasingly involved were the Mexican American Legal Defense and Education Fund and the Southwest Voter Registration Education Project. By the early eighties, these local, state, and national organizations had improved the general political situation of Latinos on the Eastside.[11]

TELACU's "Political Machine"

Because of TELACU's status as a nonprofit community development corporation, direct involvement in political campaigns always threatened to create problems with the CDC's funding sources. While organizations such as the Southwest Voter Project remained officially nonpartisan, their functions much more clearly entailed political participation. TELACU's economic focus, with its reliance on government contracts and private sector partnerships, put the CDC in an especially delicate situation when it came to political campaigns. Nevertheless, from its earliest support for Nava in 1968 through the Congress of Mexican-American Unity, TELACU was heavily and necessarily involved in politics, a pattern that would continue, though usually through its members' independent participation or through surrogate groups. Unfortunately, this pattern would add to the controversy surrounding the CDC.[12]

TELACU carried out its behind-the-scenes political involvement in a number of ways. So much of its business relying on government contracts, TELACU made sure it lobbied politicos faithfully, both Anglo and Latino, though it tied itself firmly to the Democratic party. A steady stream of politicians visited TELACU's facilities and participated in its events. These visits helped the CDC gain notice for its accomplishments as well as gain more funding; in turn, the visits gave the politicians publicity and campaign contributions of various sorts. Political contacts naturally occurred more often during election years, but since TELACU kept close ties with local, state, and national officials, election campaigns and visits were constant.[13]

A gubernatorial campaign year, 1974 naturally called for contacts of many kinds, especially since Esteban Torres and East LA incorporation appeared on the ballot. That spring Torres, no longer directing TELACU, endorsed Ed Edelman for the board of supervisors, a judicious decision since the latter subsequently became the most powerful official directly affecting the Eastside. Torres also publicly endorsed Ruben Ayala of San Bernardino and Alex García for the state senate, wise moves since the two won office. That such connections directly affected TELACU's efforts is evident; for example, in the December after the election, Supervisor Edelman appeared with David Lizarraga, informing the public of TELACU's food stamp distribution program. An electoral off-year, 1975 still found TELACU members meeting with officials, such as Assembly Speaker Leo McCarthy and state health and welfare Secretary Mario Obledo, discussing TELACU's transportation programs and similar matters.[14]

During 1976, a presidential election year, TELACU became more directly involved politically, but again through surrogate organizations, such as ACTIELA in the earlier incorporation effort. That year TELACU created two organizations to advance its political interests and those of the Chicano community. These organizations were People for TELACU State Action, a political action committee registered to solicit funds for local and state campaigns, and Voter Organization through Education (VOTE), a technically nonpartisan group formed to register voters.[15] These groups helped keep TELACU in touch with some of the most prominent politicians, local, state, and national.

TELACU's Political Action Committee

Listing an office on Wilshire Boulevard as its headquarters, People for TELACU formally registered with the state on June 23, 1976. Despite continual registration until August 1980, the organization only functioned during its first summer of official life. Actually, People for TELACU carried out only one major activity, a formal fund-raising dinner—a noteworthy event nonetheless. Only three days after the organization's registration with the state, People for TELACU held a private reception and dinner in honor of numerous elected officials at the Beverly Hills home of prominent Westside Democratic supporter Leo Wyler. The formal host was David Lizarraga, and the honorees made up a veritable "who's who" of California's leading Democratic representatives: Congressman Edward Roybal, Senate Majority Leader David Roberti, Senator Alex García, Assembly Speaker Leo McCarthy, Assembly Majority Leader Howard Berman, Assembly Majority Whip Joseph Montoya, Assemblyman Terry Goggin, Supervisor Edmund Edelman, and California Democratic party Chairman Charles Manatt.[16] Even though it communicated through a political action committee, TELACU clearly kept in touch with California's powers-that-be.

A variety of people from around the Los Angeles area made the one-hundred-dollar-per-plate donation and more. They included representatives of large institutions, such as Union Oil Company of California, Chemical Bank, Commonwealth Bank, and Coopers and Lybrand CPA. But other businesses also contributed: Bell Best Pies, Jason D. Groode Enterprises, Ian Caterers, Atlas Aquarium Engineering, Stone Outfitting, W.R. Company, and Norman F. Swanton Associates. A couple of companies whose names indicated Mexican-American ownership were donors too, Martínez Chevron and John L. Espinosa Realty. Representatives of community service groups, such as Cleland House and the Ayúdate Project, attended as did a number of individuals, including Gregory Villanueva, an architect involved in several TELACU projects.[17] Because many of the smaller businesses hailed from the Eastside, TELACU clearly sought to bring Eastside Chicanos into contact with traditional Westside power brokers. In this way, Mexican Americans would gain greater access, not only to politicians, but to the political arena.

Voter Registration for Jimmy Carter

Of somewhat longer duration than People for TELACU, Voter Organization through Education formed another of the CDC's legal political "fronts." Founded on August 26, 1976, VOTE resulted from informal conversations held at the Beverly Hills fund-raiser. The organization lasted about a year, long enough to participate in the 1976 presidential campaign and the Los Angeles municipal elections of the following spring. In setting up VOTE, TELACU was influenced by the San Antonio–based Southwest Voter Registration Education Project, the nonprofit organization funded by the Ford Foundation that had such dramatic success registering Mexican Americans in Texas. With this technical assistance and with the sponsorship of leading Democratic politicians, VOTE launched its efforts during Jimmy Carter's 1976 campaign. Co-chairmen of the committee were David Lizarraga and Leo Wyler. A partnership began to form between the Latino Eastside and the liberal Jewish Westside, long a wing of LA Mayor Tom Bradley's coalition.[18]

TELACU hired political consultants Winner, Lovell, Taylor & Associates to put the VOTE proposal together. This group, experienced in Democratic campaigns, had both the expertise and the contacts to help launch the new organization. Leslie Winner had helped manage Edmund Muskie's campaign for president in California in 1971–72; locally, she had managed a campaign for LA City Council in 1974. She had also served on Jerry Brown's staff during his time as secretary of state. In 1976 John Lovell was manager of the Jimmy Carter presidential campaign in southern California and had once worked as a student coordinator in Bobby Kennedy's Senate drive. He had also served on the staff of Supervisor Ed Edelman. Rick Taylor had once been on the national staff of presidential candidate George McGovern.[19] Clearly, this group could provide the political expertise VOTE needed to register the right kind of voter.

TELACU set up an executive committee for VOTE, including honorary chairmen and honorary members, as well as regular members. U.S. Senators Alan Cranston and John Tunney, Congressman Ed Roybal, and Supervisor Ed Edelman held the honorary chairs. State Senator Alex García, Assemblymen Richard Alatorre, Joseph Montoya, and Art Torres, and LA Deputy Mayor Grace Montañez Davis served as honorary committee members. Clearly, these positions gave prestige to the organization by allowing its letterhead and publicity to list prominent support. In addition, the list made it obvious that the Democratic party completely backed this "nonpartisan" organization. The twenty or so regular committee members were less prominent, though important members of the community, such as TELACU officials. These lesser lights included Gloria Molina, aide to Assemblyman Torres, Armando Rodríquez, president of East LA College, and Grace Castro Nagata, former director of TELACU communications.[20]

Despite the luminaries on VOTE's letterhead, a professional staff carried out the real work of the organization. Generally following the recommendations of Winner, Lovell, Taylor & Associates, the staff included a coordinator and field directors; the former would be Tom Castro, the latter Ron Noblet and Rachel Ruiz. The political consultants also recommended a preliminary budget—to be funded by TELACU, Wyler, and other Democratic contributors—of $114,000 per year, two-thirds of which would go to the consultants and directors, with the rest going to standard expenses, such as telephones, postage, and rent. In 1976 VOTE first planned a registration drive in unincorporated East Los Angeles, then a "get-out-the-vote" campaign in the days immediately preceding the November general election. An innovative aspect of the registration drive, one indicating TELACU's social concerns, was the recruitment of female gang members to register voters.[21]

During the first two weeks of September 1976, this unconventional force completed 90 percent of the voter registration. Rachel Ruiz had close ties with the young women of the colonia and consequently succeeded in soliciting their strong support for the effort.

Since these women knew their neighborhoods well, they carried out their task on a barrio basis, rather than on the conventional precinct basis. Though nominally volunteer workers, the registrars received fifty cents per voter card submitted, as compensation and as an incentive. Door-to-door registration was most arduous, but most effective in getting to know the community. Registration at shopping centers and social gatherings garnered many new voters, but resulted in less direct knowledge of the community, information vital to getting out the vote on election day. TELACU also funneled job trainees to VOTE, trainees paid under the federal Comprehensive Employment and Training Act (CETA), a program administered locally by the county through the CDC. In other words, TELACU used federal funds to pay workers of a nonpartisan organization to register voters who would overwhelmingly vote Democratic. Although such questionable activities contributed to TELACU's controversial image, VOTE's registration drive netted 30,000 new voters, an obvious success for the community.[22]

In terms of getting the electorate to the polls, VOTE proved just as successful, encouraging a local turnout of 75 percent in the 1976 presidential election. Volunteers canvassed the barrios door-to-door and by telephone to get voters to the booth, a process that began about two weeks before election day. Volunteers were so thorough that they contacted each voter face-to-face in fifty key precincts at least once and telephoned each household within the same area a minimum of three times by election day. Indeed, volunteers stopped calling when some residents complained of being reached once too often. On election day TELACU itself provided most of the workers for the get-out-the-vote campaign. The CDC closed down for the day, and about forty of its employees volunteered to make phone calls, drive people to the polls, and do the many other tasks necessary for a successful turnout. Casa Maravilla, Cleland House, and local Catholic high schools also contributed volunteers. Although Jimmy Carter lost California to Republican Gerald Ford, Carter won 82 percent of the Latino vote, no small portion of it from East Los Angeles. Without a doubt, this constituency had earned some consideration from President Carter's new administration.[23]

Political Self-Criticism

The 1976 campaign taught VOTE and TELACU members a good deal about themselves and their relationship to the community, including much that disturbed them. Ron Noblet and Rachel Ruiz, field directors of VOTE, found a persistent problem in their dealings with individuals and other organizations in the barrios—a negative image of TELACU and consequently of VOTE. According to the field directors' report on the election,

> One of the problems we had . . . in the area was that the people other than [in] top administrative positions knew little or nothing about VOTE and tended to discount it. VOTE is seen as an arm of TELACU and is therefore painted with the same brush of suspicion. We found this suspicious attitude prevalent throughout East Los Angeles, in most agencies, public and private, and in lower administrative levels. We feel that this suspicious attitude tinged with ignorance and fear, is a normal feeling toward the "big boy on the block."

While the analysis of the problem at this point lacked deep insight, it did reveal the serious public relations problem haunting the CDC. Because the field directors had extensive contact with opinion on the street, their observations were damning—obviously, ordinary people in East LA disliked TELACU. Unfortunately, the directors' seeming denial of VOTE's links to TELACU further fed that suspicion. Moreover, the reasons they inferred for the "suspicious attitude" toward TELACU—fear, ignorance, and resentment—were superficial.[24] Why did TELACU elicit such feelings?

In a later section of their report, Noblet and Ruiz interpreted TELACU's image problem more critically. They argued that much of the CDC's staff had lost its sense of dedication to the community and needed a program of political education to revive that dedication. Especially in need of such motivational training were the administrators of TELACU Industries and the Community Planning and Development Corporation. These divisions had sent virtually no volunteers to VOTE on election day, suggesting an unwillingness to mingle with the community. Indeed, the report charged these administrators with feeling "paternalistic and condescending toward the community." Certainly, condescension would elicit resentment from the residents of the barrios. In addition the report argued that "lower echelon staff" felt alienated from the CDC at large and consequently "Less than 50 percent of the people feel the commitment to community that TELACU, as a community development corporation must have to be relevant and succeed." Apparently, the officers of the CDC had lost contact not only with the community, but with their own rank and file. The report went on to ask rhetorically, "If the people within TELACU are unaware of or have forgotten the goals and aims of the organization; if they lose sight of themselves as individuals within the organization, then how can they possibly give full enthusiasm or support to VOTE?"[25] The question cut to the heart of difficulties the CDC would experience in subsequent years. Indeed, could a leadership that had apparently become self-centered lead an organization of alienated workers toward the goal of self-determination for an entire community?

Another serious charge leveled at TELACU by Noblet and Ruiz concerned the status of women in the CDC as a whole. The field directors claimed that female TELACU employees did not volunteer in great numbers for VOTE, a potentially serious handicap since women formed the backbone of both organizations. The reason, according to the report, was pervasive male chauvinism. The CDC as a whole tended to treat women "as second rate humans" in three ways. First, the male administrators often displayed open hostility; second, they devalued the ideas of women; and third, they constantly interrupted the input of women at meetings. The field directors recommended a reevaluation of the role of women at the CDC, a reevaluation that would hopefully lead to a complete change of attitude. Despite the successes of Maggie Aparicio's Business Development Office and the awards granted by TELACU to outstanding local women, the CDC had obviously not solved its internal problems with sexism.[26] The progressive public image TELACU sought to promote with regard to sexual equality seemed less than candid.

Despite these serious criticisms, the field directors' report on the 1976 presidential election concluded on a somewhat positive note; after all, the registration and get-out-the-vote campaigns had been successful:

One of VOTE's strengths during the campaign was its willingness and ability to act as a liaison to all community and political groups [sic] One of the reasons for this was VOTE's non-partisan image which allowed for a broad base of allies. It is essential that we keep this image of non-partisianship [sic] for at least another year; i.e. early 1978. . . . the more groups that do not feel threatened by VOTE, the better . . .

VOTE had succeeded in unifying the community politically, despite the suspicious connections with TELACU. VOTE had also somehow projected a "non-partisan image" successfully, despite its open connections to the Democratic party.[27] Unfortunately, VOTE's image, like TELACU's as a whole, remained enigmatic for even as VOTE hoped to gain the trust of the community, an element of dissimulation entered the picture. Did VOTE expect to become openly partisan at some future date? If so, was it presenting a false image to the community at present? Such questions reflected the overall problem TELACU and its affiliates had in their relations with the public.

Mayor Tom Bradley's 1977 Campaign

Success in the presidential election of 1976 encouraged TELACU and other supporters of VOTE to involve the organization in the Los Angeles municipal election of April 1977. The target area therefore changed from unincorporated East LA to the eastern barrios of the city of Los Angeles—Lincoln Heights, El Sereno, and Boyle Heights. Although VOTE continued its registration activities, it stressed a get-out-the-vote drive because in local elections victory meant encouraging a generally apathetic electorate to vote. Though VOTE remained nonpartisan, TELACU had three political goals for the organization. The first and second were to reelect Democrats Burt Pines and Tom Bradley to the nonpartisan offices of city attorney and mayor, respectively. The third was to encourage voters to elect several nonpartisan candidates for the board of a new health services agency, which the federal government had recently established to meet the health needs of the area.[28] The third aim involved TELACU's long-term plans for a medical center on the Eastside and showed that the CDC had not completely forgotten the basic needs of the community.

In January 1977 VOTE held preliminary meetings with the Pines and Bradley campaigns to coordinate strategy. Semiweekly meetings continued with Grace Montañez Davis, deputy mayor of Los Angeles and Mayor Bradley's liaison with the Chicano community. Since municipal elections in California remain officially nonpartisan, close cooperation between VOTE and these campaigns was legal. Indeed, VOTE became a formal part of these campaigns in separate meetings on February 4, 1977. On that date George Pla— "TELACU's director of economic development and [at that point] VOTE's operations director"—together with Tom Castro, Rachel Ruiz, and Ron Noblet, met the managers of the Pines and Bradley campaigns. At these meetings VOTE agreed to run the campaigns and the get-out-the-vote drives for Pines and Bradley in Lincoln Heights, El Sereno, and Boyle Heights. In return Pines offered VOTE $8,500, with an unspecified amount coming from Bradley. In late February Pines met for discussions with David Lizarraga and made a tour of TELACU's facilities.[29] Without a doubt TELACU had become an informal but important supporter of the Democratic party in the Los Angeles area.

Indeed, in an unofficial capacity, several members of VOTE had attended the convention of the state Democratic party at the end of January 1977. Those attending were David Lizarraga, Roy Escarcega, George Pla, Ron Noblet, Richard Polanco, Carlos García, and Rachel Ruiz—all members of VOTE or TELACU. At the convention these people succeeded in having their candidate, Bruce Corwin, chosen southern section chairman of the state party—a post Lizarraga would fill a few years later. In an interoffice memorandum following up on the convention, VOTE coordinator Tom Castro discussed the importance to TELACU of the political contacts made in Sacramento:

> The State Party apparatus and the party officers represent a significant potential resource for TELACU. The State Party activists, officers, and fundraisers are influential and well-connected individuals. Among their ranks are included many influential businessmen, and a good number of the "movers and shakers" in Los Angeles and California. I can foresee these people being helpful to TELACU; political appointments and economic development activities, just to name a few.
>
> These resources will only be available to us, however, if we cultivate

them. For a little money and time we can accomplish this. Our task is all the ... easier because a "demand" exists for TELACU and its activities. As Chicanos become a greater and greater proportion of California's population, the power structure "needs" Chicanos it can relate to. Our role is not to become their "house Mexicans," but rather to be prepared to sit down at the bargaining table to negotiate for our people.[30]

As we have seen, TELACU already had many contacts in the party and among contributors and would soon receive appointments not only in Sacramento, but Washington. In reality TELACU officials had become de facto representatives of the Chicano community in the party because they had learned the inner workings of the political system. With their technical expertise they could discuss economics and politics on an equal basis with the powers-that-be. TELACU officials were indeed integrating into the system, but doubts about their dedication to the community remained.

The April 1977 municipal elections turned out well for VOTE. Both Bradley and Pines won reelection, thereby guaranteeing TELACU a voice in city hall. In the election for the board of health service agency, candidates supported by VOTE won five of the seven seats. Turnout in an area traditionally indifferent to local elections equaled that of the city as a whole, indicating that VOTE had had a positive effect. This success resulted from VOTE's ability to recruit volunteers from key elements of the community. In addition to TELACU employees, college students, senior citizens, and members of the East LA Jaycees volunteered. The Chicana Nurses Association took a special interest in the campaign because of the health issues involved. César Chávez and two hundred members of the United Farm Workers also joined the fray, the former receiving a special tour of the soon-to-be demolished Goodrich Tire plant.[31] Indeed, TELACU had shown the ability to gather grass-roots support, as well as skill in cultivating prominent power brokers.

In early June of 1977, VOTE organizers hoped to make the group permanent. Since it already had an office at Soto and Brooklyn on the Eastside and an experienced staff, VOTE expected the voter education and registration operation to continue. In fact, organizers foresaw "Establishment of a precinct captain system" headed by volunteers from local neighborhoods. Interestingly, the organizers were developing "a concept similar to the 'Daley Machine'" of Chicago, designed to call up volunteers to saturate the area rapidly. Comparison with the boss system in general had been made during the campaign itself in a letter encouraging voters to go to the polls. In the letter John Echeveste, TELACU's director of communications, issued an invitation:

> to witness firsthand the workings of a political machine of sorts as it combs through the precincts of East Los Angeles in an attempt to get every registered voter out to the polls.
> The "machine" is VOTE, Voter Organization Through Education, a non-partisan, non-profit educational communittee [sic] set up by The East Los Angeles Community Union (TELACU) to increase political awareness in the Chicano community.

The unwise comparison would come back to haunt the CDC. Because of the popular association of political machines with corruption, critics would examine TELACU in the same dim light. The fact that the boss system had historically given ethnic groups access to employment as well as political office had been forgotten. TELACU had obviously hoped to connect itself with the machine's positive past, but that past had become too obscure. In any case, by the end of June TELACU decided to discontinue VOTE because funding proved a problem in non-election years.[32]

Hispanic Democrats

After the discontinuation of VOTE, TELACU's political activities revolved around lobbying the Carter administration for Mexican-American appointments—a successful effort, as we have seen. Political appointments, however, syphoned off some of the CDC's major talent. For example, in early 1978, George Pla, TELACU's liaison with VOTE, was appointed director of Business and Economic Development by Governor Jerry Brown. Curiously, this left TELACU politically disorganized during Brown's reelection campaign in 1978. TELACU nevertheless proved influential as candidate Brown appeared at the CDC's "Domingos Alegres" program, in May just before the primary. In July U.S. Senator Alan Cranston, long supported by the CDC, also made an appearance at Nueva Maravilla with TELACU officials. During this period, David Lizarraga, as a Carter appointee to the National Commission on Neighborhoods, remained extremely busy, which may explain the temporary slowdown in the CDC's grass-roots electoral activities.[33]

David Lizarraga, Democratic Party "Boss"

In early 1979 the situation changed somewhat when Lizarraga, freed of his service to the Carter administration, won the chairmanship of the southern section of the state Democratic party. In this position Lizarraga gained responsibility for coordinating fundraising and general electoral strategy for the party throughout southern California. This meant, of course, that he would make major decisions regarding party endorsements and financing for candidates for the numerous offices throughout the region.[34] This consequently meant that Chicanos would have greater opportunities to get the money and connections needed to win political office. Needless to say, Lizarraga's selection to so powerful a post was a coup for TELACU and the Chicano community. TELACU could certainly claim leadership in the movement for Chicano self-determination, as well as credit for Mexican-American integration into the democratic system.

The 1980 Presidential Campaign

One of Lizarraga's major duties was, of course, preparation for the 1980 presidential campaign, for both the primary and the general election. He also clearly had responsibility for getting out the Latino vote. As part of the latter effort in early 1979, he helped form a new organization called Hispanic American Democrats (HAD). This organization would operate on a nationwide basis with branches at the regional and state levels. Because of the national contacts made by TELACU during the Carter administration, Hispanic American Democrats included individuals from throughout the nation and from varied Latino groups. Headquarters were located in Washington, D.C., with regional offices in New York City, East LA, and Coral Gables, Florida—obviously, in the population centers of the major Latino subgroups, Puerto Ricans, Mexican Americans, and Cuban Americans, respectively.[35]

The bylaws of Hispanic American Democrats stated its intentions. Following the broad stategy necessary for a presidential campaign, the organization embraced all Latinos, not just Mexican Americans. Moreover, it sought to integrate these groups into the power structure of the national Democratic party. The organization was to

> provide a politically unified and directed voice for the Hispanic communities within the United States that is attentive to the needs and well-being of the Hispanic people; . . . by causing to bring about effective Legislative State and/or Federal action, as an official representative within the Executive Committee body of the Democratic National Committee.

Revisions in Democratic party rules during the George McGovern presidential campaign of 1972 had permitted greater participation of nontraditional groups. Hispanic American Democrats exemplified those changes. Its governance indicated the new organization intended to become a functioning component of the Democratic party: "In every instance, rules and regulations promulgated by HAD should parallel DNC [Democratic National Committee] rules and regulations."[36]

Unfortunately, unlike VOTE, Hispanic American Democrats relied on a top-down strategy because of the breadth of the presidential campaign. The organization sought to recruit "hispanic leaders (community, political, labor, and business) throughout the country so that these persons can become the nucleus of HAD in their respective communites." Elected officials would serve on the national council; regional and state councils included their respective elected officials and other prominent individuals. The national convention would have delegates apportioned by the Hispanic populations of the various states. Local chapters were formed by interested individuals or from existing organizations. From its inception HAD naturally had the support of prominent elected officials: Assemblyman Richard Alatorre and Congressman Ed Roybal of California, Representative Baltasar Corrada of Puerto Rico, and Congressman Robert García of New York. The organization also set up a nationwide network of prominent local people supposedly to reach the grass roots. David Lizarraga became national chairman of

HAD, and in addition to these duties, took on the task of organizing the California branch, appropriately assigned the acronym CHAD.[37]

Hispanic American Democrats essentially operated for the duration of the 1980 presidential campaign. During the primaries HAD, like the rest of the Democratic party, split over the candidacies of Jimmy Carter and Edward Kennedy. Having become part of the regular party establishment, Lizarraga and much of HAD's leadership leaned toward the president; unfortunately for HAD, the Latino electorate had a sentimental attachment to the Kennedys, especially in California, which the senator won.[38] Garnering votes for Carter at the grass-roots level proved difficult. At best HAD succeeded in gaining financial support through direct mailings, but lacked an organized campaign like VOTE to operate successfully in the barrios.

During the general election of 1980, HAD and the Democratic party in general won the Latino vote for Jimmy Carter, but not by the overwhelming margins of the past. The charismatic Ronald Reagan, former governor of California, in carrying the state made inroads into the traditionally Democratic Latino constituency, even in southern California. Carter's failure to win reelection ended an important period of Mexican-American influence in Washington. TELACU's hard-won appointments in the federal government disappeared with the Carter administration. While President Reagan would also appoint Hispanics to his administration, obviously they would be Republicans or at least supporters of his policies.[39] TELACU and the Democratic Latino majority once again found themselves without a voice at the White House.

Historic Victories on the Eastside

Despite this setback, TELACU and other Latino groups saw the potential for major political gains in the near future because of the rise of the Latino population. Having actively participated in the census of 1980, TELACU recognized the impact the new figures would have on the reapportionment of political bodies. The CDC geared its political efforts to take advantage of redistricting, especially in the 1982 midterm elections. In these efforts the CDC's contacts in Sacramento and within the state Democratic party proved invaluable. Chief among these contacts were Assemblymen Richard Alatorre and Art Torres, who after nearly a decade in the statehouse had gained seniority and moved into powerful committee positions. Having supported the successful bid of Willie Brown, a black, for assembly speaker, Alatorre received the powerful chairmanship of the assembly's Elections and Reapportionment Committee. Since this committee would redraw California's legislative and congressional districts, Alatorre could now enhance Latino representation, especially on the Eastside. Alatorre and Torres could also facilitate the appointment of Latinos to various commissions and, more importantly, influence who the party would support for various offices.[40] As a longtime supporter and ally of Alatorre, TELACU had also positioned itself to gain political advantage, particularly through Lizarraga's chairmanship of southern California's Democratic party.

The Pivotal 1982 Elections

In the two years between the elections of 1980 and 1982, there was a flurry of political activity in California among Mexican Americans, naturally including the members of TELACU. Besides lobbying on redistricting, TELACU supported Governor Brown's appointment of Cruz Reynoso to the state Supreme Court, an appointment severely criticized by increasingly powerful conservative voices in the state. This appointment, of course, signified the restoration of Mexican-American representation at the highest levels of state government. In early 1982 the euphoria over the impending political rise of Latinos even led a Mexican American to run for governor. Mario Obledo, California's former health and welfare secretary, decided to run for the office being vacated by Jerry Brown. Obledo, however, lacked the support of Brown and the Democratic establishment, which lined up behind LA Mayor Tom Bradley. Needless to say, Latino politicos, such as Alatorre and Torres, kept their distance from the maverick Obledo campaign. They considered his drive premature and believed it might discourage more viable candidates for statewide office in the future.[41] TELACU, of course, aligned itself firmly with the establishment.

Indeed, the Latino Democratic establishment was planning carefully for the future, especially of the Eastside. Prominent politicos realized that the opportunity of a century had arrived, and if Mexican Americans were to take full advantage of it, they needed viable candidates and a coordinated strategy. Since the selection of candidates would naturally create some resentment, the leadership needed to coordinate its decisions to minimize disunity, win the general elections, and serve the constituents. The first step taken demonstrated the difficulties involved. Art Torres, with the blessing of Assembly Speaker Willie Brown, decided to run against fellow Mexican-American Alex García for the state senate. Although García had pioneered the Chicano advance into the legislature, he had become ineffective and had made the serious mistake of supporting Reagan in the previous presidential election. Though García still had powerful allies, such as César Chávez, the Alatorre-Torres team decided to challenge the senator as they believed he no longer served the party or his constituents.[42]

A more important move to improve the representation of Mexican Americans came about through the influence of Alatorre and Torres on Governor Brown. When a position on the state Court of Appeal opened up, they convinced him to appoint Congressman George Danielson to the seat. This left the predominantly Mexican-American Thirtieth Congressional District open to Latino candidates on the Eastside. In February 1982 the *Los Angeles Times* noted the importance of this change for the ethnic politics of the area:

> A wide-ranging struggle has now begun from East Los Angeles through much of the San Gabriel Valley. It involves possession of two congressional seats, one of them created through reapportionment [and Alatorre's influence], two Assembly seats and Garcia's state Senate seat. If Latinos win the two congressional seats, they will triple, from one to three, the number of Latino congressmen from Los Angeles County.[43]

Tripling the Greater Eastside's congressional delegation represented the opportunity of a century and would certainly stand out as a major victory in the Mexican-American drive for self-determination.

Over the previous decade, Congressman Ed Roybal, state Senator Alex García, and Assemblymen Alatorre and Torres had been the major Chicano representatives on the Eastside, but as middle-class Mexican Americans moved into the suburban San Gabriel Valley, they too had put their own into office. Joseph Montoya of Whittier had actually joined the assembly in 1972, the same year as Alatorre, and had moved to the senate in 1978; in 1980 Marty Martínez of Monterey Park had also entered the assembly. While Mexican-American Democrats generally cooperated, Montoya and Martínez represented more multiethnic districts and could not support Chicano issues quite as strongly, at least initially. But as the Mexican-American population expanded, the suburban Democrats realized their own increasing ethnic power base and resisted the dictates of the traditional Eastside "machine."[44] These "power brokers" had to accommodate one another to assure a sweeping Mexican-American victory in 1982.

Conclave at Steven's Steak House

Fearing that political infighting might ruin the opportunities evident in the 1980 census, the key Mexican-American Democrats decided to meet and coordinate strategy. According to the *Los Angeles Times*,

> Within two days of Danielson's appointment [made February 4, 1982], a secret meeting of the area's Latino political leadership—with the exception of Garcia—was convened at Steven's Steak House in the City of Commerce, under the chairmanship of veteran Latino Rep. Edward Roybal (D-Los Angeles), to try to impose some political order in the situation.

At the conclave sat Alatorre, Art Torres, Martínez, and Montoya, in addition to Roybal and three prominent men from TELACU—Esteban Torres, David Lizarraga, and George Pla. Lizarraga, of course, remained sectional party chairman, while George Pla had served as TELACU's liaison to VOTE. Significantly, Esteban Torres with his extensive local, as well as Washington, experience had been invited as a potential candidate for office.[45] On this momentous occasion, TELACU was playing a critical role in the recovery of political self-determination for Mexican Americans, for the ramifications of this meeting would ripple well beyond East LA.

The major decisions at the meeting involved who would run for what. Suburban Monterey Park's Marty Martínez, relatively new to the assembly but with a strong base in the area, seemed most electable to Danielson's old congressional district. Of course, Esteban Torres also had a base in the district but had lost to incumbent Danielson in 1974. To avoid a clash between Martínez and Torres, the gathering convinced Torres that in the interest of Mexican Americans he should seek election in the newly created, but even more suburban, Thirty-Fourth District. Since Torres had raised his family in La Puente, within the new district, and still owned a house there, establishing residency would be no problem. This decision, however, did not receive unanimous consent because Joseph Montoya, whose senate district overlapped the Thirty-Fourth, perceived the move as carpetbagging. Montoya preferred someone with solidly suburban credentials, such as City Councilman Luis Escontrías of Santa Fe Springs. However, the conclave as a whole agreed that Torres had much more national and international experience, than any other local candidate; his qualifications for office were simply superior. Torres shortly thereafter received the endorsement of the caucus of California's Democratic delegation in the House of Representatives.[46] Montoya could not match the clout of the traditional Eastside politicos.

With the congressional candidates set, decisions on seats in the legislature followed. Once the conclave ratified Art Torres's decision to challenge Alex García for the state senate, the question of the two assembly seats to be vacated by Martínez and Art Torres remained. Charles Calderón, a Montebello school board member, received the nod to replace Martínez. As might be expected, the conclave favored candidates associated with TELACU in one way or another. The replacement for Art Torres was to be Richard Polanco, a member of the inner circle at TELACU at least since 1974. Although the selection of Calderón caused no controversy, the choice of Polanco did. Though designed to reduce infighting among Mexican Americans, the meeting at Steven's Steak House did not entirely succeed. As we have already seen, the conclave excluded Alex García, and Joseph Montoya left unhappy. The selection of Polanco created further dissension because another strong candidate decided to ignore the recommendations of the politicos and run against him. This development proved particularly significant because the candidate was Gloria Molina, the first Latina ever to contend seriously for a seat in the legislature.[47]

Assemblywoman Gloria Molina

Interestingly, Molina, like Polanco, had strong ties to the Mexican-American political establishment, including TELACU. As we have seen, TELACU had employed Molina briefly in the early seventies. From there she had gone on to serve in the campaigns and on the staffs of Tom Bradley, Willie Brown, Art Torres, and Jimmy Carter; she had obviously done her time in the trenches. However, when she sought the support of the establishment for her assembly campaign, she was denied. According to Frank del Olmo, columnist for the *Los Angeles Times*, "Many Latino political activists, most of them men, had serious doubts that a woman could win office in a Latino district."[48]

Indeed, the only meaningful difference between Polanco and Molina proved to be gender. Like Molina, Polanco had served as an aide to prominent Democrats, including Governor Brown and Supervisor Ed Edelman. Polanco had also worked for TELACU, including a period as vice president of the Community Research Group, the CDC's vaunted think tank. Both candidates had roots in the community—Polanco's deep in East LA, Molina's in the inner suburb of Pico Rivera. When it became apparent that Molina intended to run despite the decision of the conclave, the establishment tried to convince one or the other to drop out or to move to another district. The established officials even offered campaign support to the one who would move, but to no avail. With so few differences between the candidates, the campaign focused on endorsements, a situation that created factionalism as the two sought support from individual leaders of the establishment. Indeed, even longtime allies Alatorre and Torres split over this race; the unity achieved at the conclave dissolved, though not acrimoniously.[49] The dissension, on the other hand, undermined the notion that the Eastside establishment, including TELACU, constituted a political machine. The politicos were hardly bosses.

Molina succeeded in convincing Ed Roybal and Art Torres to break with the conclave's recommendation for Polanco. This move benefited her immensely because she gained the support of the area's venerable congressman and the support of the assemblyman whose district she sought. Polanco retained the backing of TELACU, where he had recently worked, and of Alatorre, whom Molina alienated by claiming his endorsement prematurely. Ultimately, bright and articulate Molina convinced the electorate she could do the job. In winning she shattered the myth that the Mexican-American community would not elect a woman to office.[50] This victory was only the first of many that would lead the independent Molina to the top of Los Angeles politics.

Congressmen Esteban Torres and Marty Martínez

Despite the conclave's failure to maintain unity behind Polanco, the decisions made at Steven's Steak House proved excellent. All of the candidates selected at the meeting proved viable. Charles Calderón joined the assembly, Art Torres defeated Alex García for the state senate, and though Molina defeated Polanco, the latter would win an assembly seat in 1986. Most importantly, the Greater Eastside's congressional delegation jumped from one to three. Both Marty Martínez and Esteban Torres won seats in Congress. Twenty years after Edward Roybal's first election to that body, he was joined by fellow Mexican Americans from the Greater Eastside. Though still underrepresented in virtually all government bodies, the Mexican-American colonias had clearly progressed.[51]

Democratic Integration

The election of Congressman Esteban Torres especially demonstrated that TELACU was providing the political leadership to recover the self-determination of the Chicano community. Throughout the years, and most evidently in 1982, the CDC had in one way or another assisted virtually every Mexican-American elected official in gaining the positions necessary to empower the Eastside. Despite the imagery of boss rule and machine politics, TELACU and Mexican-American officeholders had played the electoral game according to the formal and informal rules of American politics. These rules allowed political action committees, nominally nonpartisan registration drives, and back-room deals. Although TELACU's nonprofit, nonpartisan status had made its political involvement controversial, the CDC acted through legitimate third parties, again in time-honored tradition. Indeed, TELACU and Mexican-American politicians had learned the techniques required to integrate fully into the nation's democratic system, a system immersed in ethnic politics from its inception. But even as the East Los Angeles Community Union shared in the electoral triumph of 1982, and even as *The Pride of Our Heritage* took shape on the facade of TELACU's new headquarters, the federal government and the *Los Angeles Times* were conducting major investigations into every phase of the CDC's activities.[52]

8. The TELACU Center. Modern black stone-and-glass headquarters of the East Los Angeles Community Union. Photograph by author, 1997.

SEVEN

TELACU Under Investigation

Recovery Threatened

In 1982 the crowning edifice of the Eastside's new industrial park neared completion—the TELACU Center, an attractive five-story office building of lava rock and black glass. The facade of this structure would soon display *The Pride of Our Heritage*, the epic mural depicting the history of Mexican-American Los Angeles. As the new headquarters of the East Los Angeles Community Union, this veritable monument would signify the institution's increasing strength. However, before the building reached completion, TELACU's very existence was threatened by the institutions that had sustained it—agencies of federal, state, and local government. From its inception the community development corporation had infiltrated the political institutions of the capitalist system in hopes of freeing East LA from what TELACU interpreted as internal colonialism. However, in 1982 as the CDC steadily advanced toward its objectives of political self-determination and socioeconomic integration, the system seemingly retaliated. Amassed in the attack were the United States Department of Labor, a multitude of other government agencies, and the *Los Angeles Times*.[1]

Federal auditors probed deeply into TELACU's finances and operations, uncovering a plethora of questionable practices on the part of the CDC.[2] In the meantime the *LA Times* revealed these practices to the public, seriously damaging TELACU's reputation. Because the CDC advocated self-determination while accommodating the sytem, the image of TELACU had been enigmatic from its beginnings. After that its close relations with big unions, big government, and big business had made the CDC suspicious to other activists and ordinary people in East LA. But the controversy of 1982 produced an even more negative image of TELACU. While most of the charges resulted from a misunderstanding of TELACU's legal structure and overall purpose, the issues raised were not simply questions of legality or imagery, but of ethics. For the investigations questioned the fundamental value of TELACU to the community, by revealing that TELACU's management disproportionately enjoyed the benefits of the CDC's success. Despite this, TELACU's overall history demonstrated that the CDC had moved the Eastside toward significant political and socioeconomic recovery, progress now threatened.

Federal Audit

TELACU's troubles began in early 1980 when Jerome Gold, a former employee, charged that the CDC had violated the provisions of the Comprehensive Employment and Training Act (CETA). As participants in a jobs program, CETA workers were paid for work with private and public employers with federal money funneled through local governments. Since government provided their salaries, these workers could not participate in partisan activities. Gold charged, among other things, that since 1976 TELACU had illegally used CETA workers to solicit votes for Democrats, including Jimmy Carter. TELACU immediately labeled Gold a disgruntled employee fired for reasons unconnected with his accusations. Though TELACU reached a settlement with Gold after he appealed to the state, his earlier complaints to Los Angeles County officials reached the Department of Labor, the federal office ultimately responsible for CETA.[3]

The Department of Labor decided that the situation warranted an audit, which began in April 1980. This audit continued for two and a half years and expanded beyond the original areas of inquiry to touch on all public and private funding connected with TELACU from October 1, 1976, to September 30, 1979. Although audits by both private accounting firms and government agencies were normal operating procedure for organizations like TELACU, the duration, scope, and method of this particular audit created increasing tension between the CDC and the government. Because the audit had originally involved only CETA contracts, David Lizarraga and his staff resented the decision to expand into other areas of the CDC's operations. TELACU especially resented the government's audit of federal funds involved in for-profit ventures because, the CDC argued, such funds lost their public character once they entered the private sector. Despite TELACU's initial objections on these grounds, it decided to provide some information for the audit after discussing the matter, in late 1980, with the U.S. Community Services Administration. This agency, the major federal funding source for CDCs, suggested cooperation, a suggestion that TELACU could hardly refuse.[4]

The Department of Labor's auditors, Don B. Byrd and A. J. Bodero, met repeatedly with TELACU management, especially Executive Vice President George Pla, General Counsel Carlos J. García, and Senior Vice President Jess García. Problems nevertheless continued as mutual suspicion poisoned the relationship. In early 1981 the two parties had agreed to *cooperate*, but apparently disagreed on the meaning of the term. TELACU's executives agreed to provide documents requested by the auditors while the latter agreed to provide biweekly progress reports. Despite this, the executives interpreted the progress reports as simply more requests for documentation while the auditors became increasingly dissatisfied with the amount of information received. TELACU's executives became irritated that requests for information never indicated the specific concerns of the auditors, in other words, the purposes of the inquiry. Lizarraga and his executives suspected a fishing expedition. When TELACU management complained that providing documentation was taking an inordinate amount of staff time, the auditors suspected intentional lack of cooperation. By mid-1981 Byrd and Bodero ceased their requests and progress reports and decided to continue the audit via an alternate route. The federal auditors continued by examining the "workpapers" of three accounting firms that had previously conducted audits of TELACU. Byrd and Bodero finished the on-site review on October 23, 1981, though they would not make the complete report public for another year.[5]

A sample listing of social program costs by Byrd and Bodero themselves indicates that TELACU's executives always responded to the auditors' requests, though frequently with only partial documentation. Management claimed its staff at times could not supply the documents because they were in use, lost, or nonexistent. Ultimately, TELACU's managers argued they had supplied 80 percent of the papers requested, but the auditors claimed they received only about 50 percent.[6] Whatever the exact amount, the documentation including the workpapers obtained by the Department of Labor created further problems for the CDC. From TELACU's perspective, that the auditors gathered such troublesome evidence indicated that the CDC's staff had hidden nothing; from the auditors' perspective, the evidence suggested they had only seen the tip of the iceberg. In either case TELACU soon faced trial by the media.

Shattered Image in the *LA Times*

As early as April 1980, the press knew about the audit of TELACU, but in early 1982 the *Los Angeles Times* apparently received a tip that the auditors had uncovered serious problems. Assigned the story, investigative reporters Claire Spiegel and Robert Welkos published a three-part series in March, with many follow-up articles appearing in later months. Although a summary of the auditors' report did not surface until May and the full report not until much later, the *Times* gained access to much of the material through apparent leaks. Though the auditors denied leaking the information, a comparison of the final audit report with the earlier news stories indicates that the *Times* had an inside source. In a matter of weeks, on their own the newspaper reporters could not have accumulated the data that had taken the auditors years to compile, especially since TELACU had denied the reporters access to its records.[7] In any case at the end of March, the story became public well before the audit report appeared.

The *Times*'s investigative series dealt a shattering blow to TELACU's image and threatened the CDC's very survival. The headline to the first article suggested the impact the series would have, "Anti-Poverty Agency Leaving Barrio Behind: East L.A. Community Union's Spending Runs into Millions, and Now Official Suspicion." A shotgun blast of allegations followed—over fifty in the first article alone. The accusations spread across several broad categories: political corruption, financial mismanagement, conspicuous consumption, and poor community service.[8] While the articles alleged some illegal activity, essentially the series challenged the fundamental ethics of TELACU's board, its management, and its entire operation.

Political Corruption

In a companion article to the first in the series, the *Times*'s charges of political corruption basically involved misuse of government-paid workers and campaign contributions. The former centered on the already public charges that TELACU had used CETA workers in the campaigns of such Democrats as, Mayor Tom Bradley, Congressman Ed Roybal, and President Jimmy Carter, accusations refutable due to the legally nonpartisan status of TELACU's voter registration organization. However, additional charges surfaced regarding possibly illegal contributions of over $60,000 made by the CDC to a variety of Democratic officeholders, including many in positions to influence TELACU's funding. To the *Times* the contributions seemed illegal because federal law prohibited corporations from engaging in such activities, especially with government funds. TELACU responded that the applicable laws were California's, which permitted corporate contributions, and that the funds came from corporate profits, in other words, private and not government funds.[9] As TELACU's major line of defense, this argument rested on the underlying principle that to promote the self-determination of a community a CDC required independence. If government strictly controlled the budgets of CDCs, their underlying purpose disappeared.

Despite TELACU's generally credible defenses, the impression of political corruption set firmly because of the vivid details provided by the *Times*. For instance, the newspaper claimed that CETA workers during the 1976 get-out-the-vote campaign received precinct packets with photographs of Jimmy Carter and Walter Mondale on the cover. When asked to comment on this, a TELACU spokesman declined, naturally leaving the impression of misconduct. Another specific noted by the *Times* was a special bank account set up for a committee called the Friends of David Lizarraga. A $10,000 bank loan guaranteed by TELACU Industries and paid off by several other subsidiaries had been deposited in the account for use as political contributions.[10] While the account contained private funds and thus proved legal, its very name suggested venality. The hint of political corruption, justified or not, badly tarnished the image of TELACU.

Financial Mismanagement

The *Times*'s charges of financial mismanagement involved poor investments far from East Los Angeles and lack of adequate financial controls. The newspaper claimed that despite TELACU's official mission to improve East LA, the organization "spent most of its venture capital on business deals . . . , in places as far away as the Midwest, the East Coast and Europe." The reporters understated the fact that TELACU usually invested in other minority enterprises, with the long-term plan of reinvesting the dividends in East LA. It was, nevertheless, true that large profits had not materialized. Indeed, in 1980 overall profits had declined to $188,000 from the previous year's $490,000, due to the unusual risk involved in minority investments. Regarding financial accountability, the *Times* cited an unnamed auditor in asserting that funds were so intermixed between companies, and from government and private sources, "that control appears to be lost." In response TELACU argued that the auditors simply misunderstood the flexibility inherent in the operations of a community development corporation. On the other hand, the *Times*'s reporters did reveal a fundamental problem with the board of directors when George Pla acknowledged that it sometimes failed to oversee management adequately.[11]

Repeatedly, the vivid details the *Times* used to illustrate its charges did more harm to TELACU's image than the general charges themselves. For instance, in the series' second part, which focused on investments, the reporters discussed TELACU's involvement in Michigan Peninsula Airways, "a minority-owned air cargo company." After investing $100,000 in the company, TELACU bought and leased a DC-8 for the business, a plane without "any navigational equipment." Though the airline's management had dreamed of flying planes to South America and elsewhere, the company sank into debt, and TELACU's stock became worthless. TELACU's standard reply was that such investments involved risk, but the picture painted by the *Times* suggested incompetence. Another example concerning the problem of accountability proved similarly damaging. José Elizondo, a board member, admitted he "felt ill-equipped to evaluate complex business deals." As a maintenance man, he represented blue-collar East LA; indeed, he and several other board members held their seats for that very reason. But despite training programs in business, they only rarely challenged the professional expertise of the full-time managers.[12] The impression set that the corporate managers ran TELACU as if they, rather than the community, owned the CDC.

Conspicuous Consumption

Most damaging to TELACU's corporate image, however, were the accusations of conspicuous consumption and possible embezzlement on the part of both the board and managment. The *Times* charged that TELACU functionaries pocketed money illegally from their positions in the CDC and led extravagant lifestyles. The reporters claimed TELACU president David Lizarraga borrowed thousands from the corporation in order to make personal investments. Although the government would later judge this practice legal due to the private character of the funds, the readers of the *Times* must certainly have inferred a conflict of interest in the executive's behavior. The newspaper also charged that TELACU staff spent unnecessarily high sums on luxurious surroundings, expensive travel, and fancy automobiles. TELACU's response that the business world demanded such trappings for participation drew little sympathy. For the *Times* had labeled TELACU an "anti-poverty agency," not a community development corporation engaged in business.[13]

The *Times*'s vivid illustrations of alleged embezzlement and conspicuous consumption particularly besmirched TELACU's reputation. For example, in describing the loans for Lizarraga's personal investments, Spiegel and Welkos reported that "his name was sometimes 'whited-out' on TELACU ledgers." Clearly, the reporters were implying that the staff covered up illegal activity since they offered no interpretation of this descriptive comment. Descriptions of the apparent extravagance of TELACU functionaries had the longest effect on the CDC's image. One particularly illustrative example supported the adage that a picture is worth a thousand words. In the opening column of their series, the reporters noted that "TELACU Industries . . . operated out of a lavish office suite decorated with a $10,000 table and a $400 wastebasket." Other, similarly sensational descriptions of the CDC's physical surroundings appeared throughout the series. With regard to corporate travel, the *Times* noted, "TELACU's . . . expenditures have ranged from a trip to Mexico City for the board of directors and their guests to a $25,000 bill for travel and other expenses . . . to Switzerland and Lebanon." TELACU justified the former as a reward for the unpaid service of the directors, and the latter as a business trip in search of financing for a hotel project that later proved impractical. Again TELACU's explanations were credible for a business corporation, but seemed dubious for what the *Times* constantly called an antipoverty agency. No doubt, readers inferred that antipoverty officials driving around in Mercedes-Benzes must be corrupt.[14] TELACU's defense that the corporate culture required business suits and expensive cars had some merit, but the overall image remained negative.

Poor Community Service

The imagery of conspicuous consumption proved particularly shocking when juxtaposed with TELACU's mission of community service. Headlining the final part of its series "Giant Anti-Poverty Agency Did Little to Create Jobs," the *Times* charged that TELACU had violated its pledge to serve the community, especially with regard to employment. The reporters described TELACU's job-training programs, real estate projects, and loan programs as ineffective and self-serving. According to the *Times*, "Much of the money spent on job training has not yet been audited, but more than 50 program violations were reported in a 1979 county audit of $1.1 million." On the other hand, the reporters did recognize that TELACU's home-repair projects and their job trainees were generally well received by community residents. Regarding TELACU's vaunted real estate projects, however, the newspaper criticized TELACU Industrial Park for not creating enough employment because tenants generally brought their work forces with them. TELACU countered that it could not force the companies to employ locals, but implied that in the long run they would do so. Additionally, the *Times* indirectly criticized TELACU for placing all of Community Thrift & Loan's branches outside of East LA, but failed to explain that the thrift used deposits from suburban branches to make small loans to the businesses and residents of redlined East LA.[15]

Again the illustrations used by the *Times* to support its allegations of poor community service by TELACU proved even more harmful than the assertions themselves. Regarding job programs, the investigative reporters pointed out that Joe L. González, chairman of the CDC's board of directors, had once enrolled himself and his wife in a TELACU program funded by CETA. González answered that he "was having hard times financially several years ago"; the *Times* juxtaposed this disingenous response with the information that he currently owned "an export-import company and two art galleries." Concerning the industrial park, the *Times* reported that one labor-intensive tenant subsidized by TELACU produced skateboards "four or five years behind the times," hardly conducive to the image of technical expertise promoted by the CDC. Finally, regarding loans arranged by the Business Development Center, the then retired Maggie Aparicio commented that the "taco stands, restaurants, [and] body-and-fender shops" of East LA received much less assistance than clients in Orange County because to qualify for this federal aid businesses had to have at least $100,000 in sales.[16] The *Times*'s portrayal of TELACU's service to the community was indeed bleak, if one-sided.

David Lizarraga, "Plutocrat"

Ultimately, the *Los Angeles Times* painted a picture of an "antipoverty agency" that enriched its officials far more than it assisted the community. Perhaps the most graphic illustration of this theme was the reporters' description of David Lizarraga's lifestyle: "He owns a home with a service entrance and a boat parked in the driveway on 11 acres of land in the Covina Hills. He also owns another house in Ontario, a Brentwood condominium and desert land in San Bernardino County. . . ." Though his salary remained undisclosed, apparently he received compensation on the scale of chief executive officers in the business world, not on that of common bureaucrats. This point revealed a fundamental difference of perception between the newspaper and the CDC. The former imagined TELACU as a wayward government welfare agency, the latter perceived itself as a business corporation contracting with government.[17] While a major purpose of TELACU was to develop East LA economically, its managers increasingly perceived that purpose according to the "trickle-down" theories just then becoming popular nationally. If TELACU's management did well, the entire community eventually had to benefit.

Public and Official Reaction

Following the series in the *Los Angeles Times*, the letters to the editor revealed a generally hostile public reaction toward TELACU, as we might expect. In one letter, an Anglo reader from La Puente commented bitterly, "As I read the articles my sense of outrage grew and grew." A Latina from Los Angeles echoed the sentiment, "I am truly angered that the officials in that agency have taken so much money for themselves so callously while parading as a community-service organization." On the other hand, TELACU did have its defenders. For example, a Chicano from Compton trenchantly remarked,

> Mexican Americans have long been told to learn how to negotiate the system. What is happening to TELACU's leadership proves that once they learn, they had better be super-clean. . . . For while the sins of the founding fathers and their progeny are forgiven . . . Mexicans, blacks

and other suppressed minorities are kept in their place—especially if they show signs of having learned how the game is played.[18]

It did seem that the *Times* and the general public expected TELACU's Mexican-American officals to participate in the system as benign social reformers—not as assertive politicians or aggressive capitalists.

Government Contracts Canceled

In response to the *Times*'s series and public opinion, government bodies that had contracts with TELACU began to review them. The Federal Communications Commission took the first action of this type in mid-April 1982. The FCC temporarily revoked earlier permission for sale of a television station to TELACU and a group of Virginia businessmen, including several prominent politicians. The station, located in Hartford, Connecticut, appeared on the market at a low price under federal regulations designed to encourage minority ownership of broadcasting facilities. Criticism of the sale concerned the fact that TELACU officials would personally gain stock without putting up any of their own funds and that the consortium purchasing the station seemed insufficiently "minority." The FCC acknowledged that it took action "in light of certain information . . . highlighted" by the newspapers.[19]

More serious still was the reaction of the Los Angeles City Council, which had contracted with TELACU to hire CETA workers. After publication of the *Times*'s investigative articles, apparently city administrators met secretly with A. J. Bodero, one of the auditors from the Department of Labor, who briefed them on the contents of the still unpublished audit report on TELACU. At the late April meeting the auditor ran through many of the same charges that the *Times* had published, including the claim that $47 million, more or less equaling the total assets of TELACU, was in question. Though the auditors later admitted that they had exaggerated the figure to draw attention to TELACU's misconduct, the city became concerned over its liability for such a large amount. On May 14 the city unilaterally canceled its contracts with TELACU. The direct impact of the canceled city contracts was not that severe since they were due to expire in a few months; furthermore, these contracts only involved about fifteen CETA employees, whom the city transferred to other accounts. While the cancellation ended the financial liability of TELACU as well as the city, the CDC's reputation suffered again.[20] This remained a serious matter to an organization whose dealings with government and business required good faith.

Community Health Threatened

In one other area the threat to TELACU directly affected the community as well. The scandal threatened to undermine the TELACU Family Health Foundation, established in Highland Park in 1981, because the city of Los Angeles became concerned over the funds it had contributed to the medical center. Fearing TELACU's mismanagement of that facility, the city seemed ready to pull out of that financial arrangement. Since such a funding cut would hurt the very physical health of the community, TELACU began to separate itself from the foundation. By the end of 1982, the separation was complete, and the facility had been renamed the Arroyo Vista Family Health Center. However, TELACU of necessity canceled its plans to put up a new building for the health center.[21] Curiously, TELACU had to abandon its most ambitious social service project because of the charges that the CDC inadequately served the Eastside.

In late April 1982 after the city's secret meeting regarding its CETA contracts with TELACU, state Senator Alex García entered the fray. García, whom TELACU opposed for reelection, released a statement to the press, calling for an investigation of the CDC by the state's Small Business Development Board. Since TELACU and its subsidiaries had received over $2 million within the previous two years from the state, García's call meant more trouble for the CDC. As a member of the board, García's opinion carried some weight. In his press release, García commended the *Los Angeles Times*, not so much for uncovering a situation already under audit, but "for placing this story in its proper social and moral context." He went on to condemn TELACU's activities, adding a few suspicions regarding state funds along the way. García's efforts would fail, however, as the state board in June unanimously declined to conduct a full investigation, concluding that García's charges were "politically motivated and unfounded in fact." García nevertheless proved right about one thing: "The recent press reports on TELACU have tapped an undercurrent of suspicion. . . . That suspicion is now widespread."[22] The public's suspicious attitude toward TELACU concerned not simply its legal and financial activities, but its moral principles.

The next body to question TELACU's reputation was the Los Angeles County Board of Supervisors, which also had CETA contracts with the CDC. After also receiving a briefing from the Department of Labor auditors, the supervisors on May 25 met with TELACU officials to discuss the CETA contracts. TELACU's executives had finally been briefed by the auditors, but only a few hours before facing the supervisors. Like the LA City Council, the supervisors seemed most concerned about liability for the $47 million figure bandied about by the auditors. The supervisors forgot the specific purpose and value of the contracts at hand and also decided to cancel. Though the county planned to reassign the CETA workers, TELACU found itself once again losing face. TELACU lost contracts, not because of specific violations, but because of general charges that it had scarcely had a chance to answer, having only recently received a summary of the audit report. The eventual conviction of Joe L. González, former chair of TELACU's board, for false statements concerning his CETA employment, partially vindicated the contract cancellations. However, without a doubt the city and county reconsidered the contracts in the first place because of the *Times*'s investigative series.[23] The media had put TELACU on trial.

Legal Battles

Following the *Times*'s series, the FCC, the city, the state, and the county had reviewed and in most cases revoked contracts with TELACU, but the CDC's problems persisted. TELACU had had a longstanding disagreement with the U.S. Small Business Administration, which flared up again during the audit by the Department of Labor and especially after the media publicized the issue. As we have seen, in late 1975 TELACU had succeeded in obtaining a license for a Minority Enterprise Small Business Investment Company (MESBIC), an entity designed to provide capital for disadvantaged businesses. With the license the SBA advanced $700,000 to get the new MESBIC off the ground. Thus appeared TELACU Investment Company, a subsidiary placed under the management of Leonard Rutkin, a former New York stockbroker and part-time consultant to the CDC. While Rutkin seemed well qualified, he had had personal financial problems for years; indeed, a former partner commented, "He gave the impression he knew what he was doing, but he couldn't handle money." Rutkin, moreover, was accustomed to a lavish lifestyle.[24]

TELACU Investment Company Besieged

In 1978 the inspector general of SBA had ordered an audit of TELACU Investment Company that unearthed five violations. Most serious of these was that the company had borrowed money using its assets as collateral without SBA approval. TELACU had not revealed this fact while applying for and receiving another $700,000 from the SBA. More damaging, however, was that Rutkin and his vice president tried to cover up the matter when questioned by the auditors. After the audit uncovered the deception, the federal government decided not to prosecute the officials, apparently deciding that the original infraction had been unintentional. Moreover, "The investigation disclosed that none of T.I.C.'s assets were diverted to any of its officers or the officers of the TELACU organization."[25] SBA, nevertheless, placed the company on informal probation and advanced no further funds.

At this point, Rutkin naturally lost the confidence of TELACU's central management and resigned in May 1979. On his departure he stated that except for a few problem areas, TELACU Investment Company remained healthy and should resist SBA's threats to liquidate it. He regretted the misunderstandings with the CDC and wished to negotiate the terms of his separation. The terms negotiated proved quite generous, including the continuation of several months' salary, justified as consulting fees. TELACU also made arrangements for him to pay off thousands of dollars he owed the

CDC. At his departure he continued to live at a condominium owned partially by David Lizarraga and drove away in a company Mercedes-Benz whose lease he promised to pay. Despite this favorable separation, Rutkin could not pay his debts to TELACU; apparently, his new independent consulting firm in Santa Monica did not produce enough revenue. In any case, by March 1982 when the *Times*'s series reported on Rutkin's activities, TELACU was desperately trying to recover some $65,000 owed it by this former official.[26]

Independent of the Department of Labor audit initiated in early 1980, the Small Business Administration had continued to monitor TELACU after the problems under Rutkin's management, but the difficulties persisted. Apparently, his successor, Gustavo Paladines, proved no more competent as the SBA found even more violations and finally about December 1981 decided to liquidate the MESBIC. (The violations generally involved conflict of interest and self-dealing.) TELACU sought to avoid the liquidation, fearing criminal prosecution of the former managers might follow. The negative publicity generated by the *Times*'s investigative series made TELACU even more leery of acquiescing to the SBA's decision. In June 1982 TELACU offered to sell the MESBIC to a third party, but the SBA refused this informal settlement.[27] Consequently, the matter dragged on.

Strategy Session in Washington

The complexity of TELACU's funding sources led federal officials from a variety of agencies to meet in Washington on July 1, 1982, to discuss the ramifications of the Department of Labor's yet-to-be-completed audit report. In attendance were nearly thirty bureaucrats from the Agency for International Development, the Community Services Administration, the Department of Commerce, the Department of Housing and Urban Development, the Department of Health and Human Services, the Small Business Administration, the Department of Transportation, the Office of Management and Budget, and of course the Department of Labor. Labor's Inspector General Tom McBride presided. Each of the agencies briefly described their connections with TELACU and the actions they expected to take in light of the audit. AID and HUD reported that they had recently terminated contracts with TELACU, and other agencies continued to review theirs. Given the possible cancellations, McBride commented that the CDC might "be facing a shaky future." The officials discussed whether coordinated action might be necessary. Though no conclusion arose with regard to this, such action seemed unlikely because of the complex relationships involved. McBride noted, "on a separate track, matters related to possible criminal prosecution had been referred to the U.S. Attorney's office in Los Angeles. . . ."[28] Though these matters were not the focus of the meeting, they were certainly uppermost in the minds of TELACU's executives. The high-level meeting demonstrated the extensive federal scrutiny TELACU experienced in 1982; that the CDC survived at all surprised many in Washington, as well as Los Angeles.

Under the barrage of accusations from the media and contract terminations by government, TELACU at first retreated. To many of the charges made by the *Times*, TELACU initially had no comment. David Lizarraga, under the advice of attorneys, refused interviews with the investigative reporters. For the same reason John Echeveste, TELACU'S public relations director, also frequently refused comment.[29] Moreover, the executives' situation on publication of the story remained precarious because they did not know the specifics of the Department of Labor's audit. Unfortunately for the CDC, the initially weak response left the impression that they had something to hide. TELACU nevertheless marshaled a counterattack.

TELACU's Counterattack

As early as April 7, 1982, the *East Los Angeles Tribune* printed the following headlines: "TELACU Fires Back: Agency Cites Accomplishments in Wake of Investigative Series." TELACU issued a statement to the local community paper, and Lizarraga granted it an interview defending the CDC in general terms and listing its various projects. More important than the list, however, was the image TELACU sought to project in the *Tribune*. Though labeled an antipoverty agency by the *Times*, Lizarraga stressed that TELACU was a community development corporation. As such, the CDC had become "the prime economic catalyst for the East Los Angeles area." He pointed out that no other organization invested as much private capital in the community; indeed, at the time both the private sector and government were disinvesting in the area. TELACU's press release added that the CDC competed "in the business world alongside Bank of America, Chrysler and other corporate giants."[30] In other words, the *Times* failed to see TELACU in the context of the business world. Unfortunately for the CDC, despite the credible article, the *Tribune* had nowhere near the circulation of the *Times*.

This article began a broad offensive by TELACU, which had to hire a number of law firms to fight its battles. After the city and county cut their CETA contracts with the CDC, TELACU appealed the decisions within the judicial systems of the two bureaucracies. In both forums it argued that the governing bodies had terminated the contracts without due process, that these bodies had taken rash actions based on the one-sided briefings of the federal auditors and the *Times*'s series. However, in both cases TELACU faced the insurmountable stipulation that either party to the CETA contracts could terminate them unilaterally, within thirty days, without cause. TELACU appealed just the same, in hopes of getting its side of the story told.[31]

In late July 1982 Jess García, TELACU's senior vice president of finance, testified in hearings before county and city administrative judges. García received the best opportunity to present TELACU's side of the story in the city hearing. Although the legal issue was due process, the proceedings revealed that García and TELACU's management worried most about the adverse publicity the contract terminations had dealt the CDC, in other words the damage done to its image. During the proceedings, Joseph Connolly, counsel for TELACU, made this point evident. Although he did not accuse the city of defamation, Connolly stated, "We accuse the DOL auditors of doing that and of intimidating and stampeding the City into terminating TELACU's status as a contractor and stigmatizing it with this brand of being, lacking integrity, being dishonest and trying to cover things up. ...."³² To carry on its business, TELACU needed to recover its reputation, which indeed the government and media had injured.

The city hearing officer understood the underlying purpose of the complaint and allowed TELACU's counsel substantial latitude in presenting his case. TELACU clearly hoped to use any favorable findings from this hearing in other forums, especially against the Department of Labor. Connolly put the matter thus:

> We have been looking ... for somebody to stand up and say what these DOL auditors did and what they caused these local government officials to do violated fundamental principles of due process. ... Politicians are thoroughly intimidated by The Los Angeles Times and ... these Department of Labor auditors. ...

The counsel for the city responded that with no way of double-checking the auditors' claims, the city had to cut the contracts to prevent liability for any subsequent problems. The hearing officer ultimately agreed that the city could cut the contracts unilaterally, basically dismissing the question of defamation as irrelevant (the county hearing officer followed the same thinking). TELACU, nevertheless, decided to appeal, still hoping to repair the damage done to its image.³³

Rural Development Loan Challenged by U.S.

Even as TELACU took the offensive against the media, the city, and the county, pressure from the federal government continued. In August 1982, even before the unfavorable rulings in the city and county matters, the inspector general of the Office of Community Services conducted another audit of TELACU, an audit clearly inspired by the recent negative publicity. This audit involved $1 million from the Rural Development Loan Fund for a project to be administered by TELACU. The federal office had loaned TELACU the money in January 1981 so that the CDC could in turn lend the money to disadvantaged businesses in rural areas. Over a year and a half later, however, TELACU had only made one loan of $30,000 and that to an ineligible applicant in the suburb of Fremont, California. To make matters worse, the recipient had defaulted. TELA-

CU had kept the remaining funds in certificates of deposit earning $230,000 in interest. In addition the auditors cited other problems regarding administrative costs in their report.[34] Once again TELACU faced public charges of incompetence, financial mismanagement, and possibly even embezzlement.

In response to the audit report from Community Services, TELACU admitted making a mistake with the ineligible loan recipient from Fremont. The CDC claimed it misunderstood the loan program's definition of "rural"—hardly a credible defense. Regarding the bulk of the million dollars, TELACU replied that it had planned to invest these in an industrial park in Parlier, an agricultural community south of Fresno, California, but that after close examination had decided that the project lacked feasibility. The Office of Community Services rejected TELACU's explanations, pointing out that the CDC had not provided informative or timely reports of the Parlier plans. In November 1982 Community Services followed by terminating the rural loan contract and demanding return of all funds, plus interest.[35] TELACU thus became involved in another lengthy legal case, attempting to cleanse a public image that had by now thoroughly tarnished.

TELACU Partially Vindicated

In November 1982 the Department of Labor's complete audit report finally became available. At this point the three-volume report, including TELACU's responses and exhibits, seemed anticlimactic since much of it had leaked over the previous months. Though the audit had taken over two years, TELACU had only had a few weeks over the summer to reply; consequently, many of the CDC's specific responses seemed inadequate. On the whole, however, the final report backed away from some of the most serious allegations previously leaked to the *Los Angeles Times*. First and foremost, the $47 million figure loosely questioned earlier declined to less than $4.5 million. Second, the charge that TELACU had not achieved self-sufficiency disappeared. Third, the report dropped many specific questions, such as those involving a gasoline fund, after adequate explanation by TELACU.[36] In effect the final audit report signaled that TELACU as a whole would survive because the vast majority of its operations had passed the in-depth federal inspection.

Confirmation of this came on November 12, 1982, when the *Los Angeles Times* itself printed what amounted to a retraction of its March investigative series on TELACU. The headline read: "Poverty Agency Largely Immune from Corruption Probe: Taxpayer Dollars Invested in TELACU's Businesses Became Private Funds." The article cited Stephen Trott, the U.S. attorney in Los Angeles who had investigated the possibilities of criminal charges resulting from the Department of Labor's audit. Trott had consulted, in his own words, "every expert under the sun," and concluded that TELACU remained largely "impenetrable."[37]

As indicated in the final audit report, TELACU had won the major legal points regarding its operations. The CDC had successfully argued that federal funds invested in its ventures entered the private sector and could be spent in any way deemed appropriate by TELACU. Indeed, Don Byrd, the auditor who had complained about the CDC's lack of cooperation, admitted to the newspaper that he discovered he had "no authority to question." Byrd also admitted that the CDC's complexity had overwhelmed the auditors, thus supporting TELACU's contention that they did not understand the operation. Key to this contention was the issue of self-sufficiency. Because the auditors and the *Times* had construed TELACU as simply a welfare agency running on federal funds, they had failed to perceive it as an autonomous corporation that held private capital. The critics had not understood the Special Impact Program. Only when the U.S. attorney looked into the possibilities of prosecution did the applicable laws become clear. As Trott pointed out to the *Times*, "The way the project was set up—to act as a capital enterprise and investment operation—there's almost anything you can do."[38] Since Congress had designed the Special Impact Program to foster community self-determination, it could not permit excessive government interference in the operations of community development corporations.

Neither federal officials nor the *Times* were pleased with this state of affairs. Though the November article was virtually a retraction, the *Times* published it without apology. Indeed, the *Times* and federal officials left the distinct impression that TELACU officials were getting away with murder. Despite the general vindication, the attacks on TELACU's image continued in both the rhetoric and the content of the November article. For example, with regard to the Special Impact Program, former Inspector General William O'Connor of the Community Services Administration stated, "It's the damnedest piece of legislation I've ever seen in my life in terms of losing control of federal dollars once they were shoveled out the door." Even U.S. Attorney Trott resorted to profanity in showing his displeasure over the matter: "they're [TELACU officials] right (that) they can damn well do anything they want with it [federal money] as long as it's arguably within the scope of the project." Spiegel and Welkos, authors of the November article as well as the March series, repeated the imagery used earlier, "federal dollars . . . became private dollars—free to be spent on big salaries, fancy cars, personal loans, worldwide travel and plush accommodations, among other things."[39] The ethical issue of conspicuous consumption remained; despite winning legal vindication, TELACU had not cleared its image.

Though the November article conceded that TELACU had used the vast majority of its funds legally, the *Times*'s reporters devoted much space to those still in doubt. The $47 million loosely mentioned in the initial series vanished, but the $4.5 million still questioned in the Department of Labor's final audit report now received substantial coverage. Despite this, the *Times* did recognize that TELACU might successfully account for much of the smaller figure on a case-by-case basis before the various agencies involved. Toward the end of the article, the *Times* stressed the recent convictions of TELACU Chairman Joe González and his wife for their illegal activities in connection with CETA. "Sentenced to five years' probation and 1500 hours of community service," the two were nevertheless the only people connected with TELACU finally brought up on criminal charges by U.S. Attorney Trott. At the article's conclusion, Trott trenchantly remarked regarding his continuing investigation, "I don't know how many days God had to render the universe out of chaos, but I think even somebody with those types of powers would have trouble making order out of this."⁴⁰

TELACU Presses On Against Washington

Encouraged by its general vindication in the *Times* and by the U.S. attorney, TELACU intensified its battle with the government through the courts. As we have seen, in the spring TELACU had lost its initial confrontations over CETA with the city council and the county board of supervisors. In August and September of 1982, appeals in the city and county cases, respectively, had also been lost; the administrative law courts had ruled that the local governments could unilaterally break their contracts. But TELACU continued the process still hoping that along the way an appeals court would report tangential findings that TELACU might use in its other legal battles. At the very end of 1982, TELACU and the U.S. attorney locked horns again, this time over the Small Business Administration's Minority Enterprise Small Business Investment Company and the Office of Community Services's Rural Development Loan Fund.⁴¹

As we have seen, the SBA matter basically involved questions of self-dealing and conflict of interest by TELACU Investment Company, the MESBIC subsidiary of the CDC. SBA charged the MESBIC with making investments in other companies associated with TELACU specifically, board Chairman Joe González's art company and Congressman Esteban Torres's international trading company. The federal agency also accused the MESBIC of "making unauthorized salary and management payments," specifically the consultation fees paid to Leonard Rutkin at his separation. Ultimately, the SBA charged the CDC with ten detailed violations of regulations.⁴²

During the summer of 1982, TELACU had been on the verge of acquiescing to the SBA's liquidation of TELACU Investment Company, but the CDC backed out at the last minute. On the advice of counsel, the threat of criminal prosecution had compelled TELACU's executives to seek complete vindication. The subsequent retreat of the Department of Labor and the *LA Times* in November had further encouraged a counterattack. On December 30, 1982, the very same day the Department of Justice filed a civil suit over the MESBIC in Los Angeles, TELACU filed its own complaint in Washington, D.C. By establishing a venue more to their liking, TELACU's lawyers hoped to control the pace and possibilities for future settlement.[43] Over five years of legal wrangling followed, not concluded until well after TELACU's 1982 crisis had subsided.

Reagan Administration Attacked

As its main argument, TELACU charged that the Small Business Administration was "discriminatorily and selectively enforcing the small business laws . . . because TELACU's executive management and members of its Board of Directors . . . [were] active politically in the Democratic party." TELACU argued that the Reagan administration sought to deter TELACU's political activities and thus improve the Republican party's future success in California. TELACU believed that the executive branch sought vengeance against the CDC and that the administration wanted nothing more than to replace TELACU's officials with Reagan supporters. The fact that President Reagan in September 1981 had downgraded the Community Services Administration gave credence to TELACU's suspicions. This agency, already demoted once, had been the successor to Lyndon Johnson's Office of Economic Opportunity, the controversial heart of the War on Poverty. Of course, Community Services managed the Special Impact Program, the basic funding agency of CDCs. Community Services' operations had been cut, disbursed, or consigned to the lesser, newly created Office of Community Services, within the Department of Health and Human Services.[44] Since TELACU's problems with the SBA extended back to the Carter administration, the charge based on political persecution lacked substance. Yet the argument revealed what the CDC regarded as the underlying source of the continuing troubles with the federal government.

To make matters even more complicated, TELACU and the U.S. attorney also sued each other over the Rural Development Loan Fund monies supplied to TELACU by Community Services. In an attempt to preempt the plaintiff's position in any litigation on this matter, TELACU in late December 1982 sued the Office of Community Services in Washington, again hoping to argue a case in a more favorable venue. A short time later Community Services countersued in Los Angeles. As we have seen, the issue involved $1 million in loan funds that the federal government claimed TELACU had failed to use as required. TELACU argued that Community Services had failed to provide the technical assistance necessary for the CDC to administer the monies properly. In their testimony TELACU officials claimed that they were not clearly informed of the conditions of the rural loan program and consequently misunderstood it. This proved a disingenuous argument at best, making TELACU officials look like bunglers, rather than the technocrats they claimed to be. More convincing was their argument that the Department of Labor's audit so preoccupied them that they never had a chance to carry out the provisions of the loan program.[45]

As in the SBA lawsuit, TELACU also claimed the executive branch of the federal government, now under Republican control, conspired to undermine the CDC because of its Democratic party associations. This conspiracy defense, elaborated before the U.S. district court in Los Angeles, had several parts. TELACU argued first that the Reagan administration, by distributing incomplete reports to the press and local government, sought "To damage and destroy defendant's ability to function as a community development corporation by publicly besmirching its business reputation. . . ." Second, TELACU argued that the executive branch sought to place individuals on the CDC's board and in its management more favorable to the administration. The third argument was that Republicans hoped to improve their chances in the 1984 elections by undermining the CDC's political position. Basically, TELACU claimed the administration hoped "To reward Republican politicians and businessmen of Hispanic background in the Los Angeles area by turning over to them control of what might eventually remain of defendant's activities after the Republican Administration's attack." The conspiracy took effect, according to TELACU, through the constant threat of new audits and intensification of those already under way.[46]

The government's case was much simpler. The loan documents, which TELACU officials claimed they misunderstood, contained a provision that allowed Community Services to cancel unilaterally a specific rural loan program even if the recipients only seemed in violation of its requirements. In early January 1983 this provision had initially allowed a federal judge in Los Angeles to rule quickly against TELACU even without its presence in court. As in the CETA cases involving the city and county, the contract provisions themselves gave TELACU little hope of winning. Nevertheless, TELACU appealed again, in the vain hope of repairing its shattered image.[47] This case would drag on until mid-1985.

Closing Skirmishes

Appropriately enough, the final legal battles regarding the critical events of 1982 involved TELACU and the Department of Labor itself. The latter had, of course, launched the sweeping audit of the CDC in 1980 over alleged CETA violations. Since these violations had involved city and county contracts, most of the litigation had gone through the administrative law courts of the local governments. Curiously, the county and TELACU together filed an appeal through the Department of Labor's own judicial system. They sought to prevent the department from collecting about $150,000 in CETA funds remaining from their joint contract. In a separate action launched in late 1983, the department directly sued TELACU within the former's administrative judiciary for recovery of less than $15,000 in questioned costs, involving rental of space to certain politicians and political groups. Significantly, the amounts in these final suits were paltry sums compared with the nearly $50 million figure originally trumpeted by the Department of Labor and the *Los Angeles Times*. These cases would continue until early 1986.[48]

In the end the East Los Angeles Community Union survived the assault of government, at least financially. Of the $47 million that auditors publicly claimed TELACU had misused, they ultimately challenged less than $5 million officially. As we have seen, of the funds challenged, TELACU lost most through protracted legal battles. In mid-1983 the CDC dropped its appeal of the city case over CETA, thus admitting defeat in that matter. In early 1986 the county and Department of Labor suits were settled out of court, with TELACU returning nominal sums to the government. In mid-1985 Community Services and TELACU settled the rural loan suit with the CDC returning the $1 million with interest to the government. After keeping TELACU Investment Company in receivership for several years, in mid-1988 the SBA liquidated the MESBIC, reclaimed over $3 million, and finally ended that long legal affair.[49] Of course, Joe González had long since pleaded guilty to the charges against him. Although TELACU had lost virtually all the legal battles undertaken, it had successfully prevented government officials from challenging the vast majority of its assets in court. Because those assets remained in the private sector, TELACU had assured its financial independence.

Of course, TELACU's programs suffered because of the scandal. As we have seen, the CETA programs were scuttled, though this would have occurred anyway since the Reagan administration soon ended the jobs program nationally. TELACU's mismanagement of the MESBIC denied the community an important program for economic development when the SBA liquidated the company. TELACU's program for expanding into rural areas collapsed because of the CDC's own ineptitude and possibly federal harassment. On the other hand, the Reagan administration had also been seeking to dismantle the Rural Development Loan Fund nationwide. TELACU's international projects ended when the Agency for International Development terminated its contracts with the CDC, again on mere suspicion of wrongdoing. Even the Department of Housing and Urban Development, a longtime supporter, cut its funding of TELACU projects. As we have seen, the loss of the TELACU Health Center proved especially harmful since it had best symbolized TELACU's fundamental commitment to the Eastside. Moreover, TELACU had to close one of its most creative ventures, the Community Research Group, once more on mere suspicion.[50] TELACU could not challenge all of these losses in court because of the enormous legal costs.

Despite these losses, throughout the scandal Lizarraga and his officers had worried more about the damage done to TELACU's image. Without a good reputation they would have difficulty in their future relations with business, government, the general public, and the local community. With regard to the first two, TELACU's executives could repair the damage through face-to-face contact, but they would have more trouble changing the minds of ordinary people. Even before the scandal, TELACU had seemed suspiciously aloof to members of the local community. The *LA Times* did almost irreparable damage by reinforcing these local suspicions and extending them to the general public beyond the Eastside. Despite the virtual retraction of the *Times*'s series against TELACU in November 1982, the negative press continued into mid-1983 when the scandal had about run its course.[51]

On July 9, 1983, the *Times* reported a memorable event in the history of the East Los Angeles Community Union: the dedication of the TELACU Center, the newly completed corporate headquarters. Unfortunately for the CDC, reporter Claire Spiegel used the occasion to repeat several charges still pending, such as those involving the MESBIC and the rural loan fund. Again, more damaging than the charges themselves was the imagery she used in the article. For example, in describing David Lizarraga's new quarters, she again criticized the conspicuous consumption of TELACU's management: "He's got his own bathroom, shower and kitchenette—besides an office with plush carpeting and designer furnishings that include a gleaming round walnut desk with matching coffee table and a $400 wastebasket." And in describing *The Pride of Our Heritage* depicting what she called the "Latino heritage," the reporter repeated that the mural's designer had recently been convicted of felony charges.[52]

Ethics, Recovery, and Integration

Though TELACU had survived legally and financially, the image problem remained because the imagery brought up ethical questions. Should an organization dedicated to improving an impoverished community engage in conspicuous consumption? More importantly, did the ordinary people of East LA benefit from the CDC as much as its managers? TELACU had failed to give satisfactory answers to such questions. Despite this, the *LA Times* noted that at the dedication of the TELACU Center, César Chávez delivered a speech commending the CDC for its survival and its achievement of self-sufficiency. As a Chicano leader close to the very poor and never given to personal luxury, his supportive comments carried weight. His comments suggested that despite its imperfections, TELACU provided services to the the Eastside that no other Mexican-American organization could match, especially in economic development.[53] TELACU's contributions to Mexican-American regional recovery and national integration were considerable; and for this reason the community-owned institution deserved reevaluation and reform.

EIGHT

Resurgence of TELACU and the Eastside

Major Institution for Economic Recovery

By mid-1983 the East Los Angeles Community Union had survived the worst of its confrontation with the federal government and the *Los Angeles Times*. Although litigation would continue until 1988, TELACU much earlier concentrated on recovery from the scandal.[1] As a direct result of the scandal, the CDC retreated from the heavy political involvement of the period from 1976 to 1982. From 1983 into the nineties TELACU deemphasized voter registration campaigns, political fund-raising events, and similar activities through "front" organizations. Adverse publicity had made such actions counterproductive. Of course, individuals associated with the CDC remained politically active, and TELACU maintained the strong connections it had with politicians from city hall to Washington. But now more than ever, the CDC focused on economic development, especially real estate development.

Other groups, such as the United Neighborhoods Organization and the Mexican American Legal Defense and Education Fund, had become important and successful in the political arena, but no other Latino organization in the Los Angeles area, or elsewhere in the United States, could match TELACU's expertise in economic development.[2] Despite the damage done to its image by the federal and media charges of incompetence and financial mismanagement, TELACU had undeniable successes in an area that few other Latino organizations had dared enter. This was especially important since by the nineties, Mexican Americans were making major gains in the political arena, but in some ways losing ground economically. Politically, the Eastside was gradually becoming independent, but economically it still resembled a colony. Economically at least, TELACU remained the major institution offering the Mexican-American community a way toward regional recovery and integration with the larger society.

Revitalized Landscape

The very landscape of East Los Angeles reflected TELACU's economic influence. By the mid-eighties the area's major commercial strip, Whittier Boulevard, had revived. As we have seen, during the 1970s TELACU had been involved in several award-winning studies for the redevelopment of East LA and its major thoroughfare. The most elaborate had been the Zócalo plan, which had envisioned a plaza placed just off the boulevard, a plan obviously inspired by Mexican models. The Whittier Boulevard Revitalization Project had followed a less ambitious but more practical plan. The most important aspects of the latter had been the establishment of a local development corporation, composed of the merchants along the strip, and the formation of a revolving loan fund by TELACU and the Bank of America. The county ended the CDC's participation in the design of the project during the 1982 scandal, but TELACU's influence remained.[3]

Beginning with the original ideas drawn up by TELACU, the merchants themselves came up with a redevelopment plan to suit their own needs. The merchants' corporation then convinced the county to widen and resurface the boulevard. With monies drawn from the revolving loan fund, the merchants upgraded the facades of their many small shops uniformly from Atlantic Boulevard to the Long Beach Freeway—nearly a third the width of unincorporated East LA. Additionally, a completely new complex arose, the Plaza Colonial minimall, the first such development in the area in over forty years. This Spanish-style complex was also financed by the revolving loan fund and influenced by the Zócalo ideas of the previous decade. Highlighting the overall renewal of Whittier Boulevard, two arches now spanned the thoroughfare, proudly displaying its name and that of the community. The changes had made the boulevard more attractive and profitable; they had also provided more jobs and produced more sales and tax revenue for East LA. In the North Broadway area of Lincoln Heights, similar redevelopment had also helped make the Eastside more self-sufficient.[4] These two projects were among the best examples of TELACU's influence on the economy and landscape of the community; moreover, they were projects that everyone on the Eastside could enjoy.

Community Services

In spite of the reemphasis on economic development, TELACU continued its social service projects, though it increasingly referred to them as "community services" in order to erase any notion that it was some sort of welfare agency. As we have seen, TELACU's first activities as an organization had been youth and senior citizens' programs; these continued in both traditional and new forms during the eighties and into the nineties. More general community services, as diverse as cultural events and housing rehabilitation, also continued as part of TELACU's overall program.[5] These services, nevertheless, remained a secondary part of TELACU's operation; their relationship to the CDC's business end resembled the relationship between the activities of a nonprofit charitable foundation and its corporate parent. Though TELACU did not make the distinction so sharply, the CDC had increasingly separated the two components as it emulated business corporations more and more.

Social Services

TELACU's Youth Services Program had evolved from the summer camp project of 1968 to a more technological approach. In conjunction with the Young Men's Christian Association and American Honda, TELACU offered junior high students who had had problems with the law an innovative path back to respectability. According to TELACU's publicity, "The program seeks to stimulate positive change by using mini-bikes as a motivational tool." Youths referred to TELACU by the police, the courts, the schools, and various other community institutions were taught the safe use and maintenance of small motorcycles with the idea that this popular activity would teach a general sense of responsibility as well as a useful skill. Such a constructive pursuit carried out in small groups also allowed personal attention and taught cooperation. In addition to maintaining the machines, the youths planned and participated in competitions, camping trips, and parades with the idea that they thus developed organizing skills and self-pride. Though the program may have seemed farfetched to some, TELACU claimed a 70 percent success rate.[6] In any case, the program exemplified TELACU's technical approach to community problems, as well as its continued success in drawing corporate contributions to the local area.

A more traditional service for youth was the TELACU Scholarship Fund, established in 1984. TELACU set up the scholarships to help pay the expenses of entering and continuing college students from the Eastside. The applicants had to show both need and promise. The institutions participating were those most commonly attended by Eastside students: East Los Angeles College, the California State University campuses at Los Angeles and Long Beach, the University of Southern California, and the University of California, Los Angeles. TELACU utilized its leveraging technique even in the design of this higher education fund; for example, Cal State–Long Beach matched each TELACU scholarship on a one-to-one basis, while USC matched each two to one. This obviously expanded the benefits of TELACU's original contribution. Through 1986 a hundred students had received a total of $85,000 directly from the fund, and the numbers continued to increase. To assure the continuity of these educational efforts, in the late eighties TELACU also put together a $500,000 endowment to build "a strong core of educated professionals to lead the community in the coming decades."[7] Indeed, one of TELACU's enduring legacies would remain the development of a professional leadership. The new scholarship programs could only help but improve the CDC's image and build a loyal following among a future generation of highly skilled leaders.

While youth received renewed emphasis in the mid-eighties, senior citizens were not forgotten. The TELACU Senior Citizens'

Club, founded by Glenn O'Loane in the sixties, continued under his direction in the late eighties and remained one of the most active groups of its kind on the Eastside. Since East LA lacked a municipal government to provide such services, many seniors relied on this club for recreational and educational activities. A distinctive feature of the club remained its long-established food cooperative, which provided a full range of market products at discounts.[8] Given the low-income senior population of East LA, the cooperative served an especially useful purpose. This type of grass-roots program could only help TELACU's image among the needy.

Another project continuing to serve senior citizens and other needy people on the Eastside remained the TELACU Transit System. Founded in the mid-seventies after a study by the CDC of the area's transit needs, the system had been one of the nation's first dial-a-ride operations. In an area woefully short of quality public transportation, this dial-a-ride system offered the physically and mentally disabled, as well as the elderly, door-to-door service with a simple phone call. In addition senior citizens' clubs chartered minibuses for group excursions to recreational areas, shopping centers, and elsewhere. According to TELACU's publicity, "The distinctive fleet of beige and brown mini-buses, including lift-equipped vehicles . . . is a familiar sight on local streets." Indeed, to many in the community these clearly marked vehicles were the most visible symbols of TELACU. Though many of the buses had begun to show their age by the late eighties, they still projected a positive image of the CDC. Averaging 200,000 miles per year, the fleet of minibuses undeniably served the community.[9]

As with many of the CDC's other community services, the TELACU Transit System operated under contract with the city, county, and state. Because of this, the 1982 scandal had also threatened the system's survival, and thereafter requests for continued funding often encountered opposition based at least subliminally on the CDC's tarnished reputation. In September of 1986, controversy resurfaced in the Los Angeles City Council as this body discussed whether to grant the system $722,000 to continue its service on the Eastside. According to the *Los Angeles Times*, "The council's Transportation Committee, at the behest of Councilman Richard Alatorre, who represents the Eastside, recommended that the council award the contract to The East Los Angeles Community Union." Some members of the full council objected because TELACU Transit had scored lower than two other systems on a federal grading system of such operations. Though the leading competitor, Pacific Busing, offered more vehicles at lower cost, TELACU's defenders pointed out that its system was familiar with and owned by the community; it also had a strong affirmative action program.[10] The criticism suggested that TELACU Transit needed improvement, but the CDC's long support of Richard Alatorre proved decisive in winning the grant. Since council members effectively controlled what services their districts received, Alatorre finally steered the funds toward his supporters. Obviously, TELACU could still manipulate the political system.

Cultural Preservation

TELACU's commitment to Latino, particularly Mexican-American, cultural preservation demonstrated that the CDC's service to the community transcended antipoverty programing. Over the years TELACU's support of the visual arts had been apparent in the mural and especially the architectural projects it had promoted. The CDC had also attempted to support the performing arts through such for-profit companies as Inter-American Entertainment, a subsidiary that had failed. However, "Domingos Alegres," as we have seen, had been a perennial success. Launched in 1976, the Latino variety show of music and dance performed, free of charge, for the community every other Sunday from April to October. Cosponsored by the LA County Parks and Recreation Department, the newspaper *Noticias del Mundo*, and Spanish-language Radio KALI, the three-hour shows continued to take place in the "civic center" of East LA at the Belvedere Park amphitheater.[11]

The importance of TELACU's cultural contribution was evident not only in the centrality of "Domingos Alegres" to the life of the local community, but also in the quality and extent of the effort. TELACU recruited top Latino artists from throughout the United States and Latin America for the Sunday performances. Despite this, local artists also had opportunities to highlight their talents, allowing many to develop their careers further. By 1986 the performances had gained such an impressive following that TELACU arranged a television contract for a season of sixteen broadcasts. The series appeared nationally on Spanish-language television in eight major markets, including of course Los Angeles on KVEA-TV. This series, made possible through major sponsorship from Anheuser-Busch and Pepsi-Cola, was "the first domestically-produced program of its kind for the U.S. Hispanic audience." Of course, "Domingos Alegres" had received some international attention even earlier through the Spanish-language media, but this telecast of an entire series reached Latinos in much of the United States.[12] Through such efforts TELACU helped break down the cultural isolation of the colonias within the nation.

Although TELACU's community services and its businesses operated separately, they overlapped far more commonly in the CDC than in a regular business corporation. TELACU's Weatherization Service and its Inter-City Energy Systems exemplified this overlap. In conjunction with the Southern California Gas Company, the Weatherization Service helped low-income people save on their utility bills while conserving energy. Residents could receive "up to $500 in free weatherization services, including attic insulation, installation of low flow showerheads, water heater blankets, caulking and weather stripping." In addition, free portable heaters, fluorescent bulbs, and a money-saving energy survey were available. As a result, up to a 40-percent savings on utility bills accrued to most homes, and from the project's beginning in 1982 to 1987, over seven thousand homes received the free services. While the Weatherization Service was free and nonprofit, the for-profit Inter-City Energy Systems offered the same services for a price to those who did not qualify as low-income. Besides assisting the needy and the environment, these projects trained and employed sixty local workers in installation and sales.[13] In these projects TELACU's long experience in housing rehabilitation and real estate obviously benefited the community in multiple ways.

Real Estate and Construction

Despite the scandal of 1982, TELACU's business ventures moved ahead, especially in areas related to real estate and construction. In the midst of the scandal, TELACU had acquired the South Coast Shingle Company, a respected building supplier, family-owned for over thirty years. Since the firm could supply many of the basic needs for ventures in construction, TELACU purchased the company to assure those supplies at a reasonable price. Since the same experienced management remained in place, the company posted profits every year after its purchase. In 1985 TELACU also acquired the Air Management Company, a heating and air conditioning firm serving private residences, new residential developments, and light commercial construction projects in much of southern California. Employing about seventy workers, the company provided training and subsequent employment for East LA residents. Air Management also served as a supplier for TELACU's real estate ventures.[14]

Both of these companies were subsidiaries of TELACU Industries, the CDC's general business wing, and of TELACU Development Company, the CDC's real estate development subdivision. TELACU Development had undeniably become the core of the CDC, especially since the demise of such subsidiaries as the Community Research Group and TELACU Investment Company. TELACU Development absorbed the planning and research functions of the former, ignored the wide-ranging investment strategy of the latter, and focused on real estate. After the construction of TELACU Industrial Park, TELACU Development had become increasingly sophisticated and applied its growing technical expertise to a variety of activities. The company provided "full-service property development, construction, realty, and management services"; it specialized "in the construction and development of mid- and low-rise office buildings, master-planned office and industrial parks, and multi-tenant residential projects." Of course, the company's major initial project had been TELACU Industrial Park, which it continued to manage as it undertook a 6-acre addition to the original 48-acre complex.[15] But this was only the beginning. By the mid-eighties TELACU Development had launched several other major projects that would mark a new era in the CDC's brief history.

South Gate Industrial/Retail Park

In early 1986 building directly on its experience with its own industrial park, TELACU Development undertook a similar project on the site of an abandoned General Motors plant in South Gate, a community bordering impoverished South-Central Los Angeles. Again, because of the community union's early ties with the United Auto Workers and the automotive industry, TELACU succeeded in acquiring the site for redevelopment into an industrial and retail complex. In conjunction with Goldrich & Kest, as well as Sheldon Appel Company, TELACU demolished the old plant on the 96-acre site and by 1992 replaced it "with 1.8 million square feet of industrial, light manufacturing, and retail distribution space, and a 15-acre shopping center." TELACU leveraged the project, costing $80 million, in its usual fashion and retained 25-percent ownership. While automobile assembly had virtually disappeared from southern California, TELACU was helping fill the vacuum. Although the CDC could not directly replace the high-paying jobs of the auto assembly lines, TELACU did produce four thousand largely service jobs that helped keep the local economy alive.[16]

Tamayo Restaurant

In 1984 TELACU Development Company launched another ambitious project, a new Mexican restaurant in East Los Angeles itself. Of course, East LA had many such restaurants, but it did not have a first-class establishment. Though the area remained poor, a feasibility study had shown that a market existed for the "luncheon and banquet trade." Indeed, for years surrounding cities had catered to the trade profitably, with such restaurants as the Quiet Cannon in Montebello, Luminaria's in Monterey Park, and Steven's Steak House in Commerce. The growing Mexican-American middle class with roots in East LA indicated that the market for such dining was growing, and another elegant restaurant could succeed. With $500,000 from the Office of Community Services, $1 million from a partner in Spago on Sunset Boulevard, and another million

9. Tamayo Restaurant. Restored Eastside structure exemplifying Spanish Colonial Revival architecture. Photograph by author, 1997.

of its own, TELACU set out to establish the Tamayo Restaurant, named in honor of renowned Mexican painter Rufino Tamayo.[17]

Clearly, TELACU designed Tamayo Restaurant with cultural pride as well as economic development in mind. Indeed, as a holistic project, the restaurant gave meaning to the abstract concept of community development. For one thing, TELACU established the restaurant in a historic Spanish Colonial Revival structure built in 1927. Located next to TELACU Industrial Park, the structure had been identified as culturally significant in the heritage survey that the CDC had conducted in the seventies; the building had nevertheless seen better days and needed renovation. According to the *Los Angeles Times*, "The building at various times housed a pipe supply store, a coffee shop, the Department of Motor Vehicles, the California Highway Patrol and the Brown Berets. . . ." The building therefore reflected not simply the area's architectural heritage, but the community's diverse political history. Taking cultural preservation beyond renovation of the building, TELACU decorated the interior with examples of Rufino Tamayo's own work, which diners could appreciate as they enjoyed distinctive Mexican cuisine, such as *huachinango flameado* (red snapper) and *pavo fumaro en dos salsas* (smoked turkey). The interior also contained huge tapestries from Oaxaca and imported tile and marble, as well as an open pit in the main dining room capable of seating 165 people. Even as TELACU thus preserved the community's heritage, the CDC generated new jobs for the local population in construction and the food industry. The restaurant's incorporation of culture, history, and economics embodied the holistic ideal envisioned by proponents of community development corporations.[18]

Nevertheless, Tamayo Restaurant had its critics, some basing their positions on the negative image of TELACU resulting from the 1982 scandal. Reporting on the restaurant's opening in March 1988, the *LA Times* once again reminded its readers of the scandal, but in a more moderate tone, probably because the reporter was Latino George Ramos. According to Ramos, some activists argued "that the non-profit corporation . . . should funnel its money into pressing social needs, instead of a fancy eatery." They argued that the CDC should invest in libraries or hospitals. Although these critics did not realize that TELACU had previously established a reading program and a health center, their criticism reflected a deeper ignorance of the goals of community economic development and thus of the long-term purposes of TELACU.[19] Of course, the *Times* and even the Justice Department had misunderstood those goals in 1982. TELACU was not a simple antipoverty agency; its goals involved holistic community development, including not only social service, business development, and job creation, but such matters as cultural preservation and beautification.

The critics also complained that Tamayo Restaurant was too expensive for the low-income residents of the area since dinner entrees ranged from $12 to $22. To offset these prices somewhat, TELACU had taken care to offer lunches for as little as $5.50; it also offered Sunday brunches for families at relatively low cost. While the restaurant remained beyond the reach of many, the community as a whole benefited from the money spent by more affluent suburbanites drawn to the area, especially through business with TELACU. This, of course, meant at least one hundred new jobs.[20] Though these were again largely low-paying service jobs, the many unskilled workers in East LA preferred such work to unemployment.

The criticism was by no means universal. Community activist Lydia López commented just before Tamayo opened, "It's about time East L.A. had a place like this." She, like many others in the area, had been skeptical regarding TELACU because of the 1982 scandal, but she had changed her mind. "I think they've learned from their mistakes and they're going the extra mile," she remarked. "The restaurant is evidence of that."[21] Though TELACU often received little credit for projects, such as Nueva Maravilla and the Whittier Boulevard redevelopment, landmarks such as the TELACU Center and Tamayo Restaurant helped cleanse the CDC's tarnished image, at least in the eyes of those who did not romanticize the ascetic life.

TELACU Manor, Retirement Homes

Indeed, local criticism might have lessened had another of TELACU's current projects received nearly as much publicity as the restaurant. Even as TELACU launched Tamayo Restaurant in the late eighties, the CDC initiated a string of retirement homes in southern California. Subsidized by the Department of Housing and Urban Development, the CDC planned to construct, own, and operate TELACU Manor at different sites in the Los Angeles area. Each location would include social and recreational amenities geared to the local community. In July 1988 groundbreaking for an Eastside branch was celebrated at the site in the city of Commerce. This first complex included seventy-five units, constructed in a loose Spanish style.[22] A branch in unincorporated East Los Angeles followed. Apparently, HUD had forgiven TELACU's earlier transgressions and decided that the CDC served the needy sufficiently to receive renewed funding. Considering that Republicans had administered HUD for nearly eight years, this new funding of TELACU was certainly a vote of confidence. As expected, long before the general public, government and business perceived TELACU's image in a more positive light.

Battle for Los Angeles's Historic Plaza

Just the same, controversy seemed to follow TELACU's development efforts almost everywhere, especially in metropolitan Los Angeles. In early 1988 before the establishment of TELACU Manor, a dispute broke out over plans to redevelop the culturally significant plaza area of downtown—El Pueblo de Los Angeles Historic Park. The area embraced the *placita*, Olvera Street, and the Avila adobe—respectively, the city's oldest church, its traditional Mexican marketplace, and its earliest residence. Besides other sites important to the city's early history, the proposed redevelopment involved about seventy additional acres important to the city's later history, including Union Station and the downtown post office. The difficulties began rather quietly in 1986 when the Olvera Street Merchants Association commissioned a study concerning possible renovation of the immediate area.[23]

The shopkeepers of the Merchants Association worried that the government was not properly maintaining the popular tourist attraction. From the founding of Los Angeles, the plaza had had a concentration of Hispanics even during the mid-nineteenth century when other ethnic groups, such as the Italians and Chinese, had had a strong presence there. In the first decades of the twentieth century, the area had become dilapidated, but Anglo preservationists had revived it in the 1930s. At that time the land had been purchased by the state; the buildings had been renovated, though not always with the greatest authenticity; and Olvera Street had become a tourist attraction. Although the state owned the property, the city's Parks and Recreation Department managed it. Finally, the state decided to turn over legal title to the city in 1988. In anticipation of this, the merchants, mostly longtime Mexican-American tenants, commissioned their study in hopes of influencing the changes sure to come once the city had full power to redevelop the area.[24]

Gloria Molina Versus Richard Alatorre and TELACU

Controversy arose when two distinct redevelopment plans were proposed by competing factions at city hall and on Olvera Street itself: The Merchants Association, backed by Councilwoman Gloria Molina, and the Business Leadership of Olvera Street, supported by Councilman Richard Alatorre and TELACU. The Merchants Association sought limited development immediately around Olvera Street; Alatorre, with plans drawn up by the city's Community Redevelopment Agency, sought to revamp a much broader area, including Union Station and the post office. The merchants basically feared that a massive redevelopment, especially competing shops in the huge revamped post office, would hurt their businesses. They also feared higher taxes and rents would result. Alatorre saw his proposal as a chance for more Latino employment downtown and an increased Mexican cultural presence in the area. TELACU became involved because it planned to bid for the post office redevelopment, expecting eventually to operate the building as well. Since Richard Alatorre represented the district including the plaza, TELACU stood to gain from its long support of his political career.[25]

Mayor Tom Bradley and Other Parties

The politics of the redevelopment were extremely sensitive because of the potential magnitude of the project. In addition to the two Mexican-American factions, other parties became involved, including Mayor Tom Bradley, the city's Planning Commission, Councilman Zev Yaroslavzky, the Los Angeles Conservancy, and MCA Incorporated. Because of the importance of the project to the city as a whole, Mayor Bradley could not leave it entirely to the councilman of the district. Bradley consequently sought to play the role of mediator in the dispute. The Planning Commission would have to make decisions on the project if it became a municipal redevelopment. Councilman Yaroslavsky entered the picture because he favored slow growth and questioned any new development strongly. The Conservancy's interest was architectural preservation. MCA, the developer of Universal Studios and other major entertainment complexes, expected to compete with TELACU for the new project.[26] Just how El Pueblo de Los Angeles Historic Park and its environs changed would involve years of political haggling between these and other contending parties.

By early 1989 Mayor Bradley had temporarily reconciled the Mexican-American factions in time for his reelection campaign that year. Since Mexican-Americans formed an important part of his political coalition, he could not afford to have divisions in their ranks. To assuage the fears of the Merchants Association, the city agreed to allow them partial ownership of the property and to pay any temporary relocation costs incurred during any reconstruction. On the other hand, this meant that the larger development envisioned by Councilman Alatorre, TELACU, and their allies both old and new remained a possibility. The merchants and their growing number of supporters had nevertheless "formed an ad-hoc committee called the Los Angeles Mexican Conservancy" to protect their interests as the dispute flared again.[27] Progress on the redevelopment slowed when even more groups entered the fray.

Conflicting Cultural Images

By mid-1990 another serious issue entered the picture. As plans for El Pueblo de Los Angeles went forward, interethnic strife over conflicting historical images of the area developed. While Olvera Street had since the 1930s highlighted the Mexican heritage, city planners with the Parks and Recreation Commission began to take a multiethnic perspective on the area. For example, in a draft of the guidelines for the project, the planners included a Chinese-American museum at one end of Olvera Street and permitted storefronts on parallel streets to "reflect a different historic character." The merchants of the Mexican Conservancy complained that this would necessarily deemphasize their culture in the area. While other ethnic groups had in fact resided in the plaza area during the nineteenth century, the merchants pointed out that the Mexican heritage, a fusion of Indian and Spanish, predated the others.[28]

The members of the Los Angeles Mexican Conservancy were also upset at suggestions in the guidelines that reinforced cultural stereotypes Mexican Americans had battled for decades. The guidelines suggested that the costumes and decorations reflect the "Romance of California." Historians such as Antonio Ríos-Bustamante, a member of the Mexican Conservancy, pointed out the problems with that historical image. At the turn of the century, the cult of romantic California, promoted first by Anglo-American writers and then by local chambers of commerce, had emphasized the "Spanish" past to the almost complete exclusion of things "Mexican," even the ethnic label. Any redevelopment that revived that "fantasy heritage" would deemphasize the role of Mexicans in the city's history and again deny Mexican Americans their connection to that past. To avoid such distortions, the Mexican Conservancy argued for the importance of including Chicano historians in the planning of the project.[29] The issue was laden with meaning because it reflected the desire of Mexican Americans not only to maintain control of Olvera Street, but to control the telling of their very history. Subliminally, perhaps the entire issue also reflected their desire to regain control of Los Angeles itself.

Despite the lingering suspicions of many Latinos regarding TE-

LACU, the CDC was the most qualified developer for the plaza area. As the only major Mexican-American developer in the Los Angeles area, TELACU's bid for renovation of the plaza certainly had more merit than MCA's. Although MCA could marshal greater resources than TELACU, the former could not address the culturally and historically sensitive issues as well as the latter. With its commitment to Mexican-American self-determination, TELACU would not likely follow a misguided multicultural plan, such as that proposed by the city's Parks and Recreation Commission. The plaza renovation called for the holistic approach to development that TELACU had undertaken since its founding. The CDC had long ago learned that rebuilding communities involved more than applying new paint to old buildings; it meant sensitivity to the multifaceted needs of the community. Despite this, neither TELACU nor any other developer won permission to undertake the sweeping revitalization envisioned for the plaza.[30] Through 1993, except for refurbished Union Station, the plaza area remained largely unchanged.

Growing Political Self-Determination

Though TELACU had avoided direct electoral politics since 1982, its contributions to Latino political empowerment had borne fruit. As we have seen, the Eastside's congressional delegation that year had jumped from one to three, and Mexican Americans had succeeded in retaining their legislative seats despite a shuffling of officeholders. Prior to that year, gains had usually been temporary, with Mexican Americans having a difficult time succeeding one another in office. In the decade after 1982, important gains accrued, with the reapportionment based on the 1990 census leading to more rapid advances.[31] Though TELACU remained in the background, the progress of Mexican-American politicians generally meant progress for the CDC, as well as the rest of the community. The ties between TELACU and Richard Alatorre were just one example of the way these connections worked.

Alatorre to the LA City Council

Mexican-American politicians did not sit on their laurels after 1982. State Senator Art Torres and Assemblyman Richard Alatorre, especially, made continual efforts to improve Latino representation in the various elected bodies of the Los Angeles area. The LA City Council became a major battlefield because Latinos remained completely unrepresented in that body despite comprising 28 percent of the city's population in 1980. Not since 1962 when Ed Roybal moved from the council to Congress, had Latinos held a seat. Despite great effort, Mexican-American activists had failed to wrest the Fourteenth Council District on the Eastside from Anglo control.[32]

Anglo incumbent Art Snyder retained the seat representing the Fourteenth District for reasons that held in other areas as well. Most importantly, the legislature had drawn the district's lines in such a way that middle-class voters in predominantly Anglo Eagle Rock controlled the seat. Better educated and more attuned to the political system, they voted in greater numbers than Mexican Americans and overwhelmingly for Snyder. Moreover, enough of those Mexican Americans who did vote supported Snyder, allowing him to win reelection repeatedly. An adept politician, Snyder catered to the entire community, even taking Spanish lessons to communicate better with his constituency. In fact his performance on behalf of the district as a whole had been creditable. TELACU had had amicable relations with the councilman for years; indeed, David Lizarraga once commented that Snyder had probably never voted against a city grant proposed for the CDC. Relations with Snyder, however, became a liability as the councilman came under the increasing scrutiny of the press.[33]

In 1981 as a result of revelations made in the *LA Times*, Snyder and TELACU had come under investigation by the state's Fair Political Practices Commission over a real estate leasing arrangement. Snyder had sublet the property in East LA where the CDC had established an automobile leasing agency and a job training center. The newspaper and the state voiced concern over conflict of interest since Snyder was making money from an organization that received city funds. While the lease itself did not involve city funds or even property within the city, the state commission fined the councilman $14,000 for failing to disclose the rent paid by TELACU. To make matters worse, Snyder came under increasing attack because of personal problems with drinking and driving. At various times Mexican-American activists had unsuccessfully sought his removal by recalling him or, curiously, by securing him a judicial appointment. In 1984 they launched another effort to recall him from office, but to no avail. Nevertheless, the pressure continued as his personal problems persisted, and in 1985 Snyder finally resigned, leaving the Fourteenth District open for Latino representation.[34]

Richard Alatorre's decision to run in Snyder's old district in 1985 underscored the importance of the new opening on the city council. Since his prominence in Los Angeles assured his election, Alatorre decided to move from the assembly to the city council to gain Mexican-American representation on the latter. His move to the council also left his assembly seat to Richard Polanco, the TELACU official who had lost to Gloria Molina in 1982. As we have seen, this strategy had worked well in 1982 and would succeed again. Alatorre's move was even more important because reapportionment had become a bitter issue in the council. After constant complaints by Latinos, the U.S. Department of Justice had charged Los Angeles with violation of the Voting Rights Act. Consequently, the city council decided to redistrict, rather than undergo extensive litigation and possibly a court-ordered plan. Since Alatorre had directed reapportionment of the state legislature in the early eighties, his election to the city council made him the most experienced member in such matters. He was consequently placed in charge of redistricting the city, which meant of course that he could encourage more Latino representation.[35]

Indeed, Alatorre's move to the council generated more gains for Mexican Americans. After an acrimonious redistricting process that temporarily pitted Asian Americans against Latinos, Alatorre succeeded in creating one more safe Mexican-American seat on the council. Ironically, Larry González, Alatorre's candidate, lost the race to none other than Gloria Molina, who had also decided to leave the assembly. Once again she had challenged the "machine" to become the first Mexican-American woman on the council, as she had been the first in the assembly. She amplified her victory by leaving her assembly seat to another Latina. Lucille Roybal Allard, daughter of Congressman Roybal, parlayed name recognition and endorsements to win Molina's former seat in early 1987. Mexican Americans had thus gained two seats in the council and lost none in the legislature, a major gain in political self-determination.[36]

Since all the candidates were liberal Democrats, factionalism rather than ideology played the major role in Mexican-American politics. Gloria Molina and other populist candidates had successfully challenged what remained of the Torres-Alatorre establishment, even as they benefited from its machinations. Though TELACU had connections in both camps, it had long since identified with the establishment, a situation immediately apparent after Alatorre joined the council. Unfortunately for both the councilman and the CDC, in early 1988 Alatorre was fined by the state's Fair Political Practices Commission for attempting to steer a large contract to TELACU. Since the councilman had only recently received a $1,000 speaking fee from the CDC, the commission judged his actions improper.[37] Even after the scandal of 1982, TELACU still managed to overstep the boundaries of political propriety.

Molina to the County Board of Supervisors

Shortly after reapportionment seated Mexican Americans on the Los Angeles City Council, the county's board of supervisors came under fire. In 1988 plans for redistricting of the five-member board were criticized because they perpetuated control by Anglo males and a conservative majority of three. The Mexican American Legal Defense and Education Fund, the American Civil Liberties Union, and the U.S. Department of Justice sued the county for gerrymandering district lines and intentionally denying Latino representation. The county decided to fight the suit and eventually pushed it to the U.S. Supreme Court. The bitter redistricting battle took some curious ethnic turns. For example, longtime conservative Supervisor Pete Schabarum, claiming Mexican ancestry, argued he had become the object of discrimination. Though he had scarcely mentioned his Mexican grandmother in his twenty years on the board, he found his ancestry convenient when his San Gabriel Valley district faced dismemberment in response to Latino complaints. Schabarum finally decided not to seek reelection when it became evident that his district would end up with a Mexican-American majority.[38]

By mid-1990 the courts had ordered the board of supervisors to draw a Latino district and schedule an election. The issue became more complicated when the county insisted on an election under its own plan before final approval by the courts. In the race for supervisor of the San Gabriel Valley, Sarah Flores, a former Schabarum aide, won a plurality of the votes for his old seat, but failed to gain the majority needed to claim the nonpartisan office. Though formerly a TELACU employee, Flores did not gain the CDC's support since she had conservative views and had registered as a Republican. Flores's candidacy nevertheless demonstrated once again that TELACU provided leadership training for the community. The courts shortly declared the mid-1990 election invalid and ordered a new one under new district lines for January 1991.[39]

Since a Los Angeles county supervisor is one of the most powerful officials in California, the January 1991 election attracted some of the most prominent Mexican-American politicians. Indeed, in early November 1990, in hopes of avoiding factionalism, a private Latino political summit convened in a Pasadena hotel, a meeting reminiscent of the conclave at Steven's Steak House in 1982. This time, however, TELACU officials stayed away, indicating that the CDC had distanced itself from politics. Just the same, many of those in attendance had long ties with the organization. Among those attending and expressing interest in the office were Congressmen Esteban Torres and Ed Roybal, and city council members Richard Alatorre and Gloria Molina, as well as state Senator Art Torres. The meeting sought to assure the election of a Latino liberal to the board. Since Democrats had called the meeting, Sarah Flores did not receive an invitation. Noting the obvious, she assessed the situation, "I think they see me as the enemy. . . ."[40]

Despite the attempt at unity, the Democrats could not reach consensus on a Latino favorite. In some ways this signified political

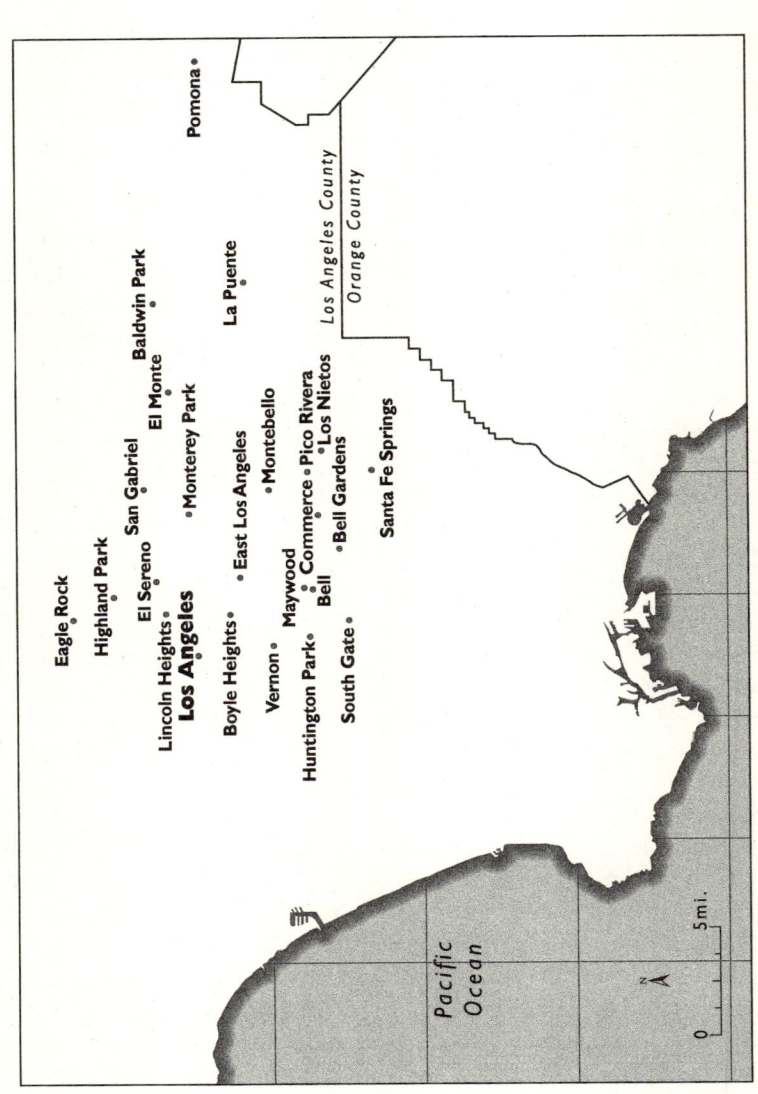

MAP 3. The Greater Eastside. Cartography by David Deis.

maturity since Democratic Mexican-American candidates felt individually strong enough to defeat any Anglo or Republican challenger in the new district. In the January 1991 election Sarah Flores lost convincingly in a field that included Gloria Molina, Art Torres, and state Senator Charles Calderón. Molina and Torres, the first- and second-place finishers, advanced to the runoff in February. That battle once again pitted the populists and Molina against the establishment and Torres. Though TELACU could take no official position, clearly its interests lay with Torres since Molina was critical of developers in general.[41] As for the community, the Latinos of the Greater Eastside had a choice between two of their most experienced and respected officeholders.

Gloria Molina once again made history by winning the election and becoming the first Mexican-American LA County supervisor in 115 years, not to mention the first woman ever. She did it by splitting the middle-class San Gabriel Valley with Torres, and taking a majority in the inner, lower-income Eastside. Her victory suggested that the "machine" politics of Torres, Alatorre, and TELACU had lost favor, especially in the barrios around East LA. Molina was an iconoclast, critical of any interest—Anglo or Latino—that did not serve ordinary people. Some of her first acts as supervisor reflected this attitude. She requested removal of security barriers to the supervisors' meeting chambers; she saw the devices as walls between the government and the people. She also refused the services of a chauffeur and an elegant county car. While this seemed like posturing to her critics, such symbolic acts could only improve her public image.[42] Had TELACU been more careful about such imagery, it might have had greater community support before, during, and after the 1982 scandal.

Molina's election in 1991 proved the greatest political victory for Mexican Americans in the Los Angeles area after 1982; they had undeniably moved toward political self-determination. Even the conviction of state Senator Joseph Montoya for bribery in early 1990 did no permanent damage to the community. It replaced him with Charles Calderón, whose assembly seat in turn went to newcomer Javier Becerra. Molina's old city council seat also went to another Mexican American, Mike Hernández.[43] Mexican Americans were again making gains and keeping the ground made in the past. Moreover, the larger number of officeholders also meant that any talk of a political machine was obsolete. Clearly, the old Torres-Alatorre-TELACU establishment of 1982 no longer controlled Mexican-American politics, if it ever had. While the "establishment" remained influential, it hardly deserved even that label any longer.

Congressman Javier Becerra

The elections of 1992 confirmed that observation. While pundits talked of a new Molina machine challenging the old Torres-Alatorre-TELACU machine for supremacy, the factions aligned themselves loosely and lacked consistent electoral power. For example, in the 1992 primary longtime TELACU allies Art Torres and Richard Alatorre backed Leticia Quezada in the race to replace retiring Ed Roybal in Congress. On the other hand, former TELACU director Esteban Torres supported Gloria Molina's candidate, Javier Becerra. Though Becerra defeated Quezada, this hardly confirmed that a new Molina machine had ascended because overall five of the seven candidates she supported lost. On the whole, neither Art Torres nor Gloria Molina displayed long coattails.[44] Because TELACU had connections in both camps, its influence diffused; the CDC no longer exercised the power it had in 1982 and earlier.

Congresswoman Lucille Roybal Allard

For Latinos as a whole, 1992 proved another strong year politically. The 1990 census had confirmed the growth of their population, and the latest reapportionment allotted them more seats in both Congress and the legislature. Although Roybal, the dean of California's Mexican-American politicians, retired, he was replaced by young Becerra, who had only two years earlier joined the assembly. In his thirties, he promised to be a political force for years to come. Even more exciting for the community's prospects was Lucille Roybal Allard's move to Congress. As a result of the 1990 census, the Eastside's representation in Congress had climbed from three to four. Roybal Allard captured the new congressional seat, assuring continuation of her father's legacy, not to mention becoming California's first Latina in Congress. Becerra and Roybal Allard joined veterans Marty Martínez and Esteban Torres in that body.⁴⁵

In the state legislature the 1992 elections brought a fresh group of Mexican-American leaders to the fore. In the assembly Latino representation from the Greater Eastside doubled from three to six members; moreover, women captured four of the six seats. With the departure of Becerra and Roybal Allard for Congress, incumbent Richard Polanco welcomed Louis Caldera, Diane Martínez (daughter of Congressman Marty Martínez), Martha Escutía, Hilda Solís, and Grace Napolitano to the assembly.⁴⁶ This crop of new Democratic leaders, many having held local municipal office, was the harvest of the early political efforts of activist Chicano groups, including TELACU. These new officeholders helped fulfill the hopes for Mexican-American self-determination on the Eastside.

The Continuing Political Struggle

Despite the impressive gains over the previous twenty years, Latinos remained significantly underrepresented. For example, although they comprised 28 percent of the state's population, in late 1992 they held only 8 of 80 assembly seats, 3 of 40 senate seats, and no statewide offices. In their Los Angeles "stronghold," the situation remained paradoxically weak; 2 of 15 council members were Mexican Americans though Latinos comprised 40 percent of the city's population. Representation on the LA school board and the community college board remained similarly weak. The situation was little better in the dozens of suburban municipalities, school districts, and college districts, many with Latino majorities, especially in the southeastern portion of LA County.⁴⁷ Though these governing bodies had served as training grounds for some Mexican-American legislators, Latinos still lacked full representation in virtually all these governments. Although Mexican Americans had progressed, they had a long way to go before recovering their historic regional position in terms of political power.

Yet even in the working-class suburbs, dramatic change was discernible. In late 1991 in Bell Gardens, a low-income suburb just south of Commerce, location of the TELACU Center, a portentous electoral revolt occurred. Over the previous two decades, Bell Gardens's population had shifted from an Anglo majority to a 90-percent Latino, largely Mexican and Mexican-American, majority. The city council had nevertheless remained overwhelmingly Anglo. Unfortunately, the city council, operating in its own interest, had undertaken commercial redevelopment that demolished hundreds of residences and planned to condemn more. Outraged by the destruction of homes, especially those of low-income residents, News for America, a new, largely middle-class group led by small landlords, organized a recall election. After registering hundreds of new voters, the group succeeded in recalling four of the five council members, leaving only a Latina unchallenged. This election emphasized what TELACU and Nueva Maravilla had long ago demonstrated—that development must not proceed without the consent and participation of the community. Although the new council remained middle class, its new Mexican-American majority promised to be more receptive to the concerns of working-class Latinos. Significantly, News for America planned similar insurgencies in surrounding communities.[48] Obviously, in terms of politics, new groups had moved to the fore, but TELACU continued to lead in economic development.

Changing Latino Los Angeles

While Mexican Americans had made major political gains since TELACU's founding in 1968, their economic situation was less clear. In some ways the situation seemed worse than a quarter century earlier because the population of Los Angeles County had changed so dramatically. The 1990 census revealed that *Hispanics*, as the increasing use of this term indicated, had become much more diverse. In 1970 the community had been overwhelmingly Mexican in ancestry, with some Cuban, Puerto Rican, and "other" Spanish-speaking residents. But as early as 1980 a sizable Central American population, especially Salvadoran, had made its presence known, and by 1990 other groups such as Guatemalans had also established communities in the county. In other words distinct Latino communities had developed in the metropolitan area, with the

Mexican-American remaining the largest and still growing due to the continual infusion of "immigrants" from Mexico.[49]

The new Latino communities, including many Mexican newcomers, had established themselves in downtown Los Angeles, southwest of the plaza, and in "black" South-Central Los Angeles. The new communities were therefore separate from the Eastside, though they met appropriately enough at the plaza. Mexican Americans, on the other hand, had dispersed to many other parts of Los Angeles County. While they remained concentrated on the Eastside and its San Gabriel Valley suburbs, only on the wealthy Westside did they not live in significant numbers. Mexican Americans, as a result of precedence, became the leading Latino group in the community, providing virtually all the political leadership, a situation that other Latinos might not always appreciate.[50] Moreover, economic competition between the Latino communities seemed to be growing.

The Continuing Economic Struggle

The economic impact of the Latino immigrants was controversial. Some observers blamed the new immigrants, Central American and Mexican, for retarding the social mobility of the earlier Mexican-American population. Movement to the United States, they argued, tended to act as a leveler since even educated and skilled immigrants often had to start at the bottom given their language and certification problems, thus increasing competition for jobs. Other observers argued that Mexican Americans had progressed, but that gross statistics on "Hispanics" often hid the progress. For example, the small homeowners of unincorporated East LA were in an enviable position compared with the immigrant renters of South-Central Los Angeles. Moreover, the extensive movement of Mexican Americans out of the Eastside to scattered suburbs suggested social mobility. However, statistics indicated that even U.S.-born Latinos, overwhelmingly Mexican American in Los Angeles, had done poorly in the economy of the eighties. According to a UCLA study, wage discrimination had actually worsened. Mexican-American men in 1986–87 earned only 78 percent of the wages made by Anglo men with the same training and experience; in 1969 the figure had been 90 percent. As a result, homeownership by U.S.-born Latino males had also declined, not a good sign for Mexican-American recovery.[51]

More serious in the late eighties than the seeming problem of immigration was the changing economy. Many unionized jobs—at B. F. Goodrich, Uniroyal, and similar plants—had disappeared, breaking several rungs in the ladder to the middle class. Even though metropolitan Los Angeles acquired new jobs in high-tech industries and light manufacturing, the former often required advanced training and the latter lacked the high pay and especially the benefits necessary for full membership in the middle class. Again, older suburb Bell Gardens exemplified the pattern. When nearby unionized plants, such as General Motors's in South Gate, closed, they were replaced by low-paying light industry, which led to the exodus of middle-class Anglos. The real median income of families in the area fell by half between 1970 and 1990, as immigrants from Mexico and Mexican Americans from the Eastside moved into the area, drawn by the new, but low-paying industries. They found employment, but no longer an unbroken ladder to the middle class. The paradox of the Greater Eastside was that it had developed new industries and new employment, as TELACU had hoped, but the benefits remained uneven.[52]

The 1992 Riots

In the early nineties the situation only worsened as recession gripped California with a consequent rise in racial tensions. In early 1992 rioting broke out in South-Central Los Angeles, spreading to many other parts of the county. Clearly, the socioeconomic problems that had led to the establishment of the Watts Labor Community Action Committee and the East Los Angeles Community Union had persisted. Although the unrest compared in many ways with the Watts riot of 1965, the situation differed in that Latinos as well as African Americans became involved, reflecting the changing demographics of South-Central. According to early estimates, fifty percent of those arrested, a third of those killed, and at least a third of those who lost businesses were Latino. Interestingly, only a few isolated incidents occurred on the Eastside, despite the fact that the issue was police brutality, long a complaint in the area. Analysts suggested that East LA's longtime residents had a greater stake in their neighborhoods than the recent immigrants of South-Central. Possibly, East LA residents, even disgruntled youth, recognized that Whittier Boulevard, Maravilla, and the entire community had experienced improvements since its own riots in 1970. On the other hand, shortly after the beginning of the violence in South-Central, a small contingent of the National Guard had moved in to enforce the peace in East LA.[53] As in 1970, the riots and the occupation suggested that internal colonialism continued in both South-Central and the Eastside.

A Vision of Reconstruction and Integration

In any case, the East Los Angeles Community Union could claim some credit for the stability. The CDC had long ago seen that economic development was one long-term solution to ethnic unrest on the Eastside, even if that development would not soon replace the high-paying jobs of the past. Like city redevelopment agencies throughout the Greater Eastside, TELACU had helped counteract plant closings and commercial decline, but its efforts had been ethnic and political as well—holistic in a way government redevelopment agencies could not be.[54] Like business corporations, TELACU had started subsidiaries, constructed buildings, and created jobs, but its ventures were community-owned, cooperative in a way private businesses could not be. TELACU thus remained a major institution offering the Mexican-American community a route toward socioeconomic recovery and integration into the larger society. Despite TELACU's controversial image, community development corporations in general offered a distinct vision of social reconstruction and national integration.

CONCLUSION

TELACU's Larger Significance

Landmark to Recovery of the Chicano Homeland

In the twenty-five years following the founding of the East Los Angeles Community Union in 1968, unincorporated East LA and the entire Eastside saw physical improvements which TELACU could justifiably claim as products of its efforts, in whole or in part. As we have seen, the Nueva Maravilla project replaced notorious slums with new housing that remained a model of redevelopment two decades after construction. This project stimulated redevelopment of the surrounding area, as the Maravilla Neighborhood Development Project and the Belvedere Park expansion reclaimed key sections of East LA from blight. Whittier Boulevard and Brooklyn Avenue, the community's major commercial strips, also underwent complete face-lifts; indeed, in 1993 the latter was renamed in honor of the recently deceased César Chávez. While TELACU mainly affected the landscape of East LA proper, the greater part of its original "special impact area," the rest of the Eastside also benefited from the physical changes promoted by the community development corporation. The North Broadway revitalization in Lincoln Heights, the TELACU Center in Commerce, and the new industrial park in South Gate were only a few of the more obvious physical improvements stimulated by the CDC in Greater East Los Angeles.[1] Through such projects, the East Los Angeles Community Union earned its own place as a landmark in the local community.

The changes promoted by TELACU in the major public landscapes of East LA inspired greater pride in the image and heritage of the community. Moreover, this urban renewal occurred without major dislocation of the area's residents or shopkeepers; in fact, they had constant input regarding the changes taking place in their neighborhoods.[2] The redevelopment projects had thus evinced not only the ethnic pride, but the self-determination of the Mexican-American community. Furthermore, TELACU demonstrated how the very space of the Eastside could be recovered politically, culturally, and especially economically. Ironically, using the technical expertise of capitalism, the community could recover its land collectively. Housing rehabilitation, urban planning, real estate development, architecture—Mexican Americans needed to master these and many other fields to regain the land and the wealth arising from it. Ideally, applying this knowledge as a community offered the greatest benefits for the community. Through the technical knowledge of cooperative institutions such as TELACU, the Mexican-American community could recover its historic place in Los Angeles and a better place in the nation. Finally, beyond the Eastside, such ethnic, self-help, cooperative, and integrative institutions offered a distinct vision of social reconstruction to those looking to transcend a defunct collectivism and an unsatisfactory capitalism.

An Imagist Evaluation of TELACU

Of course, TELACU had by no means solved all the problems of East LA or the Eastside. Unemployment, crowded housing, low educational attainment, residential blight, and the other ailments of impoverished neighborhoods persisted in many barrios and in some ways became worse. For example, in East LA unemployment stood at 7.2 percent in 1970, but at 11.5 percent in 1990; meanwhile, the proportion of the population below the poverty line stood at 19.4 percent in the former year and at 24.2 in the latter. These figures suggested that TELACU and many other institutions were losing the battle against joblessness and poverty. On the other hand, the U.S.-born in East LA had dropped by over 10,000 people, from 72 to 51 percent of the population. As these Mexican Americans moved out, they were replaced by about 30,000 mostly Mexican

Conclusion 255

immigrants.³ The constant movement out of East LA into the suburbs hid a certain amount of upward mobility due at least partially to the efforts of institutions such as TELACU.

While CDCs could not solve all the social problems of the Eastside, TELACU's success argued for more of its sort of community economic development. As a business by 1993, TELACU with $300 million in assets had become the second largest minority firm operating in the Los Angeles area. Nationally, it had climbed to twenty-first in revenue among the five hundred Latino firms listed in *Hispanic Business*. Such growth meant TELACU by that year employed 1,500 people; although this number paled in comparison with East LA's unemployed (5,900 in 1990), these figures argued for further development.⁴ Moreover, as we have seen, TELACU had stimulated jobs beyond its own subsidiaries and social service agencies through leveraging and by encouraging other companies to move into the area.

Although TELACU had helped stimulate employment on the Eastside, the CDC's forte in the nineties remained real estate development. Despite constant criticism of TELACU's role as a developer, its revitalization of public spaces and rehabilitation of housing had helped maintain property values, including those of small homeowners. In 1990 nearly 40 percent of East LA residences were occupied by their owners, the most stable component of East LA's population. From 1970 to 1990 homeowners who had remained in the unincorporated area had seen the value of their residences rise by at least seven times, well beyond the rate of inflation. While this increase reflected the general rise in the value of southern California real estate, the efforts of TELACU had certainly helped East LA keep up. With the substantial decline in real estate values during the recession of the early nineties, TELACU's redevelopment efforts were even more important in keeping the area attractive to residents and buyers.⁵

Beyond such general statistics, TELACU's full impact was difficult to measure because of the complexity inherent in the CDC's holistic approach. For example, it was difficult to quantify the effects of TELACU's often leveraged activities, leveraged in terms not only of financing but of influence. As we have seen, though the community union played a critical role in gaining direct participation of the barrio in the redevelopment of Maravilla, the funding came entirely from government. In the case of the Whittier Boulevard revitalization, the merchants' local development corporation carried out the project, but the plans and the very organization originated with TELACU. Financially, TELACU had only retained 25-percent ownership of the industrial park in South Gate, but the CDC had instigated the redevelopment of the General Motors site. Of course, the importance of TELACU's promotion of architecture, painting, entertainment, and other cultural activities defied measurement, as did the institution's symbolism. Unfortunately, the difficulties in assessment contributed to the CDC's poor public image, a situation necessitating more humanistic evaluation.[6]

When compared with other Mexican-American organizations, TELACU fared well in some respects, but not in others. Despite its training programs, housing projects, and other social services, TELACU did not empower the poor so thoroughly as did the United Neighborhoods Organization, the grass-roots group that forced insurance companies to cease redlining the Eastside in the 1970s. Nor did TELACU have the judicial and legislative impact of a group such as the Mexican American Legal Defense and Education Fund, whose lawsuits in defense of Latinos led to the reapportionment of several governing bodies.[7] But compared with other organizations, the CDC could claim to be foremost in economic development. While private Latino companies of various sorts engaged in business, none engaged in the broad economic development necessary for the improvement of entire communities. While Latino businesses trained entrepreneurs and managers with the expertise needed in the private sector, TELACU sought to train leaders with the same skills, but with a knowledge of government and a community orientation. These leaders required a holistic perspective, not narrowly confined to one business or one government agency for that matter. Though the scandal of 1982 indicated that TELACU had strayed from its original cooperative orientation, the economic services performed by the CDC, especially in real estate, could not be matched by any other Latino organization.

Neocolonialism on the Eastside?

Despite this commendable service, the scandal of 1982 indicated that TELACU needed reform. After the scandal TELACU dropped its more controversial political activities, but it never undertook the major structural changes necessary to bring the CDC closer to the community. As we have seen, activists had originally conceived of community unions as mass membership organizations on the model of labor unions. By the time of TELACU's founding, this ideal had been abandoned, and the organizing committee became the entire institution for the sake of efficiency. Organizing mass participation seemed impractical for an institution that planned to carry out highly technical activities. When TELACU became a federally funded community development corporation, membership on its board opened to include representatives of other community groups, but this remained short of mass participation.[8] As TELACU moved away from the labor union model to a business model, wider participation seemed less likely to develop.

Some of the precursors of TELACU in community development, such as Progress Enterprises in Philadelphia, had drawn wider participation by asking local people to invest in the corporation. Although such investment clearly embodied the principles of free enterprise, TELACU never followed this approach. Although the community legally owned the holding company that formed TELACU's core, there were no individual stockholders; the community as owner was an abstraction. The stockholders could not meet because they did not exist as individual people. This meant of course that they could not vote, nor could they collect dividends. The board of directors, comprised of representatives of union locals and local organizations, represented the community. The board, however, was weak because many of the members lacked expertise in business since they necessarily reflected the working-class people of the community. This naturally meant that management had an excessive amount of power, especially the president and chief executive officer.[9]

In most business corporations, the chief executive officer and management hold the power. The stockholders and the board, less aware of the operating details of the enterprise, generally accept management's decisions. If and when the company begins to lose money, the board and stockholders step in to assure accountability. While they play an essentially negative role, it provides a modicum of democracy. In the case of TELACU, the lack of stockholders and dividends eliminated even this democratic element. Given often unsophisticated directors with no individual shares in the enterprise, accountability was minimal. David Lizarraga, TELACU's president for nearly twenty years by 1993, could almost run the operation as if it belonged to him and his executives alone.[10] This structure did not change after the 1982 scandal. Indeed, since the scandal initially left the CDC with fewer government contracts, even the oversight of various government agencies declined as the CDC became by design increasingly independent. TELACU's minimally democratic structure fueled much of the suspicion directed at the organization. Had a wide assortment of people in the community received even small annual dividends, the public would more likely have had interest and trust in the CDC.

Another matter causing TELACU's negative public image was the compensation of management. In an area suffering from unemployment and low wages, the high salaries commanded by TELACU executives hardly endeared them to the people of East LA. Given that dividends were not distributed in the community, the personal investment portfolios put together by TELACU managers as a result of the CDC's ventures seemed self-serving to say the least. In its defense, TELACU competed in a market with government agencies and businesses for highly qualified architects, urban planners, lawyers, entrepreneurs, and other technocrats. To hire and retain such talented professionals, TELACU had to compensate them well. Given the capitalist system in which the CDC operated, it could not hope to retain high-quality personnel by relying solely on the latter's dedication to the community.[11] Such an expectation might be appropriate for a charity, but not for an institution competing in the business world.

Most likely, the issue of compensation would have caused less trouble had TELACU engaged in less conspicuous consumption. The public display of fancy cars and expensive suits reported by the

Los Angeles Times had most tarnished TELACU's image in 1982. The financial questions were complex and difficult to understand, but the public could see extravagance in the midst of poverty. While it could be argued that the corporate world required an image of power and wealth, this remained a dubious claim. Businesslike simplicity in dress and transportation exemplified efficiency and would more likely earn the respect of the community, where TELACU also needed to function. The elaborate exteriors of TELACU's buildings could be appreciated by the entire community since they symbolized the power and resources of East LA, but plush offices smacked too much of personal luxury.[12] A more ascetic lifestyle would have done wonders for TELACU's public image.

Indeed, the ostentation of some TELACU managers brought to mind the elites of many Third World nations. Having politically liberated their nations from colonialism, these elites too often acquired the lifestyles of the former colonial masters, leaving the masses in the same poverty and powerlessness they had previously experienced. Though this neocolonial situation resulted from the continuing economic control exercised by the metropolis, the native elites suffered little; in fact, they benefited from their higher status in the newly independent nations. Since East LA had not become an incorporated city, the analogy with an independent nation is weak; nevertheless, as the community won greater political representation, TELACU executives had become the area's elite.[13] The Mexican-American Eastside needed TELACU's economic expertise to escape colonialism, but only if the subsequent state was an improvement for the whole community and not simply a small group at the top.

Symbol of Ethnic Recovery and Global Integration

TELACU had long ago learned that escaping colonialism and recovering self-determination for the Eastside were not sufficient for full prosperity. Only integration into the national and world economies would allow for the local area and Mexican Americans to fulfill their potential. Economically, TELACU had learned that confining its activities to East LA would suffocate its efforts. Its

10. The Portals. A mixed-use business complex under construction, with the Jefferson Memorial in the foreground and the Capitol in the background, Washington, D.C. Photograph by author, 1997.

original special impact area, only a bit larger than unincorporated East LA, had been too constricting. In the late seventies TELACU had convinced the federal government to allow it to operate throughout California and eventually wherever it could invest profitably. While early ventures of this sort through TELACU Investment Company had failed miserably, the CDC persisted.[14] TELACU invested in other minority firms both regionally and nationally, bringing back profits from investment opportunities unavailable at home. In so doing, the CDC also assisted disadvantaged minorities in other parts of the country. For TELACU had also recognized early that social and cultural interaction on an equal footing in the larger society was preferible to a provincial separatism.

In the decade following the 1982 scandal, two projects evinced TELACU's renewed drive toward self-determined economic integration—one in San Antonio, Texas, and the other in Washington, D.C. The San Antonio project grew directly out of the defunct Hispanic American Coalition for Economic Revitalization. As we have seen, the coalition had sought to unite Mexican-American community development corporations to train other Latino community-based groups in economic development. When HACER's funding disappeared, TELACU continued bilateral contacts with the other CDCs. Of these contacts, the relationship with MAUC, the Mexican American Unity Council, bore fruit. In the mid-eighties the two Mexican-American CDCs undertook development of a 90-acre industrial park on a prime site intersected by a freeway in Southeast San Antonio. On completion in 1994, the project was expected to cost $66.5 million and offer employment to several thousand Tejanos.[15] Certainly, East LA was in no greater need than Southeast San Antonio. If TELACU could most profitably invest in Texas, its efforts were worthwhile. Indeed, by spreading its expertise, TELACU paradoxically exemplified an integrative spirit by encouraging Mexican Americans throughout the Southwest to join more closely in their drive for self-determination of the Chicano homeland.

Symbolically, the most noteworthy of all TELACU's "integrated" investments was in the Portals, a mixed-use project, at the gateway to the U.S. capital from National Airport. Beginning in 1980, TE-

LACU had joined Washington, D.C.'s Anacostia Economic Developement Corporation and the Harlem Commonwealth Council in a three-way partnership called the Eastcoast Development Corporation. This partnership hoped to pool its resources to invest in projects on the scale of the largest private developers. After looking over several opportunities, Eastcoast decided to join a larger consortium in the competition for the right to redevelop one of the most blighted sites in southwestern Washington. The Western Development Corporation, a major Anglo-American developer, led the consortium, with several wealthy African-American individuals as the other associates. Though holding less than an 8-percent share, TELACU once again demonstrated the advantages of leverage in the struggle for economic power. Since the site remained one of the most desirable locations for redevelopment in the nation, competition intensified, but the consortium finally won after five years of bureaucratic delays. The $600 million development would include office buildings, shops, restaurants, a first-class hotel, recreation and health facilities, and a community center. The project was also expected to employ 9,500 people. Located near the Jefferson Memorial, in a direct line to the Capitol, the new development would be in a modernized Greco-Roman style, befitting its surroundings.[16]

No landmark could better symbolize the integrative spirit that TELACU had long advocated. People of various economic and ethnic backgrounds were showing that they could work together in a holistic approach to change the nation's very capital. Despite its radical beginnings, TELACU had long practiced such accommodation with the system, and despite the 1982 scandal, its approach had succeeded. TELACU and other CDCs offered the nation a successfully tested model of cooperative economic development, a model that Robert Kennedy, Walter Reuther, Martin Luther King, and César Chávez had advocated twenty-five years earlier.[17] While this model could not end poverty and its attendant problems, it offered a vision of self-sufficient communities equitably integrated into larger regional and national bodies for mutual improvement.

In the aftermath of the Los Angeles riots of 1992, the United States briefly rediscovered the CDC and related institutions. In that election year, the candidates discussed urban problems to an extent not heard in well over a decade. Once again solutions were sought, but in the conservative political climate of that period, the broad federal programs necessary to end poverty, unemployment, poor health care, and similar national problems continued in ill repute. On the other hand, the purely private sector approaches promoted by Republican administrations in the previous decade had only allowed the seemingly intractable problems of the inner cities to worsen. As President Bill Clinton took office in 1993, the climate seemed better for renewed cooperation between the private and public sectors, for a reconsideration of institutions, such as employee-owned companies, credit unions, and community development corporations. As nonprofit, cooperative institutions that operated between government and business, CDCs like the East Los Angeles Community Union offered an alternative in a world where many had rejected the extremes of collectivism, but still suspected capitalism. While credit unions and CDCs could not solve the nation's deepest socioeconomic problems, the joint experience and practical results would help prepare society for the larger cooperative efforts necessary for the progress of the national and global communities.[18]

Despite its failures, the East Los Angeles Community Union remained a powerful symbol in the historical development of Mexican Americans. Chicanos—longtime residents of the Southwest, an indigenous people—had lost their homeland in the most recent cycle of conquest, but they were recovering. Gradually, they were building or taking over the institutions that controlled their fortunes and moving toward a society integrated on an equitable basis. Increasingly, the colonial analogy seemed incomplete. Indeed, East LA, the Chicano Southwest, and Mexican Americans needed to throw off colonialism, not for the sake of separation, but to integrate into the larger world as autonomous entities. In the nineties the model of defiant, independent, but impoverished Cuba no longer sufficed. Neither independent isolation nor forced integration had proven viable. Cuba, the dismantled Soviet Union, as well as the old European empires, had demonstrated the futility of those models. Instead, the European Union with its politically and culturally autonomous states voluntarily integrated into an increasingly cooperative whole showed greater promise. Without losing their cultures and self-determination, minorities and all peoples needed to integrate into such larger and freer political and economic systems, on an egalitarian basis.[19]

Reference Matter

Notes

Introduction

1. Matusow, pp. xiv, 395–96, 410.
2. Muñoz, pp. 59, 86.
3. Matusow, p. 408; and Parachini, *TELACU*, p. 14.
4. Parachini, *TELACU*, p. 25; Durham, p. 6; Parachini, *Political History*, pp. 37–39; and *CDCs*, pp. 19, 64, 28–31.
5. *CDCs*, p. 21; "TELACU Annual Progress Report, 1986–1987: Meeting Tomorrow's Challenges Today," TELACU Center, Commerce, Calif.; for another example of the importance of land in the ideology of CDCs, see Perry, *Building a Model Black Community*, p. 13.
6. "A Framework for Greater East Los Angeles Industrial Development," Sept. 1978, pp. 21–24, Greater East Los Angeles Overall Economic Development Program, Central Files, TELACU Center; and Ríos-Bustamante and Castillo, pp. 2, 129.
7. F. J. Weber, p. vii; and Steiner, pp. 124, 119, 34–36, 61–63.
8. Steiner, pp. 49, 8–9; and "The Greater East Los Angeles Cultural Heritage Survey," Aug. 1979, vol. 3, sites 3, 20, TELACU Papers, Special Collections, John F. Kennedy Memorial Library, California State University, Los Angeles.
9. Frank Martínez and Joe L. González, *Orgullo de Nuestra Herencia/The Pride of Our Heritage*, mural in ceramic tile, 1983, TELACU Center; and David C. Lizarraga, quoted in "1983 Progress Report," TELACU Center.
10. "1983 Progress Report"; and "*Orgullo de Nuestra Herencia/The Pride of Our Heritage*," leaflet with photograph and description of mural, TELACU Center.
11. "*Orgullo*"; and J. R. Chávez, "Image," pp. 41, 44–45.
12. J. R. Chávez, "Image," pp. 41, 44–45; and "*Orgullo*."

13. Acuña, *Occupied America*, pp. 5–6; "*Orgullo*"; and Raigoza, p. 76.
14. Sopher, p. 133; J. R. Chávez, *Lost Land*, p. 1; "*Orgullo*"; and "1983 Progress Report."
15. "1983 Progress Report"; memorandum, David C. Lizarraga to Grace Nagata, 13 March 1975, TELACU: Correspondence/Inter-Office, Central Files.
16. Smith, p. vii; and Meinig, p. 172.
17. Smith, p. vii; for criticism of this approach, see Kuklick, pp. 435–50.
18. Slotkin, pp. 6–8; and "Proposal to the Executive Director and Management Staff of TELACU," Jan. 1976, pp. 1–6, TELACU: Correspondence/Inter-Office.
19. Weyr, pp. 171–74.
20. Parachini, *TELACU*, pp. 13–14, 25; and Matusow, p. 125.
21. See Hayden, p. 32; Blauner, pp. 51–75; and Barrera, *Race*, pp. 218–19.
22. See Fanon, pp. 223–32; Memmi, pp. 145–53; Freire, pp. 48–49; Malcolm X, "*Young Socialist* Interview," p. 161; and Carmichael and Hamilton, pp. 2–32.
23. Barrera, Muñoz, and Ornelas, p. 297; Tijerina, pp. 217–18; and untitled biography under Torres, Esteban, 1974–1977, Central Files.
24. J. R. Chávez, "Image," p. 41.
25. Ibid., and "*Orgullo*."
26. "*Orgullo*"; Claire Spiegel and Robert Welkos, "Anti-Poverty Agency: Leaving Barrio Behind," *Los Angeles Times*, 28 Mar. 1982, pt. 1, p. 1; and "Report of Audit: The East Los Angeles Community Union," 8 Nov. 1982, vol. 1, p. 109, U.S. Department of Labor Investigation, Central Files.

Chapter 1

1. Herbal stores and butcher shops.
2. "The Community, the Need and the Origins of TELACU," pp. 13–17, 10, TELACU: Company Summaries, 1969–, Central Files, TELACU Center, Commerce, Calif.; cf. the figures with those for the Southwest in Grebler, Moore, and Guzmán, pp. 181, 208, 154, 255, 249, 252.
3. Parachini, *TELACU*, pp. 14–15.
4. *CDCs*, pp. 14–15; Hernández, pp. 31–33; and Essien-Udom, pp. 63–64, 164–66.
5. Essien-Udom, 63–64, 164–66; *Muhammad Speaks* (Chicago), 15 Jan. 1963.
6. Malcolm X, *Autobiography*, p. 263; see also Garnett, pp. 2–3, 19–23.
7. Essien-Udom, pp. 172, 260–62; and *Muhammad Speaks*, 15 Jan. 1963, Dec. 1961.

8. *Muhammad Speaks*, Feb. 1962, Dec. 1961; Essien-Udom, pp. 250, 60–61; and Bell, pp. 47, 176, 183–84.

9. *CDCs*, pp. 65–67; and Sullivan, p. 23.

10. *CDCs*, pp. 65–67. 11. Ibid.

12. Matusow, p. 125. 13. Sundquist, pp. 85, 60–63, 83.

14. Ibid., 60–62; and *Congressional Record*, 87th Cong., 1st sess., 1961, 107, pt. 3: 3586–87.

15. Sundquist, pp. 60–62; and Department of Commerce, Area Redevelopment Administration, *Planning for New Growth–New Jobs*, Bookshelf of Community Aids, ARA Pub. no. 62-A, pp. 4–5, 8–9.

16. Department of Commerce, p. 23; and Matusow, p. 100.

17. Sundquist, pp. 105–7, 110; and Matusow, p. 102.

18. Sundquist, pp. 61, 100–101.

19. Ibid.; and Harrington, pp. 12, 158.

20. Kennedy, pp. 37, 35; see also Brown, pp. 46–69.

21. For the following information on the origins of the War on Poverty, I am deeply indebted to Matusow, pp. 107–9, 97–127; see also "The Office of Economic Opportunity During the Administration of Lyndon B. Johnson," Nov. 1963–Jan. 1969, vol. 1, Lyndon B. Johnson Library, University of Texas, Austin.

22. Matusow, pp. 110–11. 23. Ibid., pp. 118–19.

24. Ibid., pp. 119–21. 25. Ibid., pp. 121–23.

26. Levitan, pp. 112–13.

27. "Officers," pp. 1, 3, CCAP Background, box 1, Citizens' Crusade Against Poverty, Walter P. Reuther Library of Labor and Urban Affairs, Wayne State University, Detroit, Mich.

28. Barnard, pp. 160, 204–5; and *Milwaukee Journal*, 16 June 1968.

29. *Milwaukee Journal*, 16 June 1968; *Chicago's American*, 15 Jan. 1967; and "Shriver Showdown Nears," 30 Dec. 1965, p. 2, folder 4, box 326, UAW President's Office—Walter P. Reuther, Walter P. Reuther Library.

30. "Shriver Showdown"; "Statement of Policy and Program," pp. 8–9, CCAP Background; "Community Unions," 23 May 1969, p. 5, folder 2, box 341, UAW President's Office; and Barnard, pp. 204–5, 214.

31. "At our last IUD convention . . . ," pp. 1–2, folder 11, box 326, UAW President's Office; Bullock, pp. 119, 129; and Marks, pp. 19–23.

32. "At our last," pp. 1–2; and Marks, pp. 22–23.

33. "At our last," p. 1.

34. Ibid.; and Marks, p. 21.

35. Quoted in Reuther, p. 380; and "At our last," pp. 1–4.

36. "Director's Report to the Board and Friends of CCAP," 31 Dec. 1968, pp. 4, 2, CCAP: Merger with Center for Community Change, box 1, Citizens' Crusade Against Poverty.

37. Ibid., p. 4.

38. "Current Status of CCAP Training Programs—Summary," 17 Sept. 1968, pp. 3–4, 1968 Reports on Training Programs, box 4, Citizens' Crusade Against Poverty.

39. Ibid.; and Meier and Rivera, pp. 261–62.

40. Meier and Rivera, pp. 261–62; Day, pp. 29–31; LeRoy Chatfield to Jack Conway, 13 Feb. 1968, pp. 1–3, folder 10, box 326, UAW President's Office; and "Current Status," p. 3.

41. Meier and Rivera, p. 279.

42. Ibid., pp. 262–63.

43. "At our last," p. 2; Glenn O'Loane, interview by author, 13 July 1989, East Los Angeles.

44. O'Loane interview; and Glenn O'Loane, quoted in *TELACU Today* (Los Angeles), Jan. 1978.

45. Parachini, *TELACU*, pp. 13–14; and O'Loane interview.

46. *TELACU Today*, Jan.–Feb. 1980; and George Solís, interview by author, 25 July 1989, Commerce, Calif.

47. Solís interview.

48. *Rank and File* (Pico Rivera, Calif.), Oct. 1968.

49. Ibid.; O'Loane interview; and O'Loane, quoted in *TELACU Today*, Jan. 1978.

50. *Rank and File*, Oct. 1968.

51. O'Loane interview.

52. "The East Los Angeles Community Union: Prospectus," 13 Sept. 1972, TELACU: Company Summaries, 1969– , Central Files; and untitled biography under Torres, Esteban, 1974–1977, Central Files.

53. Torres biography.

54. Ibid.

55. Parachini, *Political History*, pp. 19–21.

56. CDCs, p. 71; and Parachini, *Political History*, pp. 21–22.

57. CDCs, pp. 71–74.

58. Ibid.

59. Ibid.

60. Parachini, *Political History*, pp. 40–41.

61. Brown, pp. 65–66.

62. Kennedy, pp. 42–43.

63. Robert F. Kennedy, "A Program for the Urban Crisis," quoted in Brown, p. 68.

64. "Kennedy Is Dead, Victim of Assassin," *New York Times*, 6 June 1968, sec. 1, p. 1; and Robert F. Kennedy, [Denver speech, 5 Apr. 1968], quoted in Brown, p. 63.

65. Newfield, pp. 298–99; and "Shooting Victims Recover," *New York Times*, 16 June 1968, sec. 1, p. 32.

66. Parachini, *Political History*, pp. 51–53; and *Congressional Record*, 90th Cong., 2d sess., 1968, 114, pt. 17: 22132–37.

67. "The Community," pp. 17, 7–8; and Esteban Torres, quoted in Torres biography.

Chapter 2

1. Matusow, p. 342; Muñoz, pp. 60, 64; *Belvedere* (Calif.) *Citizen*, 23 May, 6 June 1968; and Doug Shuit and Dial Torgerson, "*Mexican-American Parade*: Southland Observances Pay Final Respects to Kennedy," *Los Angeles Times*, 9 June 1968, sec. B, p. 1.
2. Untitled biography under Torres, Esteban, 1974–1977, Central Files, TELACU Center, Commerce, Calif.; and Barrera, *Race*, pp. 218–19.
3. Torres biography; for much information in this chapter, I am indebted to Marín, p. 176.
4. Corwin, pp. 270–73; and Romo, pp. 62, 65–67.
5. Kelsey, p. 328, 335; Steiner, p. 35; "First Census," pp. 33–35; and Ríos-Bustamante and Castillo, pp. 36, 33, 24.
6. Kelsey, pp. 332–34; Steiner, pp. 38, 36, 28; "Whittier Narrows Flood Control Basin Historic Resources Survey," 1976, pp. 8–9, 11, Museum of the San Gabriel Historical Association, San Gabriel, Calif.; Griswold del Castillo, pp. 4–5; and Ríos-Bustamante and Castillo, pp. 51, 24–25.
7. Geary, pp. 17, 24–25; and Jones, pp. 177, 194.
8. Engelhardt, p. 121; and Ríos-Bustamante and Castillo, p. 18.
9. Geary, pp. 153–56; Ríos-Bustamante and Castillo, p. 79; see map in Harlow, p. 20.
10. Griswold del Castillo, pp. 25–28; and Pitt, pp. 32–35.
11. Griswold del Castillo, pp. 45–46.
12. Pitt, pp. 85–86; and Robinson, p. 106.
13. Harlow, p. 20; Docket no. 371, Board of Land Commissioners in California, 1856, Records of Department of Justice, Record Group 60, National Archives, Washington, D.C.; and "Abstract of Title of . . . Rancho Rosa de Castilla . . . 1844–1884," MS HM 31537, Gillette & Gibson Collection, Henry E. Huntington Library, San Marino, Calif.
14. Pitt, p. 296; Camarillo, pp. 119–20; and Barrera, *Race*, p. 5.
15. Griswold del Castillo, pp. 47, 49, 51; and Camarillo, p. 119; cf. Mazón, p. 95.
16. Pitt, p. 249; Griswold del Castillo, p. 148; and Romo, p. 65.
17. Romo, pp. 80–81, 169–70; and G. J. Sánchez, pp. 198–99.
18. Acuña, *Community*, pp. 104–5, 126, 129, 86; Balderrama, pp. 3–4; and Romo, p. 170.
19. Barrera, *Race*, pp. 218–19.
20. J. R. Chávez, *Lost Land*, pp. 134–35, 143, 8, 147–48, 22.
21. Ibid., pp. 142–43, 139, 129–30; and Marín, pp. 152–54, 79.
22. Marín, 6–7, 202.

23. For the following account of the student walkouts in East LA, I am most indebted to Rosen, pp. 135–37; see also Marín, 152, 157.

24. Rosen, pp. 137–39.

25. Ibid., pp. 138–40; and Gómez-Quiñones, pp. 24–28.

26. *Belvedere Citizen*, 19 Jan. 1967; 22, 29 Feb. 1968; and Marín, p. 202.

27. *Belvedere Citizen*, 7 Mar. 1968; *La raza* (Los Angeles), 4 Sept. 1967, 10 Feb. 1968; and Rosen, pp. 142–44.

28. Rosen, p. 145; and *Belvedere Citizen*, 7 Mar. 1968.

29. *Belvedere Citizen*, 7 Mar. 1968; and Muñoz, pp. 66–67.

30. *Belvedere Citizen*, 11 July, 27 June, 7 Mar. 1968; and Marín, pp. 116, 77–78.

31. *Eastside Journal* (Belvedere, Calif.), 30 May 1968; and *Belvedere Citizen*, 14 Mar., 11 July, 18 July, 5 Sept., 24 Oct. 1968.

32. "Lists of organizations . . . ," Jan. 1970, Congress of Mexican-American Unity (CMAU), 1970–1971, Central Files; *Belvedere Citizen*, 24 Oct. 1968; and *Eastside Sun* (Los Angeles), 14 Aug. 1969.

33. "An Introduction to the East Los Angeles Community Union," TELACU: Company Summaries, 1969– , Central Files.

34. Ibid.

35. Ibid.; Payne and Ratzan, p. 46; and *East Los Angeles Gazette*, 10 Nov. 1968.

36. *East Los Angeles Gazette*, 10 Nov. 1968; see, for example, Rendón, p. 295.

37. *East Los Angeles Gazette*, 10 Nov. 1968.

38. *Belvedere Citizen*, 24 Oct. 1968; "An Introduction"; and "The East Los Angeles Community Union: Prospectus," 13 Sept. 1972, TELACU: Company Summaries, 1969– .

39. *Belvedere Citizen*, 24 Oct. 1968.

40. Ibid.; Gordon Moreno, interview by author, 25 July 1990, Commerce, Calif.; and "An Introduction."

41. "An Introduction"; see also *East Los Angeles Tribune*, 27 Feb. 1969.

42. "An Introduction."

43. Ibid.

44. *Belvedere Citizen*, 24 Oct. 1968.

45. "An Introduction"; and "The East Los Angeles Community Union: Introduction," p. 7, TELACU: Company Summaries, 1969– .

46. "An Introduction."

47. "Sitsum No. 1," 31 Aug. 1971, p. 1, TELACU Matress Company, 1971–1974, Central Files; and *Eastside Journal*, 8 May 1969.

48. "Sitsum No. 1," pp. 1–3.

49. TELACU internal memorandum, quoted in Parachini, *TELACU*, p. 16.

50. Muñoz, pp. 68, 73, n. 51; Rosen, p. 146; Marín, pp. 89–90; and Moreno interview.
51. *La raza*, 15 Nov. 1967; *Belvedere Citizen*, 23 May 1968; and Rosen, pp. 148–50.
52. *Belvedere Citizen*, 17 Oct. 1968; Marín, pp. 105–6, 108; and Rosen, p. 150.
53. Moreno interview.
54. Davis, pp. 334–35; and *La raza*, 9 Nov. 1969.
55. *La raza*, 9 Nov. 1969; "Church vs. Catóicos," pp. 20–22; *Eastside Journal*, 19 Feb. 1970; *Belvedere Citizen*, 2 Apr. 1970; "Bar Admits Man Cited in Protest," *Los Angeles Times*, 26 Apr. 1973, pt. 2, p. 2
56. "Church Response," p. 27; see also *Belvedere Citizen*, 9 July 1970.
57. For the following account of the East LA riots, I am most indebted to Morales, p. 100.
58. "Lists of organizations"; and *Belvedere Citizen*, 12 Feb., 12 Mar. 1970.
59. J. R. Chávez, *Lost Land*, 143, 147; "Spiritual Manifesto," p. 84; Guzmán, pp. 12–15; and Marín, pp. 202, 204.
60. Marín, pp. 205–6; Muñoz, p. 86; see also D. Sánchez, pp. 3–4.
61. *Belvedere Citizen*, 9 July 1970.
62. Marín, p. 208; *Belvedere Citizen*, 27 Aug. 1970; *Eastside Journal*, 30 July 1970; and Moreno interview.
63. Morales, 101–7.
64. Ibid.
65. Ibid., p. 104; and Marín, pp. 214–16.
66. Jerry Buhlow and John Kumbula, "Damage in Wilmington Rioting Being Assessed," *Los Angeles Times*, 1 Sept. 1970, pt. 1, p. 3; and Morales, p. 107.
67. Letter to the editor, *Eastside Sun*, 3 Dec. 1970, reprinted in Morales, pp. 97–98.
68. Muñoz, pp. 117–19; and letter to the editor, *Los Angeles Times*, 23 Jan. 1971, reprinted in Morales, p. 117.
69. *Los Angeles Herald Examiner*, 20 May 1979.

Chapter 3

1. Photographs in Whittier Boulevard Study, 1 Sept. 1970, Central Files, TELACU Center, Commerce, Calif.
2. Much of this chapter rests on the seminal work of Parachini, *TELACU*, p. 18; and idem, *Political History*, p. 39.
3. Gene Blake, "Five Violent Groups Shared in $6 Million Gifts, Senators Told," *Los Angeles Times*, 20 Mar. 1970, pt. 2, p. 1; and "Statement by Esteban E. Torres, Executive Director, the East Los Angeles Community Union," TELACU: Correspondence/Inter-Office, 1969–1976, Central Files.

4. Parachini, *TELACU*, pp. 17–29.

5. Morales, pp. 117, 119; Parachini, *TELACU*, pp. 18–19; and "The East Los Angeles Community Union: Introduction," pp. 11–12, TELACU: Company Summaries, 1969– , Central Files.

6. "Sitsum No. 2," 8 Sept. 1971, TELACU Service Center, 1970–1971, Central Files; and Parachini, *TELACU*, p. 65.

7. "Sitsum No. 2" and "Sitsum No. 5," 1[7] Sept. 1971, TELACU Service Center; and Parachini, *TELACU*, pp. 28–29.

8. Parachini, *TELACU*, pp. 16–19; "Community Union: Introduction," pp. 9–10; and Marín, p. 199.

9. Parachini, *TELACU*, 19, 66; and "Director's Report to the Board and Friends of CCAP," 31 Dec. 1968, p. 1, CCAP: Merger with Center for Community Change, box 1, Citizens' Crusade Against Poverty, Walter P. Reuther Library of Labor and Urban Affairs, Wayne State University, Detroit, Mich.

10. "Barrio Housing Plan," quoted in Parachini, *TELACU*, p. 20; and "Fact Sheet," Aug. 1974, p. 7, TELACU Company Summaries.

11. Acuña, *Community*, pp. 58–60, 80; and "Barrio Housing Plan," quoted in Parachini, *TELACU*, p. 21.

12. Parachini, *TELACU*, pp. 19, 21; and "Cleland House Vehicle Maintenance Company," [28 Aug. 1972], p. 1, Cleland House, 1972, Central Files.

13. "Barrio Housing Plan," quoted in Parachini, *TELACU*, pp. 20–21.

14. Ibid., p. 25; and Parachini, *Political History*, pp. 51–52, 55, 60, 64.

15. Quoted in *Eastside Sun* (Los Angeles), 16 Oct. 1969; and Parachini, *TELACU*, p. 25.

16. Parachini, *TELACU*. p. 25; and idem, *Political History*, pp. 71, 76–77.

17. David Lizarraga to Ray Carrasco, 12 May 1972, and Jack M. Harper to Esteban Torres, 22 May 1972, Maravilla Housing Project, 1970–1974, Central Files; see also Parachini, *TELACU*, p. 22.

18. José Amaya, Ronald de la Torre, and Henry Toscano to Esteban Torres, 12 May 1972, Maravilla Housing Project.

19. See Pilar Hernández to Arnold Martínez, 16 May 1973, Maravilla Housing Project; and Parachini, *TELACU*, p. 23.

20. Parachini, *TELACU*, p. 23; Jack M. Harper to Esteban Torres, 1 Feb. 1972, Maravilla Housing Project; see also Louis Kanaster to editor, *Los Angeles Times*, 11 Apr. 1982, pt. 5, p. 4.

21. "Nueva Maravilla: A Program for the Modernization of Public Housing," and Harper to Torres, 1 Feb. 1972, Maravilla Housing Project.

22. "Maravilla Progress Schedule," Maravilla Housing Project; and Parachini, *TELACU*, pp. 19–20, 25.

23. "Special Impact Operational Funding," quoted in Parachini, *TELACU*, pp. 25–26.

24. Ibid.; see Harvey, pp. 172, 174.

25. Parachini, *TELACU*, p. 26; Marín, p. 186; see also Johnson, pp. 55–56.

26. Marín, p. 186; Parachini, *TELACU*, pp. 65–66; Arthur M. Miller to Alexander Grant and Company, 15 Aug. 1978, UAW Debt, 1975–1980, Central Files; "Special Impact Refunding," quoted in idem, *TELACU*, p. 29; for federal guidelines regarding *self-sufficiency*, see Carlos J. García to Robert L. Gámez, 19 Apr. 1976, TELACU: Correspondence/General Outgoing, 1968–1976, Central Files.

27. Parachini, *TELACU*, p. 26; "Fact Sheet," p. 14; "Community Union: Introduction," pp. 3–4; for discussion of democratic representation in community-based organizations, see Ambrecht, pp. 183–84; and Kelly, pp. 134, 142–52.

28. Parachini, *TELACU*, p. 25; and idem, *Political History*, pp. 77–78.

29. Parachini, *Political History*, pp. 78–79.

30. Harvey, p. 172; Morison, pp. 68–69, 93, 85, 340; and Allen, pp. ix–xi.

31. Parachini, *TELACU*, pp. 14–15, 26; Moynihan, p. 137; and "Fact Sheet," p. 14.

32. Harvey, p. 172; Parachini, *TELACU*, p. 27; and Raigoza, p. 209.

33. My account of the history of incorporation most closely follows Jorge García, "The Incorporation of East Los Angeles, 1974, Part One," p. 30, East Los Angeles—Incorporation, Pamphlet Files, Chicano Resource Center, County of Los Angeles Public Library, East Los Angeles.

34. Miller, pp. 41–47; cf. Elliott, pp. 122–23, 201–4, 141.

35. Raigoza, pp. 61–62; Acuña, *Community*, p. 87; and J. García "Part One," p. 31.

36. Raigoza, p. 64; minutes, 6 Oct. 1970, and Esteban E. Torres to members, 23 Nov. 1970, Congress of Mexican-American Unity (CMAU), 1970–1971, Central Files.

37. J. García, "Part One," p. 31; and Macías, "History," p. 16.

38. J. García, "Part One," p. 31; Torres, "Birth," pp. 13–14; and "East Los Angeles: A Brief History," pp. 19–20.

39. [Esteban Torres, anon.], interview by James José Raigoza, in Raigoza, p. 209; cf. Fanon, pp. 223–32; and Memmi, pp. 145–53.

40. Torres interview in Raigoza, pp. 209–10.

41. Ibid.; see Larson, pp. 207, 303–4, 215; and Christopulos, pp. 138–39, 167–68.

42. Torres, "Birth," p. 14; and "El Zócalo: A Community Design Project," Aug. 1975, p. 2, El Zócalo, Reports-Proposals, TELACU Center.

43. Macías et al., *Study*, p. 33; James F. Hayes [& Associates] to Ad

Hoc Committee for the Incorporation of East Los Angeles, 23 Feb. 1973, and minutes of the Local Agency Formation Commission of Los Angeles County, 8 Aug. 1973, pp. 18–21, 6, East Los Angeles: Incorporation or Annexation Documents, Chicano Resource Center.

44. J. García, "Part One," pp. 31–32; and Parachini, *TELACU*, p. 27.

45. "Maravilla Progress Schedule"; Cheri Weiss to George Pla, 8 June 1973; and memorandum, Carlos J. García to Esteban E. Torres, 16 Feb. 1973, Maravilla Housing Project; see also *Belvedere* (Calif.) *Citizen*, 1 Aug. 1974.

46. Parachini, *TELACU*, pp. 28–29, 40–41; and "Fact Sheet," pp. 10–11.

47. Parachini, *TELACU*, p. 27; "Maravilla Progress Schedule"; *Belvedere Citizen*, 7 Mar. 1974; and "Special Impact Refunding Proposal for Oct. 1, 1974–Sept. 30, 1976," TELACU Center.

48. J. García, "Part One," pp. 31–32; for comment on the break between Esteban Torres and militants in the congress, see idem, *"Forjando Ciudad,"* p. 230.

49. J. García, *"Forjando Ciudad,"* pp. 230, 210–12; "Spiritual Manifesto," p. 84; J. R. Chávez, *Lost Land*, pp. 141–42; for federal reaction to La Raza Unida Party's controversial CDC in South Texas, see "The Zavala County Economic Development Corporation," 23 Nov. 1976, Transition Reports—Community Services Administration (1), pt. II-J, box 37, John O. Marsh Files, Gerald R. Ford Library, University of Michigan, Ann Arbor.

50. J. García, "Part One," pp. 32–33; idem, *"Forjando Ciudad,"* pp. 258, 262; and Santillán, pp. 167–69.

51. J. García, "Part One," p. 32.

52. Ibid.

53. Ibid., p. 33; *Belvedere Citizen*, 7 Mar. 1974; *Eastside Journal* (Belvedere, Calif.), 13 June 1974; and Parachini, *TELACU*, p. 27.

54. J. García, "Part One," p. 33; and "Sample Ballot, General Election, County of Los Angeles," 5 Nov. 1974, pp. 10–12, East Los Angeles: Incorporation or Annexation Documents.

55. J. García, "Part One," p. 33; see also "Recount Results: Proposed Incorporation of the City of East Los Angeles, Measure X," 19 Dec. 1974, East Los Angeles: Incorporation or Annexation Documents.

56. J. García, *"Forjando Ciudad,"* p. 313; Parachini, *TELACU*, p. 27; and *Forum* (San Diego), Jan. 1987.

57. J. García, *"Forjando Ciudad,"* pp. 222–23; Parachini, *TELACU*, p. 26; and Marín, p. 199.

Chapter 4

1. Quoted in *Belvedere* (Calif.) *Citizen*, 5 Dec. 1974; for a different opinion regarding TELACU's credit for the Nueva Maravilla project, by a

former executive director of the Los Angeles County Housing Authority, see Louis Kanaster to editor, *Los Angeles Times*, 11 Apr. 1982, pt. 5, p. 4.

2. For much of the framework of this chapter, I am indebted to Parachini, *TELACU*, pp. 27, 30; "Economic Catalyst for the Eighties," progress report, [1979–1981], p. 2, TELACU Center, Commerce, Calif.

3. Parachini, *TELACU*, pp. 27, 30; *TELACU Today* (Los Angeles), June 1981; *Forum* (San Diego), Jan. 1987; for doubts regarding TELACU's benefits for its working-class community, see Acuña, *Community*, pp. 251–53, 263, 267.

4. Quoted in *Forum*, Jan. 1987.

5. Untitled TELACU brochure, [1976], TELACU (The East Los Angeles Community Union), Pamphlet Files, Chicano Resource Center, County of Los Angeles Public Library, East Los Angeles; that TELACU's management early exhibited a patronizing attitude toward women is evident from references to "the girls in the office" in memorandum, Esteban E. Torres to all TELACU staff, 16 Mar. 1971, TELACU: Correspondence/Inter-Office, 1969–1976, Central Files, TELACU Center.

6. *Belvedere Citizen*, 8 Aug., and 12 Dec. 1974.

7. Parachini, *TELACU*, p. 32.

8. Barrera, Muñoz, and Ornelas, p. 297; untitled biography under Torres, Esteban, 1974–1977, Central Files; and Parachini, *TELACU*, p. 33.

9. Parachini, *TELACU*, pp. 34–35.

10. Ibid.; and Community Thrift & Loan proposal, 7 Jan. 1976, Reports-Proposals, TELACU Center.

11. Community Thrift & Loan proposal; and Parachini, *TELACU*, p. 36.

12. Parachini, *TELACU*, p. 37; for criticism of the federal government's early MESBIC program, see Hetzel, pp. 76–78.

13. Parachini, *TELACU*, pp. 38, 73–75; and Community Thrift & Loan proposal.

14. Community Thrift & Loan proposal; Parachini, *TELACU*, pp. 39–40; and Marín, p. 199.

15. Parachini, *TELACU*, p. 36; later, criticism would be leveled at Aparicio's operation for funding companies largely outside of East LA, but federal guidelines restricted the direct assistance her office could give the "mom-and-pop" businesses in the immediate area—see Claire Spiegel and Robert Welkos, "Giant Anti-Poverty Agency Did Little to Create Jobs," *Los Angeles Times*, 30 Mar. 1982, pt. 1, p. 1; and Hetzel, p. 72.

16. *Belvedere Citizen*, 3 Jan., 25 Apr. 1974; 27 Feb. 1975; and Parachini, *TELACU*, pp. 57–58.

17. *Belvedere Citizen*, 8 Aug. 1974; 2 Oct. 1975; and 31 Aug. 1977.

18. Ibid., 24 Apr. 1975.

19. Ibid.

20. Ibid., 24 Apr. 1975, and 5 May 1976.

21. Ibid., 23 Jan., 5, 12, 19, 26 June, 3, 17, 31 July 1975; Molina's later reputation as a maverick and feminist was already well established during her stint as a job developer for TELACU—see memorandum, Joe M. Pérez to Roy Escarcega, 8 Sept. 1972, TELACU: Correspondence/Inter-Office.

22. *Belvedere Citizen*, 28 Aug., 16 Oct., 4 Dec. 1975; 2, 16, and 28 June 1976.

23. Parachini, *TELACU*, pp. 32, 36–37, 65; and *East Los Angeles Tribune*, 5 Jan. 1983.

24. Parachini, *TELACU*, p. 37; and Claire Spiegel and Robert Welkos, "Anti-Poverty Agency: Leaving Barrio Behind," *Los Angeles Times*, 28 Mar. 1982, pt. 1, p. 1.

25. Parachini, *TELACU*, p. 38; and Community Thrift & Loan proposal.

26. Community Thrift & Loan proposal.

27. Ibid.; and "Economic Catalyst for the Eighties," p. 5.

28. Untitled TELACU brochure; and Parachini, *TELACU*, pp. 40–41.

29. Parachini, *TELACU*, pp. 42–43, 65; for an example of the services provided by one spin-off company, see Leonard Rutkin to Daniel M. López, 7 Feb. 1977, First Southwest Capital, Inc., 1976–1981, Central Files.

30. Parachini, *TELACU*, pp. 41–42; see also "Community Planning & Development Corporation," brochure, TELACU (The East Los Angeles Community Union).

31. "Community Planning & Development Corporation"; Parachini, *TELACU*, p. 41; see also *Belvedere Citizen*, 17 Jan., 28 Mar., 18 Apr., 10 Oct. 1974; and 5 May 1976.

32. *Belvedere Citizen*, 5 June 1975; Parachini, *TELACU*, pp. 41, 68–69; and untitled TELACU brochure.

33. Parachini, *TELACU*, pp. 41, 66, 68; *Belvedere Citizen*, 25 July, 19 Sept. 1974; see also "El Zócalo: A Community Design Project," Aug. 1975, El Zócalo, Reports-Proposals.

34. *Belvedere Citizen*, 2 Oct., 18 Dec. 1975; 11 Oct. 1978; and "Unincorporated East Los Angeles Environmental Assessment Program," TELACU Center.

35. "Environmental Assessment."

36. *Belvedere Citizen*, 28 Sept. 1977; 25 Oct. 1978; 28 Mar. 1979; "Staffing Proposal Addendum," 7 Jan. 1980, pp. 1–3, Whittier Boulevard LDC, Reports-Proposals; see also Hetzel, pp. 78–80.

37. Parachini, *TELACU*, pp. 45–46; *TELACU Today*, Jan. 1978; and Bullock, pp. 117, 119, 124.

38. *Belvedere Citizen*, 14 Jan. 1976; *TELACU Today*, June 1978; and "Addendum," 31 July 1979, Addendum: TELACU Overall Economic Development Plan (1977) for Period 1978–1983, Reports-Proposals.

39. Parachini, *TELACU*, p. 19; Mann, pp. 97–98; and David C. Lizarraga to Edward R. Roybal, 26 Aug. 1975, TELACU: Correspondence/General Outgoing, 1968–1976, Central Files.

40. Lizarraga to Roybal, 26 Aug. 1975; Parachini, *TELACU*, p. 44; "Addendum," 31 July 1979; later it would be charged that TELACU paid too much for the Goodrich property—see Spiegel and Welkos, "Giant."

41. Parachini, *TELACU*, pp. 44, 65; and "Addendum," 31 July 1979.

42. "Addendum," 31 July 1979; "For Lease: New Multi-Story Office Building," brochure, [1986], TELACU Center; Spiegel and Welkos, "Giant"; "TELACU: Translating Unmet Community Needs into Economic Opportunities," typed circular, [1986], p. 3, TELACU Center.

43. Sanford, pp. 228–29, 248–50; "Economic Catalyst for the Eighties," pp. 12–13; and "1983 Progress Report," TELACU Center.

44. "Economic Catalyst for the Eighties," p. 20; *Belvedere Citizen*, 31 Mar. 1976; "Business Plan," 21 Sept. 1979, pp. 1, 6, Business Plan for Inter-American Entertainment Co., Ltd., Reports-Proposals; criticism would later be leveled at the company's executives for imitating Hollywood's luxurious lifestyle, thereby contributing to the venture's failure—see Robert Welkos and Claire Spiegel, "Far-Flung Empire Is Built on Federal Grants," *Los Angeles Times*, 29 Mar. 1982, pt. 1, p. 1.

45. David C. Lizarraga to Gerrold K. Mukai, 1 Aug. 1979, Addendum.

46. Cf. the divisions in the organization chart (revised 4 Apr. 1976) in Parachini, *TELACU*, pp. 70–72, with those described in "Addendum," 31 July 1979, and listed in *TELACU Today*, Mar. 1981; for the next corporate restructuring, see organization chart in *TELACU Today*, June 1981.

47. "Addendum," 31 July 1979.

48. Ibid.

49. Ibid.; David C. Lizarraga to Gloria Molina, 20 Mar. 1981, TELACU Family Health Center, 1981–1982, Public Relations and Advertising, TELACU Center; and Syyed T. Mahmood and Amit K. Ghosh, eds., "Handbook," Feb. 1979, Handbook for Community Economic Development, Reports-Proposals.

50. "Addendum," 31 July 1979; and "A Framework for Greater East Los Angeles Industrial Development," Sept. 1978, pp. iii–iv, 84–85, Greater East Los Angeles Overall Economic Development Program, Central Files.

51. "Addendum," 31 July 1979.

52. Ibid.; the Uniroyal plant and Union Station were finally redeveloped in the early 1990s by government and business without TELACU's participation.

53. Art Seidenbaum, "East L.A. Accents the Positive," *Los Angeles Times*, 24 June 1977, pt. 4, p. 1.

Chapter 5

1. For a rosier description of the area, see Art Seidenbaum, "East L.A. Accents the Positive," *Los Angeles Times*, 24 June 1977, pt. 4, p. 1.
2. Marín, pp. 179–81; and "Addendum," 31 July 1979, Addendum: TELACU Overall Economic Development Plan (1977) for Period 1978–1983, Reports-Proposals, TELACU Center, Commerce, Calif.
3. "Addendum," 31 July 1979; and "Final Report: Technical Assistance Project," p. 1, Hispanic American Coalition for Economic Revitalization (HACER), 1980–1983, Central Files, TELACU Center.
4. "Addendum," 31 July 1979; and *TELACU Today* (Los Angeles), Nov. 1977, Sept.–Oct. 1979.
5. *TELACU Today*, Sept. 1977.
6. David C. Lizarraga to Andrew Young, 4 Jan. 1977, Voter Organization Through Education (VOTE), 1977, Central Files; and Cyrus Vance to Joseph B. Montoya, 8 Jan. 1977, Art Torres to Vance, 17 Dec. 1976, Alex P. García to idem, 27 Dec. 1976, Edward R. Roybal to idem, 29 Dec. 1976, Juan Arzube to idem, 30 Dec. 1976, Jimmy Carter to Tom Bradley, 7 Jan. 1977, Torres, Esteban, 1974–1977, Central Files.
7. Quoted in *El sol de México*, 19 Jan. 1977, my translation.
8. *Eastside Journal* (Belvedere, Calif.), 26 Jan. 1977; and Lizarraga to Young, 4 Jan. 1977.
9. *TELACU Today*, May–June, Sept., Nov. 1977; *Belvedere* (Calif.) *Citizen*, 14, 28 Sept., 9 Nov. 1977; and "VOTE Progress Report," 1 June 1977, Voter Organization Through Education.
10. *TELACU Today*, Sept. 1977.
11. Ibid.
12. Quoted in *TELACU Today*, Nov. 1977.
13. *Belvedere Citizen*, 5 May 1976; and David C. Lizarraga, quoted in *TELACU Today*, Mar.–Apr., May–June 1978.
14. "Community Development Organization and Economic Development: A New Strategy for Building Capacity," and David C. Lizarraga to Tommy Espinoza, 8 June 1979, Hispanic American Coalition for Economic Revitalization.
15. "Final Report: Technical Assistance Project," pp. 2–3; for information on the early Denver CDC, see *Denver Post*, 21 Mar., 5 May 1974.
16. "Final Report: Technical Assistance Project," pp. 2–3; Parachini, *Political History*, pp. 70–71; and *Belvedere Citizen*, 5 May 1976.
17. For the following description of the Spanish Speaking Unity Council, I am indebted to Bethell and Boris, pp. 28–29.
18. Ibid.; see the *San Francisco Chronicle*, 20 Jan. 1977, for a brief biography of Arabella Martínez, a founder and early executive director of this CDC.
19. Bethell and Boris, pp. 28–29.

20. Ibid.; see also Ledezma, pp. 22–27.

21. "History of the Mexican American Unity Council," typescript, [1977], MAUC Center, San Antonio, Tex.; Frank del Olmo, "Two Latino Activists Travel Separate Paths," *Los Angeles Times*, 29 July 1983, pt. 1, p. 1; I. M. García, pp. 16, 19, 23, 41, 227–28; and Richard Avena, "One Last Vote for Willie Velásquez," *Los Angeles Times*, 18 June 1988, pt. 2, p. 8.

22. "History of the Mexican American Unity Council"; and Juan Patlán, quoted in *San Antonio Express-News*, 11 Oct. 1981.

23. *San Antonio Express News*, 11 Oct. 1981; and "History of the Mexican American Unity Council."

24. "History of the Mexican American Unity Council."

25. "Overview of the Mexican American Unity Council," and "Mexican American Unity Council: 1986 Annual Report," MAUC Center.

26. "The Report of the Task Force on Community-Based Development," Sept. 1987, p. 19, Chicanos por la Causa, Phoenix, Ariz.

27. Ibid., pp. 19–20; and "Housing Counseling Program," circular, Chicanos por la Causa.

28. "Report of the Task Force," p. 20.

29. Quoted in ibid., p. 19.

30. Quoted in ibid., p. 20; "Chicanos por la Causa, Inc.," circular, Chicanos por la Causa.

31. Quoted in "Report of the Task Force," pp. 20–21.

32. Ibid.; and "Rural Development Loan Fund," circular, Chicanos por la Causa.

33. "Report of the Task Force," pp. 21–22; "CPLC's Tucson Office," circular, Chicanos por la Causa; see also Treviño and Ruiz.

34. "Siete del Norte Community Development Corporation," typescript, Siete del Norte, Embudo, N.Mex.

35. Ibid. 36. Ibid.
37. Ibid. 38. Ibid.

39. Ibid.; see also Brieter, p. 40.

40. Carlson, pp. xiii–xv; D. J. Weber, p. 24; and Rosenbaum, pp. 150, 156–57.

41. Lizarraga to Espinoza, 8 June 1979; and memorandum, Luis López to Curtis McClinton, 23 Jan. 1980, Hispanic American Coalition for Economic Revitalization.

42. Debbie Rycroft to David Lizarraga, 11 July 1983, Hispanic American Coalition for Economic Revitalization; and "Final Report: Technical Assistance Project," pp. 3–4.

43. "Final Report: Technical Assistance Project, pp. 19, 21–22; and John Juárez to Debbie Rycroft, 27 July 1981, Hispanic American Coalition for Economic Revitalization.

44. David C. Lizarraga to John Hay Whitney Foundation, 10 Apr. 1981, idem to Landrum Bolling, 13 Mar. 1981, idem to Robert M. Frehse,

Jr., 3 Mar. 1981, and memorandum, Carlos J. García to Saad Hafiz, 14 Jan. 1982, Hispanic American Coalition for Economic Revitalization.

45. Quoted in *TELACU Today*, June–July 1980.

46. Ibid.

47. Ibid.

48. *TELACU Today*, Sept.–Oct. 1979.

49. "The Greater East Los Angeles Cultural Heritage Survey," Aug. 1979, 3 vols., TELACU Papers, Special Collections, John F. Kennedy Memorial Library, California State University, Los Angeles.

50. Arnold I. Kisch to Celestino M. Beltrán, 31 Dec. 1979, TELACU Family Health Center, 1981–1982, Public Relations and Advertising, TELACU Center; and *TELACU Today*, Mar. 1981.

51. *TELACU Today*, Mar. 1981.

Chapter 6

1. For a map of proposed changes that were generally implemented at the civic center, see the *Los Angeles County Reporter*, 30 May 1973; *Belvedere* (Calif.) *Citizen*, 26 Jan. 1977; 5, 12 Dec. 1979; 5 Mar. 1980.

2. Weyr, pp. 102–3, 105–7; Frank Sotomayor, "Latinos: Diverse Group Tied by Ethnicity," *Los Angeles Times*, 25 July 1983, pt. 1, p. 1; and *Belvedere Citizen*, 27 Feb. 1975.

3. Parachini, *TELACU*, p. 27; and Weyr, p. 105–7.

4. Pitt, pp. 201, 241, 271, 273–74; Los Angeles Public Library, 2: n.pag.; and *First Los Angeles*, p. 18.

5. McWilliams, p. 37.

6. Santillán, pp. 31, 65; and *Los Angeles County Almanac: A Guide*, pp. 28, 45, 62–63, 153.

7. Santillán, p. 31; and *Belvedere Citizen*, 19 Jan. 1968.

8. Santillán, pp. 35, 81; and Castro, p. 171.

9. Santillán, p. 75; for the chronology of the elections that follow, I am particularly indebted to Guerra and Marvick, p. 7; *Belvedere Citizen*, 31 Jan., 7 Nov. 1974; *Eastside Journal* (Belvedere, Calif.), 13 June 1974.

10. *Perspectiva* (n.p.), Mar. 1988; *TELACU Today* (Los Angeles), May–June 1978; *Belvedere Citizen*, 19 Dec. 1974; and Guerra and Marvick, pp. 7–8.

11. Guerra and Marvick, pp. 3–4, 8; *Belvedere Citizen*, 12 Mar. 1980; and Marita Hernández, "Latinos Strive to Fashion New Political Force," *Los Angeles Times*, 2 May 1982, pt. 1, p. 1.

12. M. Hernández; and *Belvedere Citizen*, 3 Sept. 1980.

13. *Belvedere Citizen*, 28 Mar., 4 July 1979; and *TELACU Today*, Sept. 1977, Jan., May–June 1978.

14. *Belvedere Citizen*, 21 Feb., 3 Jan., 11 Apr., 24 Jan., 30 May, 19 Dec. 1974; 20 Mar., 4 Dec. 1975.

15. "Committee Statement of Organization," 23 June 1976, People for

TELACU, Central Files, TELACU Center, Commerce, Calif.; and "Fact Sheet," Voter Organization Through Education (VOTE), 1977, Central Files.

16. "Committee Statement"; "Recipient Committee Statement of Termination," 19 Aug. 1980, "David Lizarraga invites ... ," 26 June 1976, People for TELACU; see also Richard Bergholz, "Democratic Dinner Official Quits," *Los Angeles Times*, 1 Mar. 1979, pt. 1, p. 28.

17. "Money Arrived—In Hand," handwritten list, People for TELACU.

18. *Belvedere Citizen*, 8, 29 Sept. 1976; "Introduction," Rachel Avila to Gwen White, 17 June 1977, "Fact Sheet," Voter Organization Through Education; and Payne and Ratzan, pp. 109, 120–21, 330.

19. "A Proposal," Voter Organization Through Education.

20. Ibid.; see letterhead, David C. Lizarraga to Andrew Young, 4 Jan. 1977, Voter Organization Through Education.

21. "A Proposal," memorandum, Tom [Castro] to Ron [Noblet] and Rachel [Ruiz], 31 Jan. 1977, "Fact Sheet," "Introduction," Voter Organization Through Education.

22. "Introduction"; "Fact Sheet"; Avila to White, 17 June 1977; and *Belvedere Citizen*, 2 Apr. 1980.

23. "Fact Sheet"; "Introduction"; Lizarraga to Young, 4 Jan. 1977; and *Political Animal* (Los Angeles), 21 Jan. 1977.

24. Memorandum, Castro to Noblet and Ruiz, 31 Jan. 1977; and "Introduction."

25. "Introduction."

26. Ibid.; and *Belvedere Citizen*, 22 Sept. 1976.

27. "Introduction."

28. "VOTE Progress Report," 1 June 1977, Voter Organization Through Education.

29. *TELACU Today*, May–June 1977; and "B.—V.O.T.E.," Voter Organization Through Education.

30. "B.—V.O.T.E."; memorandum, Tom Castro to David [Lizarraga], Carlos [García], Roy [Escarcega], George [Pla], Rachel [Ruiz], John [Echeveste], and Ron [Noblet], 28 Feb. 1977, Voter Organization Through Education.

31. "VOTE Progress Report"; and César E. Chávez to David C. Lizarraga, 11 Apr. 1977, Voter Organization Through Education.

32. "VOTE Progress Report"; Avila to White, 17 June 1977; John A. Echeveste to ... , form letter, 30 Mar. 1977, Voter Organization Through Education; cf. Robert Welkos and Claire Spiegel, "Politicking: Another Murky Area for TELACU," *Los Angeles Times*, 28 Mar. 1982, pt. 1, p. 3.

33. *Belvedere Citizen*, 1 Feb., 31 May, 12 July 1978.

34. Ibid., 25 Apr. 1979.

35. Ibid., 14 Nov. 1979; "Executive Committee Roster," and memo-

randum, David C. Lizarraga to John Echeveste, 18 Apr. 1979, Hispanic American Democrats (HAD), 1979, Central Files.

36. "By Laws," draft, 26 Feb. 1979, "Option Paper: HAD [Bylaws] Organization and Delegate Allocation Proposal," p. 4, Hispanic American Democrats; and White, pp. 187–89.

37. "Option Paper," pp. 1–2, 4–5; "Executive Committee Roster," pp. 1, 5; and Lizarraga to Echeveste, 18 Apr. 1979.

38. *Belvedere Citizen*, 28 May, 4, 11 June 1980.

39. "Many Latinos Deserted Carter," *Los Angeles Times*, 24 Jan. 1981, pt. 1, p. 17; and Richard Bergholz, "Ouster May Chill Latino-GOP Ties," *Los Angeles Times*, 3 Feb. 1982, pt. 1, p. 24.

40. *Belvedere Citizen*, 16 Jan. 1980; and *Perspectiva*, Mar. 1988.

41. Frank del Olmo, "Sophistication Changes Political Picture for Latinos," *Los Angeles Times*, 14 Jan. 1982, pt. 2, p. 7; William Endicott, "Obledo Opens Underdog Run for Governor," *Los Angeles Times*, 26 Feb. 1982, pt. 1, p. 1; and Del Olmo, "Why Obledo Got Nowhere in Campaign for Governor," *Los Angeles Times*, 3 June 1982, pt. 2, p. 7.

42. Del Olmo, "Sophistication"; *Perspectiva*, Mar. 1988; and *Belvedere Citizen*, 22 Oct. 1980.

43. Kenneth Reich, "Latino Politics Shakeup Seen," *Los Angeles Times*, 15 Feb. 1982, pt. 2, p. 1.

44. Guerra and Marvick, pp. 7–8; and Reich.

45. Reich.

46. Ibid.

47. Ibid.; Guerra and Marvick, p. 9; and Kevin Roderick, "2 Latino Candidates Fight Over a Jewel—L.A.'s 56th District," *Los Angeles Times*, 4 Apr. 1982, pt. 2, p. 1.

48. Roderick; and Frank del Olmo, "Will Gloria Molina Lead Us into Decade of the Hispanic?", *Los Angeles Times*, 11 Nov. 1982, pt. 2, p. 11.

49. Roderick.

50. Ibid.; and Del Olmo, "Gloria Molina."

51. Del Olmo, "Gloria Molina"; Guerra and Marvick, pp. 9–10; for national figures on underrepresentation as late as 1987, see *Hispanic Link Weekly Report* (Washington), 30 Jan. 1989.

52. "*Orgullo de Nuestra Herencia/The Pride of Our Heritage*," leaflet with photograph and description of mural, TELACU Center; and Welkos and Spiegel.

Chapter 7

1. "*Orgullo de Nuestra Herencia/The Pride of Our Heritage*," leaflet with photograph and description of mural, TELACU Center, Commerce, Calif.; Parra, p. 51; Claire Spiegel and Robert Welkos, "Anti-Poverty Agency: Leaving Barrio Behind," *Los Angeles Times*, 28 Mar. 1982, pt. 1, p.

1; and "Report of Audit: The East Los Angeles Community Union," 8 Nov. 1982, vol. 1, p. 1, U.S. Department of Labor Investigation, Central Files, TELACU Center.

2. "Report of Audit," vol. 1, p. 1.

3. Bullock, pp. 57–58, 116–17, 119, 124, 132–33; *Belvedere* (Calif.) *Citizen*, 2 Apr. 1980; Robert Welkos and Claire Spiegel, "Politicking: Another Murky Area for TELACU," *Los Angeles Times*, 28 Mar. 1982, pt. 1, p. 3; see also Rachel Avila to Gwen White, 17 June 1977, Voter Organization Through Education (VOTE), 1977, Central Files.

4. "Report of Audit," vol. 1, pp. 19–21.

5. Ibid., pp. 19–23, 27–30; *TELACU Today* (Los Angeles), Jan.–Mar. 1981; and "Proceedings," 29 July 1982, pp. 18, 33–34, 58, TELACU v. City of Los Angeles, 83-CET-55, Central Files.

6. "Report of Audit," vol. 1, pp. 23, 26, vol. 2, pp. 8–11; see also "Exhibits to Response to Report of Audit: The East Los Angeles Community Union," 22 July 1982, exhibit A, U.S. Department of Labor Investigation, Central Files.

7. *Belvedere Citizen*, 2 Apr., 3 Sept. 1980; "Report of Audit," vol. 1, p. 25; *Los Angeles Times*, 28, 29, 30 Mar., 15, 20, 23 Apr., 26, 27 May, 18 Sept., 12 Nov., 21, 31 Dec. 1982; 9 July 1983; and "Proceedings," pp. 18, 20.

8. Spiegel and Welkos, "Leaving Barrio."

9. *Belvedere Citizen*, 2 Apr. 1980; and Welkos and Spiegel, "Politicking."

10. Welkos and Spiegel, "Politicking"; cf. Claire Spiegel and Robert Welkos, "Poverty Agency Largely Immune from Corruption Probe," *Los Angeles Times*, 12 Nov. 1982, pt. 2, p. 1.

11. Quoted in Spiegel and Welkos, "Leaving Barrio."

12. Ibid.; and Robert Welkos and Claire Spiegel, "Far-Flung Empire Is Built on Federal Grants, " *Los Angeles Times*, 29 Mar. 1982, pt. 1, p. 1.

13. Spiegel and Welkos, "Leaving Barrio"; cf. idem, "Agency Largely Immune."

14. Spiegel and Welkos, "Leaving Barrio."

15. Claire Spiegel and Robert Welkos, "Giant Anti-Poverty Agency Did Little to Create Jobs," *Los Angeles Times*, 30 Mar. 1982, pt. 1, p. 1.

16. Quoted in ibid.

17. Spiegel and Welkos, "Leaving Barrio."

18. James R. Johnson to editor, Blanca Vargas to idem, Frank Sifuentes to idem, *Los Angeles Times*, 11 Apr. 1982, pt. 5, p. 4.

19. Quoted in Claire Spiegel, "Anti-Poverty Agency's TV Deal Held Up," *Los Angeles Times*, 20 Apr. 1982, pt. 1, p. 3.

20. "Proceedings," pp. 2, 22, 24, 44, 48, 57–58, 63–64.

21. David Lizarraga to Robert F. Higgins, 16 July 1981, idem to Don-

ald G. Galloway, 26 May 1982, idem to Parker C. Anderson, 22 Oct. 1982, Mary C. Jaramillo to idem, 30 Nov. 1982, TELACU Family Health Center, 1981–1982, Public Relations and Advertising, TELACU Center.

22. *East Los Angeles Tribune,* 23 June 1982; and "Text of Press Statement by Senator Alex P. García Regarding TELACU and the Small Business Development Board," U.S.A. v. TELACU (RDLF Lawsuit), 1982–1985, Central Files.

23. "East Los Angeles Community Union v. County of Los Angeles," 8 Sept. 1982, pp. 3–4, U.S. Department of Labor v. TELACU and County of Los Angeles, 84-CPA-2, Central Files; Robert Welkos, "County Ends Pacts with Poverty Unit," *Los Angeles Times,* 26 May 1982, pt. 2, p. 1; and "Report of Audit," vol. 1, p. 109.

24. Welkos and Spiegel, "Far-Flung Empire"; and "Report of Investigation of TELACU Investment Company, Inc.," pp. 1, 4, U.S.A. v. TELACU Investment Company (SBA Lawsuit), 1982–1983, Central Files.

25. "Report of Investigation," pp. 1, 3–4, 15–16.

26. Leonard Rutkin to David Lizarraga, 21 May 1979, memorandum, idem to Lizarraga, 14 June [1979], Lizarraga to idem, 21 April 1980, Carlos J. García to A. Hebert, 13 Sept. 1982, Rutkin, Leonard, Central Files; and Spiegel and Welkos, "Leaving Barrio."

27. Spiegel and Welkos, "Leaving Barrio"; Brian J. O'Neill to Carlos García, 6 Jan. 1982, Lloyd C. Lee to idem, 18 June 1982, J. Joseph Connolly to Walter C. Intlekofer, 10 June 1982, U.S.A. v. TELACU Investment Company.

28. "Minutes to TELACU Meeting," 1 July 1982, "List of Attendees," U.S.A. v. TELACU Investment Company.

29. Spiegel and Welkos, "Leaving Barrio."

30. Quoted in *East Los Angeles Tribune,* 7 Apr. 1982.

31. Scott M. Stahr to Carlos García, 13 Sept. 1982, "East Los Angeles Community Union v. County of Los Angeles," 8 Sept. 1982, pp. 4–5, U.S. Department of Labor v. TELACU and County of Los Angeles.

32. "Proceedings," pp. 4, 59–60.

33. Ibid., pp. 60–63; and Stahr to García, 13 Sept. 1982.

34. Memorandum, K. William O'Connor to Harvey Vieth, 16 Sept. 1982, U.S.A. v. TELACU (RDLF Lawsuit); Claire Spiegel, "TELACU Invested Money Given for Needy, Audit Says," *Los Angeles Times,* 18 Sept. 1982, pt. 1, p. 1.

35. Jess García to Spencer L. Lott, 16 Nov. 1982, Harvey R. Vieth to David Lizarraga, 29 Nov. 1982, U.S.A. v. TELACU (RDLF Lawsuit).

36. Report of Audit," vol. 1, pp. 1–10, 13; and Spiegel and Welkos, "Agency Largely Immune."

37. Quoted in Spiegel and Welkos, "Agency Largely Immune.".

38. Quoted in ibid.

39. Quoted in ibid.

40. Quoted in ibid.; see also Claire Spiegel and Robert Welkos, "$46 Million in TELACU Spending Challenged," *Los Angeles Times*, 27 May 1982, pt. 1, p. 1.

41. Stahr to García, 13 Sept. 1982; and Claire Spiegel, "U.S. Complaint Seeks $1 Million from TELACU," *Los Angeles Times*, 31 Dec. 1982, pt. 2, p. 1.

42. Spiegel, "U.S. Complaint"; and idem, "U.S. Moves to Close Poverty Agency," *Los Angeles Times*, 21 December 1982, pt. 2, p. 1.

43. Spiegel, "TELACU Invested"; Lee to García, 18 June 1982, Alvin Friedman to Jess F. García, 7 Dec. 1982, Friedman to Carlos García, 14 Jan. 1982, U.S.A. v. TELACU Investment Company.

44. "Press Release," K. William O'Connor to Don D. Byrd, 24 Aug. 1982, U.S.A. v. TELACU Investment Company; Spiegel and Welkos, "Leaving Barrio"; Parachini, *Political History*, p. 144; and Perry, *Communities*, pp. 203, 195.

45. U.S.A. v. East Los Angeles Community Union, CV 82-6870KN (TX), 21-87-146, RB45956 (section B), box 924, Federal Records Center, Los Angeles.

46. Ibid.

47. Ibid.

48. "Motion for Leave to Appeal Disallowance," 8 July 1985, U.S. Department of Labor v. TELACU and County of Los Angeles; and "Order of Dismissal," 24 Feb. 1986, U.S. Department of Labor v. TELACU, 84-CTA-15, Central Files.

49. Scott M. Stahr to Jess García, 18 July 1983, TELACU v. City of Los Angeles; Diane M. Shriver to Jess García, 10 Apr. 1985, U.S.A. v. TELACU (RDLF Lawsuit); and U.S.A. v. TELACU Investment Company, CV 82-6660-CBM (KX), 21-87-146, RB45956, box 895, Federal Records Center.

50. Reynolds, p. 325; and memorandum, Gilberto Padilla to G. de la Mora and S. Hafiz, 28 May 1982, Community Research Group (CRG), 1982–1983, Central Files.

51. Claire Spiegel, "TELACU Dedicates Offices Financed by Federal Funds," *Los Angeles Times*, 9 July 1983, pt. 2, p. 1.

52. Ibid.

53. Ibid.; and Roger Mahony, "A Voice of Justice, Following the Gospel," *Los Angeles Times*, 25 Apr. 1993, sec. M, p. 5.

Chapter 8

1. U.S.A. v. TELACU Investment Company, CV 82-6660-CBM (KX), 21-87-146, RB45956, box 895, Federal Records Center, Los Angeles.

2. Frank del Olmo, "Citizen Action Group Gives Latinos Clout on the Issues," *Los Angeles Times*, 25 Feb. 1982, pt. 2, p. 7; and Bill Boyarsky,

"U.S. Pressures Board of Supervisors to Remap for Latino Representation," *Los Angeles Times*, 7 June 1988, pt. 2, p. 1.

3. George Ramos, "Postscript," *Los Angeles Times*, 31 Jan. 1989, pt. 2, p. 3; *Belvedere* (Calif.) *Citizen*, 5 May, 9 June 1976; 28 Sept. 1977; 15 Oct. 1980; "Staffing Proposal Addendum," 7 Jan. 1980, pp. 1-2, Whittier Boulevard LDC, Reports-Proposals, TELACU Center, Commerce, Calif.; and memorandum, Gilberto Padilla to G. de la Mora and S. Hafiz, 28 May 1982, Community Research Group (CRG), 1982-1983, Central Files, TELACU Center.

4. "TELACU Annual Progress Report, 1986-1987: Meeting Tomorrow's Challenges Today," TELACU Center; and Ramos, "Postscript."

5. "Progress Report, 1986-1987."

6. *TELACU Today* (Los Angeles), Jan. 1978; and "Progress Report, 1986-1987."

7. "Progress Report, 1986-1987."

8. Glenn O'Loane, interview by author, 13 July 1989, East Los Angeles; and "Progress Report, 1986-1987."

9. "Progress Report, 1986-1987"; and Parachini, *TELACU*, p. 69.

10. Cathleen Decker, "Council Split on Dial-a-Ride TELACU Grant," *Los Angeles Times*, 20 Sept. 1986, pt. 1, p. 29.

11. Robert Welkos and Claire Spiegel, "Far-Flung Empire Is Built on Federal Grants," *Los Angeles Times*, 29 Mar. 1982, pt. 1, p. 1; and "Progress Report, 1986-1987."

12. "Progress Report, 1986-1987."

13. Ibid.

14. Ibid.

15. Ibid.; and Padilla to De la Mora and Hafiz, 28 May 1982.

16. "Progress Report, 1986-1987."

17. George Ramos, "Posh Restaurant in East L.A. Has Tongues Wagging," *Los Angeles Times*, 21 Mar. 1988, pt. 2, p. 1.

18. Ibid.; "The Greater East Los Angeles Cultural Heritage Survey," Aug. 1979, vol. 3, site 12, TELACU Papers, Special Collections, John F. Kennedy Memorial Library, California State University, Los Angeles; *Pico Rivera* (Calif.) *News*, 14 July 1988; and *CDCs*, pp. 7, 11.

19. Ramos, "Posh Restaurant"; "An Introduction to the East Los Angeles Community Union," TELACU: Company Summaries, 1969– , Central Files; and David C. Lizarraga to Gloria Molina, 20 Mar. 1981, TELACU Family Health Center, 1981-1982, Public Relations and Advertising, TELACU Center.

20. Ramos, "Posh Restaurant."

21. Quoted in ibid.

22. "Progress Report, 1986-1987"; and "TELACU Manor-Commerce, Ground Breaking Ceremony," invitation, 27 July 1988, TELACU Center.

23. Rich Connell, "Bold Plans for Union Station Area Unveiled," *Los Angeles Times*, 18 May 1988, pt. 2, p. 1; and Frank del Olmo, "It's Hard to Read the Message of Olvera Street in Laker T-Shirts and Tourist Gimcracks," *Los Angeles Times*, 20 Dec. 1988, pt. 2, p. 7.

24. Griswold del Castillo, p. 143; Tracy Wilkinson, "Renovation Plan for Olvera Street Stirs Outcry from Latinos," *Los Angeles Times*, 2 May 1990, sec. B, p. 1; and George Ramos, "Olvera St. Merchants Draft $25-Million Face-Lift Plan," *Los Angeles Times*, 1 Jan. 1988, pt. 2, p. 1.

25. Del Olmo, "Hard to Read"; and Connell.

26. Connell; and Ramos, "Olvera St."

27. Wilkinson.

28. Quoted in ibid.

29. Ibid.; see also McWilliams, pp. 35–47.

30. George Ramos, "Molina, Alatorre Clash over Plans for Olvera Street," *Los Angeles Times*, 19 June 1990, sec. B, p. 1; idem, "Reclaiming the Simple Delights of Olvera Street," *Los Angeles Times*, 18 July 1994, sec. B, p. 3; see also Acuña, *Anything but Mexican*, pp. 23–30.

31. Guerra and Marvick, pp. 8–9; *Dallas Morning News*, 20 Jan. 1991; see also Acuña, *Anything but Mexican*, pp. 43–59, 94–100.

32. Castañeda, p. 25; Guerra and Marvick, pp. 3, 9; and Erwin Baker, "Hopes Dim for Latino Council Seat," *Los Angeles Times*, 1 June 1982, pt. 2, p. 1.

33. Baker; Claire Spiegel, "Snyder Profits from Unit He Helps Fund," *Los Angeles Times*, 16 July 1981, pt. 1, p. 3; and *Los Angeles Herald Examiner*, 17 July 1981.

34. *Los Angeles Herald Examiner*, 17 July 1981; Spiegel, "Snyder"; "TELACU Response to *LA Times* Article," [17 July 1981], pp. 2, 4, Snyder Investigation, Central Files; idem, "TELACU Dedicates Offices Financed by Federal Funds," *Los Angeles Times*, 9 July 1983, pt. 2, p. 1; and Janet Clayton, "Snyder Picks the Date: 18-Year Council Career to End Friday," *Los Angeles Times*, 3 Oct. 1985, pt. 2, p. 1.

35. Clayton, "Snyder"; *Perspectiva* (n.p.), Mar. 1988; Castañeda, pp. 24–25; and Boyarsky.

36. Frank del Olmo, "Demographics Doom the Best-Laid Plans," *Los Angeles Times*, 10 July 1986, pt. 2, p. 5; *Perspectiva*, Mar. 1988; and Janet Clayton, "Allard Stresses Independence and Family Ties," *Los Angeles Times*, 14 May 1987, pt. 1, p. 3.

37. Castañeda, p. 24; and Connell.

38. Boyarsky; *Dallas Morning News*, 20 Jan. 1991; Richard Simon and Frederick M. Muir, "Schabarum Hit for Identifying Self as a Latino," *Los Angeles Times*, 7 Dec. 1989, sec. B, p. 1; and Simon and Jane Fritsch, "No Accord on Latino Choice for 1st District," *Los Angeles Times*, 10 Nov. 1990, sec. A, p. 1.

39. Simon and Fritsch.

40. Ibid.; and Kenneth Reich, "Latino Politics Shakeup Seen," *Los Angeles Times*, 15 Feb. 1982, pt. 2, p. 1.

41. Richard Simon and Jill Stewart, "Molina, Torres Head for Runoff in 1st District," *Los Angeles Times*, 23 Jan. 1991, sec. A., p. 1; Simon, "Molina Wins Historic Contest For Supervisor," *Los Angeles Times*, 20 Feb. 1991, sec. A, p. 1; and Hector Tobar, "Key Latino Group Backs Molina in the 1st District, *Los Angeles Times*, 17 Dec. 1990, sec. B, p. 1.

42. Simon, "Molina Wins"; and idem, "100 Days: Molina Shakes up Board," *Los Angeles Times*, 16 June 1991, sec. B, p. 1.

43. Maria Newman, "Verdict Taken as Blow to Latino Progress," *Los Angeles Times*, 3 Feb. 1990, sec. A, p. 27; "Final California Election Returns, *Los Angeles Times*, 7 June 1990, sec. A, p. 27; *Los Angeles County Almanac: Government*, p. 168; see also Acuña, *Anything but Mexican*, pp. 65–79.

44. *Nuestro Tiempo* (Los Angeles), 18 June 1992.

45. Ibid.; "Los Angeles County Population Figures," *Los Angeles Times*, 6 May 1991, sec. B, p. 3; and "Final California Election Returns," *Los Angeles Times*, 5 Nov. 1992, sec. A, p. 9.

46. "Final California Election Returns," *Los Angeles Times*, 5 Nov. 1992, sec. A., p. 10.

47. Ibid.; cf. "Population Figures"; *Los Angeles County Almanac: Government*, pp. 107, 87, 80–81, 167, 173, 171, 160–62; and Bill Boyarsky, "Latino Voters Could Exercise Sizable Clout," *Los Angeles Times*, 20 July 1994, sec. B, p. 3.

48. Xavier Hermosillo, "The End of 'Go Along, Get Along' for Chicanos," *Los Angeles Times*, 18 Dec. 1991, sec. B, p. 7; Mike Davis, "Latinos Rise Up in the Rust Belt," *Los Angeles Times*, 20 Dec. 1991, sec. B, p. 7; *Hispanic Link Weekly Report* (Washington), 1 Jan. 1992; see also Acuña, *Anything but Mexican*, pp. 152–54.

49. Cf. Bureau of the Census, *1970 Census of Population*, vol. 1, pt. 6, sec. 1, p. 1034; *1980 Census*, vol. 1, chap. B, pt. 6, p. 40; and *1990 Census: General Population Characteristics, California*, sec. 1, p. 28.

50. "Population Figures"; and Maria Newman, "Riots Bring Attention to Hispanic Presence in South-Central Area, *New York Times*, 11 May 1992, sec. B, p. 6.

51. L. Chávez, pp. 134–35, 138; Ruben Hernández, "'This Was about Something to Eat,'" *Los Angeles Times*, 18 May 1992, sec. B, p. 5; "Population Figures"; Ong, pp. ii, 19; however, by the mid-nineties Chicano homeownership had improved—Acuña, *Anything but Mexican*, p. 319.

52. Jill Stewart, "Two-Tier Economy Feared as Dead End for Unskilled," *Los Angeles Times*, 25 June 1989, pt. 2, p. 1; and Davis.

53. *Nuestro Tiempo*, 18 June 1992; George Ramos and Tracy Wilkinson, "Unrest Widens Rifts in Diverse Latino Population," *Los Angeles*

Times, 8 May 1992, sec. A, p. 4; see also *San Francisco Chronicle*, 6 May 1992, and Baldassare.

54. Victor Valle and Rudy D. Torres, "There's More to Power than Votes—Latinos Should Ask Pete Schabarum," *Los Angeles Times*, 23 June 1991, sec. M, p. 6.

Conclusion

1. *Belvedere* (Calif.) *Citizen*, 5 Dec. 1974; 24 Apr. 1975; 5 Dec. 1979; and TELACU Annual Progress Report, 1986–1987: Meeting Tomorrow's Challenges Today," TELACU Center, Commerce, Calif.

2. George Ramos, "Posh Restaurant in East L.A. Has Tongues Wagging," *Los Angeles Times*, 21 Mar. 1988, pt. 2, p. 1; *Belvedere Citizen*, 24 Apr. 1975; regarding community input, TELACU critic Rodolfo Acuña suspected that advisory groups, such as the Maravilla Project Area Committee, were simply rubber stamps for developers—*Los Angeles Herald Examiner*, 10 July 1987.

3. Bureau of the Census, *1970 Census of Population and Housing: Census Tracts—Los Angeles–Long Beach, California Standard Metropolitan Statistical Area*, pts. 1–2; *1990 Census of Population and Housing: California (Los Angeles County)*, summary tape file 3A; between 1970 and 1990 East LA's overall population rose from 105,033 to 126,379.

4. George Ramos, "A Developer Who Has Learned from His Mistakes," *Los Angeles Times*, 18 Oct. 1993, sec. B, p. 3; "500 Directory," p. 66; and *1990 Census*.

5. Ramos, "Developer"; *Los Angeles Herald Examiner*, 10 July 1987; *1970 Census*; *1990 Census*; Michael A. Hiltzik, "'Short Pay' Requests Rise in Slack Housing Market," *Los Angeles Times*, 25 July 1994, sec. A, p. 1.

6. Bullock, p. 129; Louis Kanaster to editor, *Los Angeles Times*, 11 Apr. 1982, pt. 5, p. 4; "Staffing Proposal Addendum," 7 Jan. 1980, pp. 1–2, Whittier Boulevard LDC, Reports-Proposals, TELACU Center; "Progress Report, 1986–1987"; and Aaron, pp. 166–67.

7. *Belvedere Citizen*, 12 July 1978; Rogers, p. 131; *Dallas Morning News*, 20 Jan. 1991; and Witherall, p. 98.

8. Parachini, *TELACU*, pp. 15, 26; for a serious critique of the CDC concept by a former CDC officer, see Berndt, p. 129.

9. CDCs, pp. 65–66; Witkin, 3: 2312–14; Parachini, *TELACU*, p. 26; and Claire Spiegel and Robert Welkos, "Anti-Poverty Agency: Leaving Barrio Behind," *Los Angeles Times*, 28 Mar. 1982, pt. 1, p. 1.

10. Chandler, pp. 312–14; Spiegel and Welkos, "Leaving Barrio"; in all fairness to TELACU, presidents of both unions and corporations have a tendency to serve long terms—Peterson, p. 71.

11. Spiegel and Welkos, "Leaving Barrio"; Small, pp. 717–18; *Dallas Morning News*, 1 Nov. 1992; and Berndt, pp. 135, 138–39.

12. Spiegel and Welkos, "Leaving Barrio."

13. Nadel and Curtis, p. 143; Berndt, p. 138; *Dallas Morning News*, 14 Aug. 1990; for a critique of the colonial analogy as applied to cities in the United States, see Block.

14. Robert Welkos and Claire Spiegel, "Far-Flung Empire Is Built on Federal Grants, " *Los Angeles Times*, 29 Mar. 1982, pt. 1, p. 1.

15. "Final Report: Technical Assistance Project," p. 2, Hispanic American Coalition for Economic Revitalization (HACER), 1980–1983, Central Files, TELACU Center; and "Progress Report, 1986–1987."

16. "Progress Report, 1986–1987"; "Partners in Bidding for the Portal Site, and Their Past Alliances," *Washington Post*, 28 Dec. 1981, sec. B, p. 4; "Agenda," 20 July 1981, p. 1, "Activity Report," 31 Oct. 1981, pp. 1–3, and minutes of the board of directors, 18 Sept. 1985, p. 1, Eastcoast Development Corporation, 1981–1985, Central Files.

17. "Progress Report, 1986–1987"; Kennedy, pp. 42–43; "Officers," p. 1, CCAP Background, box 1, Citizens' Crusade Against Poverty, Walter P. Reuther Library of Labor and Urban Affairs, Wayne State University, Detroit, Mich.; and Day, pp. 29–31.

18. Ronald Brownstein, "Clinton Offers Views on Recovery," *Los Angeles Times*, 5 May 1992, sec. A, p. 9; Berndt, p. 142; Patterson, p. 209; and Fisher, p. 149.

19. Spicer, pp. 4–8, 16; J. R. Chávez, *Lost Land*, p. 155; Barrera, *Beyond Aztlán*, pp. 175–76; significantly, Congressman Esteban Torres was instrumental in winning passage of the North American Free Trade Agreement in 1993—*Dallas Morning News*, 21 Nov. 1993.

Works Cited

In addition to books, this bibliography includes a videorecording, theses, and articles from journals and magazines. Archival sources, unpublished interviews, government publications, and articles from newspapers and newsletters are listed in the endnotes.

Aaron, Henry J. *Politics and the Professors: The Great Society in Perspective.* Studies in Social Economics. Washington, D.C.: Brookings Institution, 1978.

Acuña, Rodolfo F. *Anything but Mexican: Chicanos in Contemporary Los Angeles.* Haymarket Series. New York: Verso, 1996.

———. *A Community Under Siege: A Chronicle of Chicanos East of the Los Angeles River, 1945–1975.* Monograph no. 11. Los Angeles: Chicano Studies Research Center, University of California, 1984.

———. *Occupied America: A History of Chicanos.* 3d ed. New York: Harper & Row, 1988.

Allen, James B. *The Company Town in the American West.* Norman: University of Oklahoma Press, 1966.

Ambrecht, Biliana C. S. *Politicizing the Poor: The Legacy of the War on Poverty in a Mexican American Community.* Praeger Special Studies in U.S. Economic, Social, and Political Issues. New York: Praeger, 1976.

Baldassare, Mark, ed. *The Los Angeles Riots: Lessons for the Urban Future.* Urban Policy Challenges. Boulder, Colo.: Westview Press, 1994.

Balderrama, Francisco E. *In Defense of la Raza: The Los Angeles Mexican Consulate and the Mexican Community, 1929 to 1936.* Tucson: University of Arizona Press, 1982.

Barnard, John. *Walter Reuther and the Rise of the Auto Workers.* Ed. Oscar Handlin. Library of American Biography. Boston: Little, Brown, 1983.

Barrera, Mario. *Beyond Aztlán: Ethnic Autonomy in Comparative Perspective*. New York: Praeger, 1988.

———. *Race and Class in the Southwest: A Theory of Racial Inequality*. Notre Dame, Ind.: University of Notre Dame Press, 1979.

Barrera, Mario, Carlos Muñoz, and Charles Ornelas. "The Barrio as an Internal Colony." In *La Causa Política: A Chicano Politics Reader*, ed. F. Chris García, pp. 281–301. Notre Dame, Ind.: University of Notre Dame Press, 1974.

Bell, Inge Powell. *CORE and the Strategy of Nonviolence*. New York: Random House, 1968.

Berndt, Harry Edward. *New Rulers in the Ghetto: The Community Development Corporation and Urban Poverty*. Contributions in Afro-American and African Studies, no. 28. Westport, Conn.: Greenwood Press, 1977.

[Bethell, Thomas N., and Michele C. Boris.] *A Progress Report from America's Community Development Corporations*. Washington, D.C.: Robert A. Rapoza Associates [1986].

Blauner, Robert. *Racial Oppression in America*. New York: Harper & Row, 1972.

Block, A. Harvey. *Impact Analysis and Local Area Planning: An Input/Output Study*. Cambridge, Mass.: Center for Community Economic Development, 1977.

Brieter, Toni. "Ulibarrí Named Acting Director of Siete del Norte." *Agenda*, Sept.–Oct. 1978, p. 40.

Brown, Stuart Gerry. *The Presidency on Trial: Robert Kennedy's 1968 Campaign and Afterwards*. Honolulu: University Press of Hawaii, 1972.

Bullock, Paul. *CETA at the Crossroads: Employment Policy and Politics*. Monograph and Research Series, no. 29. Los Angeles: Institute of Industrial Relations, University of California, 1981.

Camarillo, Albert. *Chicanos in a Changing Society: From Mexican Pueblos to American Barrios in Santa Barbara and Southern California, 1848–1930*. Cambridge, Mass.: Harvard University Press, 1979.

Carlson, Alvar W. *The Spanish-American Homeland: Four Centuries in New Mexico's Rio Arriba*. Creating the North American Landscape. Baltimore, Md.: Johns Hopkins University Press, 1990.

Carmichael, Stokely, and Charles V. Hamilton. *Black Power: The Politics of Liberation in America*. New York: Random House, Vintage, 1967.

Castañeda, Ruben. "Latino Unity Stalls in East LA." *California Journal*, Jan. 1987, pp. 23–25.

Castro, Tony. *Chicano Power: The Emergence of Mexican America*. New York: Saturday Review Press/E. P. Dutton, 1974.

CDCs: New Hope for the Inner City: Report of the Twentieth Century Fund Task-Force on Community Development Corporations. With a Background Paper by Geoffrey Faux. Millwood, N.Y.: Kraus Reprint, 1974 [1971].

Chandler, Alfred D., Jr. *Strategy and Structure: Chapters in the History of the Industrial Enterprise*. M.I.T. Press Research Monographs. Cambridge, Mass.: M.I.T Press, 1962.

Chávez, John R. "The Image of the Southwest in the Chicano Novel, 1970–1979." *Bilingual Review/Revista Bilingüe* 14(Sept.–Dec. 1987–1988): 41–56.

———. *The Lost Land: The Chicano Image of the Southwest*. Albuquerque: University of New Mexico Press, 1984.

Chávez, Linda. *Out of the Barrio: Toward a New Politics of Hispanic Assimilation*. [New York]: HarperCollins, BasicBooks, 1991.

Christopulos, Diana. "The Politics of Colonialism: Puerto Rico from 1898 to 1972." In *The Puerto Ricans: Their History, Culture, and Society*, ed. Adalberto López, pp. 129–69. Cambridge, Mass.: Schenkman, 1980.

"Church Response to Demands—Fraud Wrapped Around Deceit and Hypocrisy." *La raza* 1, no. 1 (1970): 27.

"Church vs. Católicos." *La raza* 1, no. 1 (1970): 20–22.

Corwin, Arthur F. "Mexican-American History: An Assessment." *Pacific Historical Review* 42(Aug. 1973): 269–308.

Davis, Mike. *City of Quartz: Excavating the Future in Los Angeles*. Haymarket Series. New York: Verso, 1990.

Day, Mark. *Forty Acres: César Chávez and the Farm Workers*. With an Introduction by César Chávez. New York: Praeger, 1971.

Durham, Laird. *Black Capitalism*. Critical Issues in Urban Management. Washington, D.C.: Communication Service Corporation, 1970.

"East Los Angeles: A Brief History." *La luz*, Oct. 1974, pp. 18–20.

Elliott, Charles. *City of Commerce: An Enterprising Heritage*. Los Angeles: Hacienda Gateway Press, 1991.

Engelhardt, Zephyrin. *San Gabriel Mission and the Beginnings of Los Angeles*. Missions and Missionaries of California. San Gabriel, Calif.: Mission San Gabriel, 1927.

Essien-Udom, E[ssien] U[dose]. *Black Nationalism: A Search for Identity in America*. Chicago: University of Chicago Press, 1962.

Fanon, Frantz. *Black Skin, White Masks*. Trans. Charles Lam Markham. New York: Grove Press, Evergreen Black Cat, 1968.

"First Census of Los Angeles." In *Foreigners in Their Native Land: Historical Roots of the Mexican Americans*, ed. David J. Weber, pp. 33–35. With a Foreword by Ramón Eduardo Ruiz. Albuquerque: University of New Mexico Press, 1973.

The First Los Angeles City and County Directory. With an Introduction by Ward Ritchie and Early Commentaries by J. M Guinn. Los Angeles: Ward Ritchie Press, 1963 [1872].

Fisher, Robert. *Let the People Decide: Neighborhood Organizing in America*. Boston, Mass.: Twayne, 1984.

"The 500 Directory," *Hispanic Business*, June 1994, p. 66.

Freire, Paulo. *Pedagogy of the Oppressed*. Trans. Myra Bergman Ramos. New York: Seabury Press, Continuum, 1970.

García, Ignacio M. *United We Win: The Rise and Fall of La Raza Unida Party*. Tucson: University of Arizona, M[exican] A[merican] S[tudies] R[esearch] Center, 1989.

García, Jorge. "*Forjando Ciudad*: The Development of a Chicano Political Community in East Los Angeles." Ph.D. diss., University of California, Riverside, 1986.

Garnett, Bernard E. *Invaders from the Black Nation: The "Black Muslims" in 1970*. Nashville, Tenn.: Race Relations Information Center, 1970.

Geary, Gerald J. *The Secularization of the California Missions (1810–1846)*. Studies in American Church History, vol. 17. New York: AMS Press, 1974 [1934].

Gómez-Quiñones, Juan. *Mexican Students por la Raza: The Chicano Student Movement in Southern California, 1967–1977*. Santa Barbara, Calif.: Editorial la Causa, 1978.

Grebler, Leo, Joan W. Moore, and Ralph C. Guzmán. *The Mexican-American People: The Nation's Second Largest Minority*. New York: Macmillan, Free Press, 1970.

Griswold del Castillo, Richard. *The Los Angeles Barrio, 1850–1890: A Social History*. Berkeley and Los Angeles: University of California Press, 1979.

Guerra, Fernando J., and Dwaine Marvick. *Ethnic Officeholders and Party Activists in Los Angeles*. ISSR Working Papers in the Social Sciences, vol. 2, no. 11. Los Angeles: Institute for Social Science Research, University of California, 1986.

Guzmán, Ralph. "Mexican American Casualties in Vietnam." *La raza* 1, no. 1 (1970): 12–15.

Harlow, Neal. *Maps and Surveys of the Pueblo Lands of Los Angeles*. Los Angeles: Dawson's Book Shop, 1976.

Harrington, Michael. *The Other America: Poverty in the United States*. New York: Macmillan, 1962.

Harvey, Richard B. *The Dynamics of California Government and Politics*. 2d ed. Monterey, Calif.: Brooks/Cole, 1985.

Hayden, Tom. "Colonialism and Liberation in America." *Viet Report*, Summer 1968, p. 32.

Hernández, José. *Mutual Aid for Survival: The Case of the Mexican American*. Malabar, Fla.: Robert E. Krieger, 1983.

Hetzel, Otto J. "Games the Government Plays: Federal Funding of Minority Economic Development." In *Community Economic Development: Problems and Potentials for Minority Groups*, ed. John C. Weistart, pp. 68–98. Library of Law and Contemporary Problems, no. 16. Dobbs Ferry, N.Y.: Oceana, 1972 [1971].

Johnson, Darlene. "An Examination of the Extent of Community Control Through Community Development Corporations." Master's thesis, University of California, Los Angeles, 1980.
Jones, Oakah L., Jr. *Los Paisanos: Spanish Settlers on the Northern Frontier of New Spain.* Norman: University of Oklahoma Press, 1979.
Kelly, Rita Mae. *Community Control of Economic Development: The Boards of Directors of Community Development Corporations.* Praeger Special Studies in U.S. Economic, Social, and Political Issues. New York: Praeger, 1977.
Kelsey, Harry. "A New Look at the Founding of Old Los Angeles." *California Historical Quarterly* 55 (Winter 1976): 326–39.
Kennedy, Robert F. *"To Seek a Newer World."* New York: Grosset & Dunlap, Bantam Books, 1968 [1967].
Kuklick, Bruce. "Myth and Symbol in American Studies." *American Quarterly* 24 (Oct. 1972): 435–50.
Larson, Robert W. *New Mexico's Quest for Statehood, 1846–1912.* Albuquerque: University of New Mexico Press, 1968.
Ledezma, Maria. "The Spanish Speaking Unity Council: A Community Development Corporation—José Arce and Tony M. Enríquez." In *Our Barrios: Past, Present, and Future—A Look at Raza/Latinos and the Built Environment* [ed. Carlos Villaalva], pp. 22–27. Berkeley, Calif.: Chicano Architectural Students Association, 1983.
Levitan, Sar A. *The Great Society's Poor Law: A New Approach to Poverty.* Baltimore: Johns Hopkins University Press, 1969.
Los Angeles County Almanac: Government, Politics, Civics. 31st ed. Los Angeles: Republican Central Committee of Los Angeles County, 1992.
Los Angeles County Almanac: A Guide to Government and Politics. 9th ed. Los Angeles: Republican Central Committee of Los Angeles, 1970.
Los Angeles Public Library, Municipal Reference Department. *Chronological Record of Los Angeles City Officials, 1850–1938.* Vol. 2. Los Angeles: n.p., 1966 [1938].
Macías, Reynaldo [F.]. "History of East L.A." *La luz*, Oct. 1974, pp. 14–16.
Macías, Reynaldo F., Guillermo Vicente Flores, Donaldo Figueroa, and Luis Aragón. *A Study of Unincorporated East Los Angeles.* Monograph no. 3. Los Angeles: Chicano Studies Research Center, University of California, 1973.
McWilliams, Carey. *North from Mexico: The Spanish-Speaking People of the United States.* New York: Greenwood Press, 1968 [1949].
Malcolm X. *The Autobiography of Malcolm X.* Ed. Alex Haley. With an Introduction by M. S. Handler and Epilogue by Alex Haley. New York: Ballantine Books, 1973 [1964].
———. "The *Young Socialist* Interview." [Interview by Jack Barnes and Barry Sheppard.] In *By Any Means Necessary: Speeches, Interviews and*

a Letter by Malcolm X, ed. George Breitman, pp. 157–66. New York: Pathfinder Press, Merit, 1970.

Mann, Eric. *Taking on General Motors: A Case Study of the Campaign to Keep GM Van Nuys Open*. Los Angeles: Center for Labor Research and Education, Institute of Industrial Relations, University of California, 1987.

Marín, Marguerite V. *Social Protest in an Urban Barrio: A Study of the Chicano Movement, 1966–1974*. Class, Ethnicity, Gender, and the Democratic Nation, vol. 1. Lanham, Md.: University Press of America, 1991.

Marks, Marlene Adler. "The Watts Tower of Power." *New West Magazine*, 27 Feb. 1978, sec. SC, pp. 19–23.

Matusow, Allen J. *The Unraveling of America: A History of Liberalism in the 1960s*. New American Nation Series. New York: Harper & Row, 1984.

Mazón, Mauricio. Review of *Chicanos in a Changing Society: From Mexican Pueblos to American Barrios in Santa Barbara and Southern California, 1848–1930*, by Albert Camarillo, and *The Los Angeles Barrio, 1850–1890: A Social History*, by Richard Griswold del Castillo. In *Southern California Quarterly* 63 (Spring 1981): 93–97.

Meier, Matt S., and Feliciano Rivera. *The Chicanos: A History of Mexican Americans*. American Century Series. New York: Farrar, Straus and Giroux, Hill & Wang, 1972.

Meinig, D[onald] W[illiam]. "Symbolic Landscapes: Some Idealizations of American Communities." In *The Interpretation of Ordinary Landscapes: Geographical Essays*, ed. D[onald] W[illiam] Meinig, pp. 164–92. New York: Oxford University Press, 1979.

Memmi, Albert. *The Colonizer and the Colonized*. Trans. by Howard Greenfeld. With an Introduction by Jean-Paul Sartre. Boston: Beacon Press, 1967.

Miller, Gary J. *Cities by Contract: The Politics of Municipal Incorporation*. Cambridge, Mass.: MIT Press, 1981.

Morales, Armando. *Ando Sangrando (I Am Bleeding): A Study of Mexican American–Police Conflict*. La Puente, Calif.: Perspectiva, 1972.

Morison, Samuel Eliot. *Builders of the Bay Colony*. Boston: Houghton Mifflin, Riverside Press Cambridge, 1930.

Moynihan, Daniel P. *Maximum Feasible Misunderstanding: Community Action in the War on Poverty*. Clarke A. Sanford Lectures on Local Government and Community Life. New York: Macmillan, Free Press, Arkville Press Book, 1969.

Muñoz, Carlos, Jr. *Youth, Identity, Power: The Chicano Movement*. Haymarket Series on North American Politics and Culture. New York: Verso, 1989.

Nadel, George H., and Perry Curtis, eds. *Imperialism and Colonialism*. With a Foreword by Bruce Mazlish. Main Themes in European History. New York: Macmillan, 1964.

Newfield, Jack. *Robert Kennedy: A Memoir*. New York: E. P. Dutton, 1969.
Ong, Paul M. *The Widening Divide: Income Inequality and Poverty in Los Angeles*. Los Angeles: Research Group on the Los Angeles Economy, 1989.
Parachini, Lawrence F., Jr. *A Political History of the Special Impact Program*. Cambridge, Mass.: Center for Community Economic Development, 1980.
———. *TELACU: Community Development for the Future*. Cambridge Mass.: Center for Community Economic Development [1976].
Parra, Rafael. "The Emergence of Chicano Architecture: Gregory Villanueva." In *Our Barrios: Past, Present, and Future—A Look at Raza/ Latinos and the Built Environment* [ed. Carlos Villaalva], pp. 46–51. Berkeley, Calif.: Chicano Architectural Students Association, 1983.
Patterson, James T. *America's Struggle Against Poverty, 1900–1980*. Cambridge, Mass.: Harvard University Press, 1981.
Payne, J[ames] Gregory, and Scott C. Ratzan. *Tom Bradley, the Impossible Dream: A Biography*. Santa Monica, Calif.: Roundtable, 1986.
Perry, Stewart E. *Building a Model Black Community: The Roxbury Action Program*. Cambridge, Mass.: Center for Community Economic Development, 1978.
———. *Communities on the Way: Rebuilding Local Economies in the United States and Canada*. Albany: State University of New York Press, 1987.
Peterson, Florence. *American Labor Unions: What They Are and How They Work*. 2d rev. ed. New York: Harper & Row, 1963.
Pitt, Leonard. *The Decline of the Californios: A Social History of the Spanish-Speaking Californians, 1846–1890*. Berkeley and Los Angeles: University of California Press, 1966.
Raigoza, James José. "The Ad Hoc Committee to Incorporate East Los Angeles: A Study on the Sociopolitical Orientations of Mexican-American Incorporation." Ph.D. diss., University of California, Los Angeles, 1977.
Rendón, Armando B. *Chicano Manifesto*. New York: Macmillan, 1971.
Reuther, Victor G. *The Brothers Reuther and the Story of the UAW: A Memoir*. Boston: Houghton Mifflin, 1976.
Reynolds, Morgan O. "Labor Reform: A Blip on the Radarscope." In *Assessing the Reagan Years*, ed. David Boaz, pp. 321–32. Washington, D.C.: Cato Institute, 1988.
Ríos-Bustamante, Antonio, and Pedro Castillo. *An Illustrated History of Mexican Los Angeles, 1781–1985*. Monograph no. 12. Los Angeles: Chicano Studies Research Center, University of California, 1986.
Robinson, W[illiam] W[ilcox]. *Land in California: The Story of Mission Lands, Ranchos, Squatters, Mining Claims, Railroad Grants, Land Scrip, Homesteads*. Chronicles of California. Berkeley and Los Angeles: University of California Press, 1948.

Rogers, Mary Beth. *Cold Anger: A Story of Faith and Power Politics*. With an Introduction by Bill Moyers. Denton: University of North Texas Press, 1990.

Romo, Ricardo. *East Los Angeles: History of a Barrio*. Austin: University of Texas Press, 1983.

Rosen, Gerald Paul. "Political Ideology and the Chicano Movement: A Study of the Political Ideology of Activists in the Chicano Movement." Ph.D. diss., University of California, Los Angeles, 1972.

Rosenbaum, Robert J. *Mexicano Resistance in the Southwest: "The Sacred Right of Self-Preservation."* Dan Danciger Publication Series. Austin: University of Texas Press, 1981.

Sánchez, David. *Expedition Through Aztlán*. La Puente, Calif.: Perspectiva, 1978.

Sánchez, George J. *Becoming Mexican American: Ethnicity, Culture, and Identity in Chicano Los Angeles, 1900–1945*. New York: Oxford University Press, 1993.

Sanford, Trent Elwood. *The Architecture of the Southwest: Indian, Spanish, American*. New York: W. W. Norton, 1950.

Santillán, Richard. *La Raza Unida: Chicano Politics*. Los Angeles: Tlaquilo, 1973.

Slotkin, Richard. *Regeneration Through Violence: The Mythology of the American Frontier, 1600–1860*. Middletown, Conn.: Wesleyan University Press, 1973.

Small, Marshall L. "Compensating Corporate Executives." In *Advising California Business Enterprises*, ed. Wilma S. Horwitz, Betty Deal, and Norman Jensen, pp. 717–83. California Practice Handbook no. 9. N.p.: State Bar of California Through University Extension, University of California, 1958.

Smith, Henry Nash. *Virgin Land: The American West as Symbol and Myth*. Cambridge: Harvard University Press, 1950.

Sopher, David E. "The Landscape of Home: Myth, Experience, Social Meaning." In *The Interpretation of Ordinary Landscapes: Geographical Essays*, ed. D[onald] W[illiam] Meinig, pp. 129–49. New York: Oxford University Press, 1979.

Spicer, Edward H. *Cycles of Conquest: The Impact of Spain, Mexico and the United States on the Indians of the Southwest, 1533–1960*. Tucson: University of Arizona Press, 1962.

"The Spiritual Manifesto of Aztlán." In *Literatura Chicana: Texto y Contexto/Chicano Literature: Text and Context*, ed. Antonia Castañeda Shular, Tomás Ybarra-Frausto, and Joseph Sommers, p. 84. Englewood Cliffs, N.J.: Prentice Hall, 1972.

Steiner, Rodney. *Los Angeles: The Centrifugal City*. Dubuque, Iowa: Kendall/Hunt, 1981.

Sullivan, Leon H. *Build Brother Build*. Philadelphia: Macrae Smith, 1969.

Sundquist, James L. *Politics and Policy: The Eisenhower, Kennedy, and Johnson Years*. Washington, D.C.: Brookings Institution, 1968.

Tijerina, Reies López. *Mi lucha por la tierra*. With a Prologue by Jorge A. Bustamante. Vida y Pensamiento de México. Mexico City: Fondo de Cultura Económica, 1978.

Torres, Esteban E. "Birth of a City: Incorporation of East Los Angeles at the Crossroads." *La luz*, Oct. 1974, pp. 13–14.

Treviño, Jesús Salvador, and José Luis Ruiz. *Yo soy*. 60 min. Los Angeles: Interamerican Satellite, 1985. Videocassette.

Weber, David J. *The Spanish Frontier in North America*. Yale Western Americana Series. New Haven: Yale University Press, 1992.

Weber, Francis J., ed. *The Old Plaza Church: A Documentary History*. N.p.: Libra Press, 1980.

Weyr, Thomas. *Hispanic U.S.A.: Breaking the Melting Pot*. A Cornelia and Michael Bessie Book. New York: Harper & Row, 1988.

White, Theodore H. *The Making of the President, 1972*. New York: Atheneum, 1973.

Witherall, Graham. "Albert Rebel & Associates, Inc., #103," *Hispanic Business*, June 1994, p. 98.

Witkin, B[ernard] E[rnest]. *Summary of California Law: A Concise and Critical Manual of the Law of California*. Vol. 3. 7th ed. San Francisco: Bender-Moss, 1960.

Index

In this index an "f" after a number indicates a separate reference on the next page. A continuous discussion over two or more pages is indicated by a span of page numbers, e.g., "57–59." *Passim* is used for a cluster of references in close but not consecutive sequence.

A&A Camacho firm, 99
Aaron Brothers firm, 130
ACTIELA, *see* Ad Hoc Committee to Incorporate East Los Angeles
Ad Hoc Committee to Incorporate East Los Angeles (ACTIELA), 95–105 *passim*, 172f
AFL-CIO (Industrial Union Department), 27–32 *passim*
African Americans: CDCs designed to help, 41; as influence on Mexican Americans, 11, 17–20, 31, 46, 55–58 *passim*, 146; and separatism, 1, 11, 19. *See also* Black Muslims; Civil rights movement
Agency for International Development (U.S.), 162–63, 209–10, 220
Aguilar, Cristóbal, 169

AID, *see* Agency for International Development
Air Management Company, 230
Alatorre, Richard, 115, 141, 176, 185, 243; as California legislator, 170–71, 187–92 *passim*; and TELACU projects, 227–28, 236–45 *passim*
Alberto Díaz Plaza, 167
Algeria, 18
Alhambra, 93
Alinsky, Saul, 148
Allard, Lucille Roybal, 242, 246–47
Amalgamated Clothing Workers, 34f
American Civil Liberties Union, 242
Anacostia Economic Development Corporation, 262
Anheuser-Busch Corporation, 229
Annexation, 94–95, 118–19

304 Index

Antiwar movement, 1, 46, 71
Aparicio, Magdalena, 109–10, 112–15, 133, 179, 203
Aquapet, Inc., 130
ARA, *see* Area Redevelopment Administration
Aragón, Manuel, 118
Area Redevelopment Administration (ARA), 20–25 *passim*
Arizona, *see* Chicanos por la Causa
Arizona Mothers Association, 90
Arrow Truck Body Company, 63
Arroyo Vista Family Health Center, 206
Arzube, Juan, 139
Associated Southwest Investors, 157–58
Atlantic Richfield Corporation, 164
Atlas Engineering Company, 120, 174
Avelar, Jess, 35
Avellar, Emil S., 121–22
Avila, Joseph S., 60–61, 66, 80
Ayala, Ruben, 173
Ayúdate Project, 174
Aztecs, 54–55, 102
Aztlán, 54, 71, 75, 102

B. F. Goodrich, *see* Goodrich tire plant
Ballesteros, Juan, 50
Banco de San José, 114
Bank of America, 211, 224
Bank of East Los Angeles, 112, 114
Bañuelos, Romana, 116
Barrera, Mario, 10
"Barrio Housing Plan," 81–88 *passim*
Barrios, 2, 16, 248–49, 254–55. *See also* East Los Angeles
Becerra, Javier, 245, 246–47
Bedford-Stuyvesant (New York City), 39–44

Bell, 3
Bella Vista, 118–19
Bell Best Pies, 174
Bell Gardens, 247–48, 250
Belvedere Citizen, 110, 167
Belvedere Park, 131, 167, 253
Berman, Howard, 174
Bexar County Hospital District, 150
Birns, Leonard, 140
Biscailuz, Eugene, 169
Blackfeet Indian Writing Company, 120
Black Muslims, 17–19, 22, 46, 55
Black Panthers, 56
Blauner, Robert, 10
Bodero, A. J., 197–98, 205
Bolivia, 163
Boone, Richard, 31
Boston (Massachusetts), 41
Boyle Heights, 3, 48f, 53, 180f
Bradley, Tom, 60, 175, 187, 191, 199, 237; and Esteban Torres, 139; 1977 mayoral campaign of, 180–83
Brooklyn Avenue redevelopment, 253
Brophy, Bill, 170
Brown, Jerry, 171, 175, 183, 187
Brown, Willie, 187–91 *passim*
Brown Berets, 1, 55–58, 67, 69–71
Business Leadership of Olvera Street, 236
Byrd, Don B., 197–98, 214

Caldera, Louis, 247
Calderón, Charles, 190, 192, 245
California: HACER activities in, 160–61; history of, depicted in mural, 6–7. *See also* East Los Angeles; Los Angeles; Spanish Speaking Unity Council; *Agencies and offices in*

Index

California Assembly: Mexican Americans in, 171–72, 189, 191–92, 241–47 *passim*; Mexican Americans' lack of representation on, 44, 169
California Economic and Business Development Department, 160, 183
California Employment Development Project, 126–27
California Fair Political Practices Commission, 240, 242
California Highway Patrol, 72
California Hispanic American Democrats (CHAD), 186
California Senate: Mexican Americans in, 170–71, 189, 192, 240, 245; Mexican Americans' lack of representation in, 44, 169, 247
California Small Business Development Board, 206–7
California State University at Long Beach, 226
California State University at Los Angeles, 56, 226
Campesinos Unidos (Brawley), 160f
Capital Development Group, Inc., 147
Carlsbad, 121
Carmichael, Stokely, 10
Carpenter, Edward, 120
Carter, Jimmy: Latino appointments under, 138–43, 165, 183f, 191; Latino support for, 139, 175–77, 184–86, 196–200 *passim*; reelection failure of, 161–64 *passim*, 168, 186
Casa de la Raza (Santa Barbara), 160f
Casa del Sol Alcoholic Halfway House (San Antonio), 150
Casa Maravilla, 85, 90, 105, 109, 177
Castillo, Martin, 84
Castro, Sal, 59, 67f
Castro, Tom, 176, 181
Castro, Tony, 76
Castro Nagata, Grace, 176
Católicos por la Raza, 69–70
CCAP, *see* Citizens' Crusade Against Poverty
CDCs, *see* Community Development Corporations
Center for Community Change, 81
Center for Employment and Training (Salinas), 160
Central Americans, 248–49
Central Coast Counties Development Corporation (Salinas), 160
CETA, *see* Comprehensive Employment and Training Act
CHAD, *see* California Hispanic American Democrats
Chávez, César, 38, 43, 253; as Chicano leader, 1, 11, 16, 30, 33, 46, 58, 182, 188, 221–22, 262; as UFW leader, 1, 32–33, 54
Chavez Ravine, 82
Chemical Bank, 174
Chicana Nurses Association, 182
Chicano Moratorium Committee, 71–72, 75
Chicanos: activism among, 1–2, 11, 46–76, 94, 97, 135, 159, 247; basis of claims to Southwest by, 6–7, 13, 47–54; importance of land to, 2–13 *passim*, 32, 45, 47, 51, 54–55, 71, 102, 253–54, 263; as term, 58. *See also* Brown Berets; Mexican Americans; Southwest
Chicanos por la Causa (CPLC) (Arizona CDC), 145, 152–56

Chicano Youth Liberation Conference, 71
Child care centers, 147, 150
Child Mental Health Program (San Antonio), 150
Chromallay Company, 130
Chrysler Corporation, 211
Circle Associates (Boston), 41
Cisneros, Henry, 148
Citizens Committee to Incorporate East Los Angeles, 94. *See also* Ad Hoc Committee to Incorporate East Los Angeles
Citizens' Crusade Against Poverty (CCAP), 27, 30–32, 60, 81
Civil rights movement, 1, 17, 25, 32–33. *See also* Black Muslims; Riots; Voting Rights Act
Cleland House, 63, 109; and TELACU, 83, 90, 109, 174, 177
Cleveland (Ohio), 41
Clinton, Bill, 263
CMAS, *see* Congress of Mexican-American Unity
Colonialism (internal): as analogy for African Americans, 18–19, 55; as analogy for Mexican Americans, 10–11, 15, 44, 46–47, 56–61 *passim*, 71, 75–77, 165; East Los Angeles as example of, 93–94, 105, 110–11, 137f, 224, 251; incompleteness of analogy of, 263; in New Mexico, 159; and poverty in U.S., 23, 42–43; TELACU's use of analogy of, 78, 93, 95–99, 121, 135, 141–43, 162
Columbia Broadcasting System, 40
Columbus (Ohio), 41
Commerce (California), 3, 5, 93, 134. *See also* TELACU Center; TELACU Industrial Park; TELACU Manor Retirement Home

Commonwealth Bank, 119, 174
Communities Organized for Public Service (COPS), 148
Community Action Program, 20f, 25–26, 28, 92
Community Bank of California, *see* Bank of East Los Angeles
Community Credit Corporation, 113–14
Community Development Corporations (CDCs): development of, 39–44; ethnic emphasis of, 156; federal funding for, 40f, 83–85, 90–91; precursors of, 19–39, 91–92; purpose of, 91; rediscovery of, 262–63; social services provided by, 147–50, 152, 156, 158. *See also* Hispanic American Coalition for Economic Revitalization; National Congress for Community Economic Development; Special Impact Program; TELACU
Community Guidance Center (San Antonio), 150
Community Planning and Development Corporation (CPDC), 101, 123–25, 132f, 138, 178. *See also* Community Research Group
Community Redevelopment Agency (Los Angeles City), 236
Community Redevelopment Agency (Los Angeles County), 117
Community Research Group (CRG), 125, 133, 138, 145, 148, 165, 191; closing of, 220, 230; Historical Preservation Survey by, 164, 233. *See also* Community Planning and Development Corporation; His-

panic American Coalition for Economic Revitalization Community Self-Determination Act, 44, 84
Community Services Administration (U.S.): funding of CDCs by, 120, 123, 129, 146f, 153, 157, 197; in government hierarchy, 114, 217; and TELACU, 115, 119–23 *passim*, 129, 131, 135, 164; and TELACU investigation, 209, 215. *See also* Office of Community Services
Community Thrift & Loan, 108, 112–14, 120–23, 134f, 203; new building for, 123, 132
Community union concept, 27–39, 92, 257. *See also* Community Development Corporations
Comprehensive Employment and Training Act (CETA), 127; end of TELACU's involvement with, 220; and Los Angeles city and county government, 205–7, 211f, 216, 219; TELACU's use of, 126, 177, 196–97, 199, 205–6
Congress of Mexican-American Unity (CMAS), 55–59 *passim*, 66, 70; and East Los Angeles incorporation issue, 94f, 102; political influence of, 85, 170, 172; and 1970s riots, 70–78 *passim*
Congress of Racial Equality (CORE), 44, 84
Connolly, Joseph, 211–12
Construction and Rehabilitation Enterprises (New Mexico), 158
Conway, Jack, 20, 27–38 *passim*, 81
Coopers and Lybrand CPA, 174
COPS, *see* Communities Organized for Public Service

Coronel, Antonio, 169
Corrada, Baltasar, 185
Corral, Rafael, 99
Cortés, Ernesto, 148
Cortés, Hernán, 6
Corwin, Bruce, 181
Costa Mesa, 121
Council of Mexican-American Organizations, 57
CPDC, *see* Community Planning and Development Corporation
CPLC, *see* Chicanos por la Causa
Cranston, Alan, 176, 183–84
CRG, *see* Community Research Group
Crocker National Bank, 129
Cuauhtémoc, 6
Cuba, 263

Danielson, George, 188–90
Davis, Grace Montañez, 176, 181
Debs, Ernest E., 107
Delano (California), 30f
Democratic Party: and Mexican-Americans, 138–43, 170–71, 176, 184–89, 242–47 *passim*; and TELACU, 173–87 *passim*, 196, 199, 217f
Denver Community Development Corporation, 145
Development and Service Corporation, 40–41
Development Resources Consulting Group, 148
Dodger Stadium, 82
DOL, *see* U.S. Labor Department
"Domingos Alegres" program, 131, 183, 228–29

Eagle Rock, 3
East Central Citizens Organization (Columbus), 41

Eastcoast Development Corporation, 262
Eastland Center (Commerce), 132, 134
Eastland Leasing Company, 122–23
East Long Beach Neighborhood Center, 160
East Los Angeles, 3–6, 15–16, 114; annexation issues in, 116, 118–19; attempts to incorporate, 78, 92–99, 101–5, 108, 116, 118, 135, 173; as internal colony, 44, 47–54; Mexican American disfranchisement in, 168–69; "political machine" in, 171–93, 242, 245–46; redevelopment of, 116–18, 125, 253–54; as TELACU's "special impact area," 253. *See also* Barrios
East Los Angeles, Maravilla, and Belvedere Park Property Owners Association, *see* Property Owners Association
East Los Angeles Bank, *see* Bank of East Los Angeles
East Los Angeles College, 94–95, 118–19, 226
East Los Angeles Community Union, *see* TELACU
East Los Angeles Gazette, 61
East Los Angeles Labor Community Action Committee (ELALCAC), 10, 35, 37–39. *See also* TELACU
East Los Angeles Tribune, 210–11
Eastmont Parent-Teacher Association, 70
Eastside, *see* East Los Angeles
Eastside Journal, 140
Eastside Sun, 75, 94, 98, 125
Echeveste, John, 183, 210
Economic and Social Opportunities (San Jose), 160

Economic Development Administration (EDA) (U.S.), 22, 81, 129, 134, 145, 147, 159–61
Economic Opportunity Act, 26, 39–44, 91. *See also* Special Impact Program
Ecuador, 163
EDA, *see* Economic Development Administration
Edelman, Edmund, 173–76, 191
Educational Issues Coordinating Committee, 67–68
Edward Carpenter and Associates, 120
ELALCAC, *see* East Los Angeles Labor Community Action Committee
El Hoyo Association, 90
El Hoyo project, 63
Elizondo, José ("Joe"), 117, 201
El Monte, 122
El Pueblo de la Reina de Los Angeles, *see* Los Angeles
El Pueblo de Los Angeles Historic Park, 235–39
El Sereno, 3, 50, 180f
El sol de México, 140
Embudo Presbyterian Hospital (New Mexico), 156
Eppert, Luana, 63–64
Escarcega, Roy, 63, 117, 127, 143, 181
Escontrías, Luis, 190
Escuelita del Sol (San Antonio), 150
Escutía, Martha, 247
Euclid Foundation, 79
European Union, 264

Fanon, Frantz, 10, 95–96
FCC, *see* Federal Communications Commission

Federal Communications Commission (FCC), 205, 207
Federal Housing Administration (FHA), 62
Federated Group, 130
Federation of Barrios Unidos de Maravilla, 85, 90
Ferraro, John, 115
Figueroa de Ballesteros, María, 51–52
Financial institutions: and CPLC, 155; and TELACU, 109–14, 119–22, 127, 134f
First Southwest Capital, 123
Flores, Juan María, 50
Flores, Sarah, 243, 245
Food cooperatives, 126, 227
Food Stamp Outreach, 99, 122, 173. *See also* TELACU Currency Exchange
Ford, Gerald, 177
Ford Foundation funding: for Chicanos por la Causa, 153; for Citizens' Crusade Against Poverty, 30; for Southwest Council of La Raza, 152; for Southwest Voter Registration Education Project, 175; for Spanish Speaking Unity Council, 147; for TELACU, 79–81, 129, 147
"A Framework for Greater Los Angeles Industrial Development," 133–34
Franciscan missionaries, 6, 49
Freire, Paulo, 10
Friends of David Lizarraga, 200

Gangs, *see* Juvenile delinquency
García, Alex P., 173; Mexican-American opposition to, 188, 192; as state senator, 139, 170–76 *passim*, 189; and TELACU investigation, 206–7

García, Carlos J., 61–63, 65–66, 80, 109, 142, 181, 197
García, Gloria A., 164
García, Jess, 197, 211
García, Pete, 153–54
García, Robert, 185
Garfield High School (East Los Angeles), 5, 57
Garvey, Marcus, 18
General Motors plant (South Gate), 231, 250, 256
Gerrymandering, 169, 242
Glendale, 51
Glucksman, Leon, 87
GOEZ Studios, 127, 130
Goggin, Terry, 174
Gold, Jerome, 196
Goldrich & Kest firm, 99, 231
Gonzales, Rodolfo ("Corky"), 11, 55–58 *passim*
González, Joe L., 203, 207, 215f, 220; as mural artist, 12, 221
González, Larry, 241
Goodell, Charles E., 44
Goodrich tire plant, 127–30 *passim*, 135, 182, 250
Grand Central Market (Los Angeles), 5
Great Depression, 21
Greater Eastside Builders Association, 66
Griswold del Castillo, Richard, 52
Gruhle, George, 35
Guatemalans, 248
Gutiérrez, José Angel, 11

HACER, *see* Hispanic American Coalition for Economic Revitalization
Hackett, David, 24–26
HAD, *see* Hispanic American Democrats

Harlem Commonwealth Council, 262
Harrington, Michael, 25, 27
Health needs surveys, 133
Hearst Foundation, 161
Hernández, Albert A., 99
Hernández, Mike, 245
Hernández, Pilar, 86, 119
Highland Park, 3, 133. *See also* TELACU Family Health Center
High school walkouts, 46, 55–59, 67–68, 70
Hispanic American Coalition for Economic Revitalization (HACER), 138, 143–65 *passim*, 261
Hispanic American Democrats (HAD), 184–86
Hispanic Business, 255
Historical preservation surveys, 164, 233
Hollytex Carpet Mills, 63
H.O.M.E. Program, 66
Honda Corporation, 225
Honduras, 163
Hough Area Development Corporation (Cleveland), 41
Housing: and the Catholic Church, 69–70; CDCs' interest in, 91, 147–58 *passim*; in East Los Angeles, 16; studies of, 123f; TELACU's influence on, 116–18, 123; TELACU's projects involving, 62–63, 65–66, 78, 81–89, 99, 107, 109, 229, 253–55. *See also* Real estate
Hubbard Street project, 62–63, 80
HUD, *see* U.S. Housing and Urban Development Department
Huerta, Dolores, 43
Humphrey, Hubert, 43
Huntington Park, 3

IAF, *see* Industrial Areas Foundation
Ian Caterers, 174
Illinois Neighborhood Development Corporation, 120
Image: criticism of TELACU's, 12, 177–79, 198–221, 223, 233–34, 245, 257–59; Gloria Molina's, 245; of TELACU as pro-business, 115; TELACU's emphasis on, 103, 130–31; TELACU's emphasis on physical, 3, 8–9, 83, 88–89, 98, 152, 164, 253–54; TELACU's enigmatic, 2, 9, 16, 45, 64, 66, 78, 88–92, 108, 196
Imperial, Ruben, 35
Incorporation efforts, 78, 92–99, 101–5, 108, 116, 118, 135, 173
Indians, 6, 48–50, 53, 55. *See also* Mestizos
Industrial Areas Foundation (IAF), 148–49
Industrial Union Department, *see* AFL-CIO
Inter-Agency Commission on Mexican-American Affairs, 84
Inter-American Entertainment Company, 131, 228
International Business Machines, 40

Jason D. Groode Enterprises, 174
Javits, Jacob, 39–41, 84
Jews, 175
John L. Espinosa Realty, 174
Johnson, Lyndon B., 20, 25–26, 28, 84, 217
Johnson Foundation, 164
Juvenile delinquency (gangs): in Los Angeles, 35, 37, 85–86, 105, 109, 176–77; RFK's interest in, 24–25

Index 311

Juvenile Delinquency and Youth Offenses Control Act, 24
Kahlo, Frida, 65
Kaiser Foundation, 63
Kemmerer firm, 99
Kennedy, Edward M., 84, 186
Kennedy, Ethel, 84
Kennedy, John F., 20–23, 25
Kennedy, Robert F. (RFK), 16, 175; assassination of, 1, 41–46 *passim*, 68, 83; on CDCs, 20, 23, 39, 41–42, 84, 262; and CDCs' self-determination, 20–25 *passim*, 30, 40–43; and Community Action Programs, 25; and juvenile delinquency, 24–26
King, Martin Luther, Jr., 1, 17, 43, 46, 262; and Citizens' Crusade Against Poverty, 27, 30
KMEX-TV, 73
KVEA-TV, 229

Labor movement: and CDCs, 59, 61; and community union concept, 27–30, 34–35; and War on Poverty, 26–27. *See also Names of specific labor unions*
La Cocina Restaurant (Santa Barbara), 160
LAFCO, *see* Local Agency Formation Commission
Laguna Park, 72–73
La Luz, 97
Land (and Chicanos' sense of place), 2–13 *passim*, 32, 45, 47, 51, 54–55, 71, 102, 253–54, 263. *See also* Landscape; Real estate
Land banking system, 134
Land Law of 1851, 51f
Landscape: CDCs' interest in, 150–55 *passim*; TELACU's emphasis on, 3, 8–9, 83, 88–89, 98, 152, 164, 253–54
La Puente, 122
Lara, David, 35
La Raza (underground newspaper), 58
La Raza Unida Party, 78, 102–5, 148, 170, 172
Liberals, 2, 10, 26–27, 30–31, 56
Lilly Endowment, 161
Lincoln Heights, 3, 49, 180–81; revitalization projects in, 126f, 133, 225, 253
Lincoln High School, 57f, 68
Lincoln Park, 65
Lizarraga, David C., 6, 85, 140, 146, 165; business orientation of, 108–11, 113f, 119, 126, 135, 137, 211; on colonialism, 141–42, 162; and Democratic Party politics, 174f, 181–89 *passim*, 240; on National Commission on Neighborhoods, 143, 145, 184; as TELACU CEO, 108–9, 134f, 257–58; as TELACU interim director, 101–8 *passim*, 173; and TELACU investigation, 197, 201–2, 204, 209f, 220–21. *See also* Friends of David Lizarraga
Llewelyn-Davies Associates, 81
Lloyds Bank, 129
Local Agency Formation Commission (LAFCO), 98, 118
López, Jaime, 162–63
López, Lydia, 234
Los Angeles, 3, 164, 169, 172; gangs in, 35, 37, 85–86, 105, 109, 176–77; history of, 48–54; Latino diversity in, 248–49; Mexican Americans in, 1, 3, 44, 53–54, 168, 172, 186, 239, 246; parks and recreation department

of, 236–39 *passim*; political fragmentation of, 3. *See also* East Los Angeles; Los Angeles City Council; Los Angeles County; Los Angeles Unified School District; *Specific areas and agencies in*
Los Angeles City Council: Mexican American representation on, 44, 240–47 *passim*; TELACU's CETA contracts with, 205–7, 211–12, 216, 219; and TELACU Transit System, 227–28
Los Angeles Community College District, 169, 247
Los Angeles Conservancy, 237
Los Angeles County, 3, 15, 93, 164–69 *passim*, 248–49. *See also* Los Angeles County Board of Supervisors
Los Angeles County Board of Supervisors, 124, 173; on incorporation of East Los Angeles, 93, 103–5; and Mexican American representation, 44, 169, 242–43, 245; and redevelopment of East Los Angeles, 116–18, 125; and TELACU investigation, 207, 211, 216, 224
Los Angeles County Commission on Human Relations, 56
Los Angeles County Department of Regional Planning, 134
Los Angeles County Housing Authority, 86–87
Los Angeles County Parks and Recreation Program, 131, 228
Los Angeles County Regional Planning Commission, 124f
Los Angeles County Sheriff's Department, 71–72, 94

Los Angeles Mexican Conservancy, 237–38
Los Angeles Planning Commission, 237
Los Angeles Police Department, 68–78 *passim*, 251
Los Angeles Times, 73, 75, 188–91 *passim*; on Tamayo Restaurant, 233; on TELACU investigation, 193–223 *passim*, 233–34, 240, 259; on TELACU Transit System, 227–28
Los Angeles Unified School District, 117; and Mexican American representation, 57, 169–72 *passim*, 247; protests against, 46, 55–59, 67–68, 70
Lote Association, 90
Lovell, John, 175
Luminaria's Restaurant (Monterey Park), 231

McBride, Tom, 209–10
McCarthy, Leo, 173f
McDonald's franchise, 149
McDonnell-Douglas Corporation, 63
McGovern, George, 175, 185
Machado, Francisco, 169
McIntyre, James Francis Cardinal, 69
Magnolia Land Company, 87
Maine, 22
Majestic Realty, 123, 132
Malcolm X, 1, 10, 17–18
Malintzín, 6
Manatt, Charles, 174
Maravilla housing project, *see* Nueva Maravilla
Maravilla Neighborhood Development Project, 253
Maravilla Project Area Committee, 117

Maravilla Service Center, 90
Maravilla Tenants Association, 86, 90
Mardirosian, Vahac, 68
Martínez, Diane, 247
Martínez, Marty, 189–92 *passim*, 247
Martínez Chevron company, 174
Mascarel, José, 169
Massachusetts Bay Company, 17, 91–92
MAUC, *see* Mexican American Unity Council
Maywood, 3
MCA Incorporated, 237, 239
Meinig, D. W., 8
Memmi, Albert, 10, 95–96
Mendoza, Xavier, 123
Mercado (Phoenix, Arizona), 155–56
MESBICs, *see* Minority Enterprise Small Business Investment Companies
Mestizos, 6, 48–49, 159. *See also* Chicanos
Mexican-American Community Programs Foundation, 79
Mexican-American Education Commission, 68–69
Mexican American Legal Defense and Education Fund, 172, 223, 242, 256
Mexican-American Political Association, 170, 172
Mexican Americans: basis of claims to Southwest by, 6–7, 13, 47–54; Carter's appointments of, 138–43, 165, 183f, 191; educational concerns of, 56, 57–59, 67–68; history of, in Los Angeles, 47–54; immigrant experience of, 10, 48; lack of political representation of, 44, 168–69, 240, 244; Los Angeles landmarks of, 5–8, 136; network of CDCs for, 143–61; numbers of, in Los Angeles, 53–54, 168, 172, 186, 239, 246; in politics, 169–93; and United Farm Workers, 31–33. *See also* Chicanos
Mexican American Unity Council (MAUC), 145, 148–52, 261
Mexican Independence Day parade, 75
Mexican War, 7, 11, 50, 75
Mexico, 6–7, 50, 159, 165; immigrants from, in Los Angeles, 15, 49, 52f, 249, 254–55
Michigan Peninsula Airways, 201
Million Dollar Theater (Los Angeles), 5
Minority enterprises: TELACU's investment in, 120, 200–201, 261–62; TELACU's success as example of, 255. *See also* Minority Enterprise Small Business Investment Companies; *Names of specific enterprises*
Minority Enterprise Small Business Investment Companies (MESBICs), 113, 157; TELACU Investment Company as, 119, 208–9, 216–17, 220
Mobilization for Youth project (New York City), 24
Mobil Oil Corporation, 79f
Model Cities programs, 66
Molina, Gloria: on East Los Angeles issues, 118, 176, 236; elective offices held by, 191–92, 243–46 *passim*; White House appointment of, 141
Mondale, Walter, 142, 200
Montañez Davis, Grace, 176, 181
Montebello, 3, 5, 93, 118–19, 122, 134

Monterey Hills housing project, 63
Monterey Park, 3, 5, 93–95, 121, 132, 134, 189; annexation by, 118–19
Montoya, Art, 98, 118, 125
Montoya, Joseph B., 139, 174, 176, 189f, 245
Moreno, Gordon, 68–69, 109
Moreno, John, 170
Moret, Lou, 141
Mott Foundation, 164
Muhammad, Elijah, 16, 17–18
Muhammad Speaks, 18
Muñoz, Rosalio, 71–75 *passim*
Murillo, George, 117
Muskie, Edmund, 175
Mutualistas, 17

Nagata, Grace Castro, 176
Napolitano, Grace, 247
National Chicano Moratorium Committee, 71–72, 75
National Commission for Manpower Policy, 143
National Commission on Neighborhoods, 143, 145, 184
National Congress for Community Economic Development, 143, 146
National Endowment for the Arts, 124, 164
National Farm Workers Service Center, 31–33. *See also* United Farm Workers
National Guard, 251
National Institute for Mental Health, 150
National Institute on Alcohol Abuse and Alcoholism, 150
National Training Program (CCAP), 31
Nation of Islam, *see* Black Muslims
Nava, Julian, 57, 67, 170, 172

Neighborhood Development Project (East Los Angeles), 117–18, 123
Neighborhood Youth Corps, 37
New Calvary Cemetery (East Los Angeles), 5
New Left, 18, 57
New Mexico, 97, 159. *See also* Siete del Norte
News for America, 248
Newton, Huey P., 1
Nixon, Richard M., 83–84, 87
Noblet, Ron, 176, 178–79, 181
Norman F. Swanton Associates, 174
North Broadway Commercial Revitalization Project (Lincoln Heights), 126, 133, 225, 253
North Coast Opportunities (Ukiah), 160f
Northwest Mental Health Program (MAUC), 150
Noticias del Mundo, 228
Nuestro magazine, 120
Nueva Maravilla: community participation in, 82–83, 85–87, 109, 125, 248; as influence on East Los Angeles redevelopment, 116–18, 167, 253; redevelopment of, 81–83, 85–88, 99–101, 123, 256; success of, 105, 107, 183–84, 234, 251, 253. *See also* Headings beginning with "Maravilla"

Obledo, Mario, 173, 187
O'Connor, William, 215
OEO, *see* Office of Economic Opportunity
Office of Community Services (U.S.), 212–20 *passim*, 231
Office of Economic Opportunity (OEO) (U.S.), 217; CDC

funding by, 146, 149; TELACU funding by, 10, 16, 83–85, 101, 114; and TELACU structural changes, 88–90. *See also* Community Services Administration
Office of Management and Budget (U.S.), 209
Office of Minority Business Enterprise (U.S.), 112, 141
Ojo Caliente Craftsmen, 157
Olmo, Frank del, 191
O'Loane, Glenn, 33–37, 64, 109, 126, 227
Olvera Street Merchants Association, 235–37
Organization of American States, 38
Orgullo de Nuestra Herencia (mural), see *Pride of Our Heritage, The*
Other America, The (Harrington), 25
Our Lady Queen of Angels High School, 69

Pacific Busing, 228
Packinghouse Workers, 34f
Paladines, Gustavo, 209
Palomares, F., 169
Panama, 142–43, 163
Panama Canal, 142–43
Pan American Bank, 79f, 114, 116
Pasta House restaurant, 115
Patlán, Juan, 148f
People for TELACU State Action, 173–75
Pepsi-Cola Corporation, 229
Peru, 163
Pines, Burt, 180–82
Pla, George, 141, 181, 183, 189, 197, 200
Plaza de La Raza project, 65, 80, 90

Polanco, Richard, 181, 190–92, 241, 247
Political action committees, 173–75, 193
Portals (Washington, D.C.), 260, 261–62
Posadas de Colores Elderly Housing, 147
Presbyterian Economic Development Corporation, 149
President's Committee on Juvenile Delinquency, 24–26
Pride of Our Heritage, The (TELACU Center mural), 5–8, 11f, 131, 193, 195, 221
Progress Enterprises (Philadelphia), 19–20, 22, 41, 257
Property Owners Association, 94, 98
Proteus Adult Training, 160
Puerto Rico, 97

Quezada, Leticia, 246
Quiet Cannon Restaurant (Montebello), 231

Radio KALI, 228
Ramos, George, 233
Rancho Rosa de Castilla, 50–53
Rancho San Rafael, 51
Reading is Fun-damental program, 64
Reagan, Ronald, 56, 161, 165, 171, 186, 188, 217–18, 220
Real estate: Black Muslims' interest in, 17–19; CDCs' emphasis on, 42, 147–59 *passim*; Progress Enterprises' emphasis on, 19–20; TELACU's emphasis on, 3, 8, 12, 62–63, 65–67, 78, 80–106, 124, 133–35, 223, 229–39, 254f. *See also* Financial institutions; Housing; Urban planning

Reapportionment, 168, 186–88, 239–46 *passim*
Reliable Landscaping firm, 99
Republican Party, 217–18, 235, 243, 263
Restoration Corporation, 40–41
Reuther, Eric V., 60
Reuther, Victor, 38
Reuther, Walter P., 10f, 16, 38, 262; and community union concept, 27–35 *passim*
Reynoso, Cruz, 187
Ribera Ranch (New Mexico), 158
Rio Grande Alcoholism Treatment Center (New Mexico), 156
Ríos-Bustamante, Antonio, 238
Riots: in 1960s, 1, 33, 77; in 1970s, 70–75, 77–79, 94, 137; in South Central Los Angeles, 250–51, 262–63
Riverside barrio, 75
Roberti, David, 174
Rodríguez, Armando, 176
Romana's Foods, 116
Roman Catholic Church, 69–70
Roosevelt, Theodore, 142
Roosevelt High School, 57
Roybal, Edward R., 115, 139f, 176, 199, 242–46 *passim*; on Los Angeles City Council, 172, 240; medical center named for, 5, 166f; as U.S. Congressman, 127, 169–71, 174, 185–92 *passim*, 240
Roybal Allard, Lucille, 242, 246–47
Roybal Medical Center (Los Angeles), 5, 166f
Ruiz, Rachel, 176–81 *passim*
Ruiz, Raúl, 103, 170
Rural Loan Development Fund, 155, 212–20 *passim*
Rutkin, Leonard, 208–9, 216

St. Basil's Cathedral, 69–70
St. Louis (Missouri), 41
Salazar, Ruben, 73
Salvadorans, 248
Sánchez, Lucy, 35
San Gabriel Mission, 5, 9, 48–50
San Gabriel Valley, 168, 188f, 245
Santa Fe Springs, 122
Santillán, Richard, 103
SBA, *see* Small Business Administration
Schabarum, Peter, 242–43
Schrade, Paul, 28, 33–35, 37, 43, 59
Self-determination: of Black Muslims, 17–19, 55; and community union concept, 28–30, 38–39; and federal funding of CDCs, 40, 62, 85, 89–90, 106, 214f; as HACER goal, 145; of Mexican Americans, 1–3, 10–11, 38–39, 55, 57, 94, 102–3, 138–39, 254; and redevelopment and annexation issues, 116–19; RFK's support for, 20–25 *passim*, 30, 40–41; as TELACU goal, 2f, 11–13, 61, 78, 89–90, 96, 136, 168, 189–92, 239
Senior citizens, 124, 126, 147, 226–27
Separatism (ethnic), 1, 10, 17–20, 58, 61
Service Sheet Metal firm, 99
Shapell Government Housing, 99
Sheldon Appel Company, 231
Siete Building (New Mexico), 158
Siete del Norte (New Mexico CDC), 145, 156–59
Simi Valley, 121
Small Business Administration (SBA) (U.S.), 113f 119, 149, 207–9, 216–20 *passim. See also*

Minority Enterprise Small Business Investment Companies
Small Business Clinic (Spanish Speaking Unity Council), 148
Small Cities Economic Development Commission, 160
Smith, Henry Nash, 8
Snyder, Art, 118, 240–41
Soledad Church (Los Angeles), 5
Solís, George, 34, 109
Solís, Hilda, 247
Song, Al, 115
Sonora, 49
Sopher, David E., 7
Soto, Philip, 170
South Coast Shingle Company, 230
Southern California Association of Governments, 124
Southern California Gas Company, 229
Southern California Rapid Transit District, 124
South Gate, 231, 250–56 passim
South Gate Industrial/Retail Park, 231, 253, 256
South Shore National Bank of Chicago, 120
Southwest (as Mexican Americans' historic place), 2, 6–7, 11, 13, 47, 51–59 passim, 71, 76, 102, 145, 165, 263
Southwest Cable Corporation, 157
Southwest Council of La Raza, 80, 152
Southwest Voter Registration Education Project, 148, 172, 175
Soviet Union, 263
Spain, 48–49, 53
Spanish International Network, 157
Spanish Speaking Unity Council (northern California CDC), 145–50 passim, 161

"Special impact areas," 2, 21, 153; TELACU's, 3–4, 16, 133f, 253, 261
Special Impact Program, 39–44, 83–84, 88–91 passim, 111, 126, 146, 149–50, 214–15; as CDCs' funding agency, 217. *See also* "Special impact areas"
Spiegel, Claire, 198, 202, 215, 221
Stationers Corporation, 130
Steven's Steak House (Commerce), 189–91, 231
Stone Outfitting, 174
Sullivan, Rev. Leon, 19–20
Synterra, Inc., 115

Tamayo, Rufino, 233
Tamayo Restaurant, 231–35
Taylor, Rick, 175
Teamsters, 34
TELACU (East Los Angeles Community Union): accomplishments of, 2–3, 9, 253–63; and ACTIELA, 95, 101–2; audit of, 195–222; as catalyst in community projects, 86–88, 95, 99, 101, 211; as CDC, 2–3, 9, 78, 87–92, 105, 108, 135–36, 257; as compromising self-determination of, 40, 62, 85, 89–90, 106, 111; criticism of, 12, 120, 177–83 passim, 195–222, 233–34, 245, 257–59; and cultural preservation, 2, 65, 97–98, 107, 127, 130–31, 164, 228–30, 233–39, 254; as de facto government agency, 89–95 passim, 125, 137, 227; early days of, 59–64, 250; economic development emphasis of, 2–3, 12, 30, 32, 44, 47, 60–61, 76, 99, 101, 105, 135, 222–24, 248–51, 255–56; economic de-

velopment master plans of, 108–20 *passim*, 131–35; federal funding for, 2, 78–91 *passim*, 101, 105, 114, 119, 124–27, 129, 134, 137, 177, 231; goals of, 2, 3, 11–13, 61, 78, 88–90, 96, 136, 168, 189–92, 234, 239; and HACER, 160–61, 165; international ventures of, 162–63, 165; lack of stockholders or rank-and-file members of, 90, 257–58; leadership training by, 2, 64–65, 121, 243; "leveraging" by, 101, 111–12, 117, 125, 255, 262; and Mexican-American recovery of place, 2f, 11, 12–13, 45, 253–54; origins of, 2, 10–11, 33–46, 59, 64, 84; political influence of, 2, 9, 44, 57, 78–79, 117–19, 141, 167–93, 223, 227–28, 243–48 *passim*, 257; private funding for, 79–81, 129, 147, 161; real estate emphasis of, 3, 8, 12, 62–63, 65–67, 78, 80–106, 124, 133–35, 223, 229–39, 254f; scandal concerning, 12, 195–222, 224, 234, 242, 245, 256–58; social service mission denied by, 9, 44, 64, 108, 126, 132, 201–4, 210–11, 234; social services provided by, 2, 35, 37, 60, 64, 78, 87, 109, 127–33 *passim*, 206, 225–28, 234, 255; structure of, 2–3, 16, 45, 60–64, 88–90, 131–33, 135, 148, 150, 257–58; urban planning by, 122–27, 133, 137–38, 143, 254. *See also* Community Development Corporations; Community Planning and Development Corporation; Community Research Group; Hispanic American Coalition for Economic Revitalization; Image; Self-determination; *Names of persons associated with and organizations starting with "TELACU"*

TELACU Center (Commerce), 5–8, 130–31, 147, 195, 221, 234, 253

TELACU Construction Development Corporation, 80–81

TELACU Currency Exchange, 122

TELACU Development Corporation, 132, 230–31

TELACU Family Health Center, 133, 135, 164, 220

TELACU Family Health Foundation, 206

TELACU Headboard Company, 66

TELACU Home Repair Corporation, 80

TELACU Industrial Park, 108, 127–30, 134–37, 147, 165, 203, 230. *See also* TELACU Center

TELACU Industries, 120, 131–32, 178, 200, 202; subsidiaries of, 119, 230

TELACU Inter-City Energy Systems, 229

TELACU Investment Company, 112–13, 119–21, 123, 157, 216–17, 220; closing of, 220, 230; mismanagement of, 119, 196, 208–9, 261

TELACU Manor Retirement Home, 234–35

TELACU Mattress Company, 66–67, 79f

TELACU Mobil Service Center, 79–80

TELACU Resource Center, *see* TELACU Center

TELACU Scholarship Fund, 226

Index 319

TELACU Senior Citizens Club, 90, 126, 226–27
TELACU Today, 141, 165
TELACU Transit System, 227–28
TELACU Ven Cap, 123
TELACU Weatherization Service, 229
TELACU Youth Services Program, 225–26
Tennessee Valley Authority, 22
Texas, *see* Mexican American Unity Council
Theobold, Peter, 162–63
TIEMPO, Inc., 155
Tijerina, Reies López, 11, 55–58 *passim*, 159
Tiscareno, Dan, 99
Title VII (OEO) funds, 91
Todman, Terence, 140
Torres, Art, 141, 176; as California legislator, 171–72, 187, 191f, 240, 242; campaign against Alex García of, 188–90; political interests of, 118, 139, 243–46 *passim*
Torres, Esteban E.: colonial analogy used by, 11f, 46–47, 93, 95–99; and Congress of Mexican-American Unity, 57, 59–60, 70–78 *passim*, 85, 94; depicted on mural, 6, 12; and incorporation efforts, 93–99, 103f; international trading company of, 216; political career of, 101, 104, 108, 163, 173, 243, 246; political meetings of, 189f; as TELACU board member, 109, 139; as TELACU director, 37–39, 44–45, 61–67, 78, 79–80, 84–88 *passim*, 92, 101, 105, 109; UAW connections of, 38, 104, 139; and UNESCO, 141–42, 162f; as U.S. Congressman, 168, 192, 247
To Seek a Newer World (RFK), 42
Tovar, Ed, 35
Transit studies, 123f, 133, 227
Treaty of Guadalupe Hidalgo, 50
Trott, Stephen, 214–16
Tunney, John, 176

UAW, *see* United Auto Workers
UCLA, *see* University of California at Los Angeles
UFW, *see* United Farm Workers
UMAS, *see* United Mexican-American Students
UNESCO, 141–42, 162f
"The Unincorporated East Los Angeles Environmental Assessment Program," 123, 124–25
Union Oil Company of California, 174
Union Station, 135, 235, 239
Uniroyal tire plant, 134–35, 250
United Auto Workers (UAW), 63, 231; and community union concept, 30–32; and Esteban Torres, 38, 104, 139; and TELACU's origins, 10, 16, 27, 33–35, 37–38, 46, 59–60, 64, 90, 127. *See also* Reuther, Walter P.
United Farm Workers (UFW), 7; and East Los Angeles issues, 102, 182; grape strike by, 1, 31, 54, 68; as Mexican American union, 38–39, 54; and National Farm Workers Service Center, 31–32. *See also* Chávez, César
United Mexican-American Students (UMAS), 55–58, 67, 69
United Neighborhoods Organization (UNO), 148, 223, 256
U.S. Commerce Department, 112, 209

U.S. Congress, 21–26 *passim*, 113; Esteban Torres's bid for, 101, 104, 108, 168, 192; and 1851 Land Law, 51f; Mexican American representation in, 44, 168, 192, 246–47; and Special Impact Program, 39–44, 214
U.S. Forest Service, 157
U.S. Health, Education, and Welfare Department, 133
U.S. Health and Human Services Department, 155–56, 209, 217
U.S. Housing and Urban Development Department (HUD): and TELACU investigation, 209–10, 220; and TELACU projects, 86–87, 107, 123, 147, 150, 154, 235
U.S. Justice Department, 216–17, 234, 241f
U.S. Labor Department, 29, 37; TELACU investigation by, 195–98, 205–19 *passim*
U.S. State Department, 139–40, 142
U.S. Supreme Court, 242
U.S. Transportation Department, 209
U.S. Treasury Department, 116
University of California at Los Angeles, 56, 64, 134, 226
University of Chicago, 24
University of Southern California, 164, 226
UNO, *see* United Neighborhoods Organization
Urban planning, 122–27, 133, 137–38, 143, 254
Urban Planning Research Department (TELACU), 133

Vance, Cyrus, 139
Velásquez, Willie, 148
Verdugo, Julio, 51
Vernon, 3
Vietnam War, 1, 71, 84. *See also* Antiwar movement
Villanueva, Gregory, 174–75
Virgin Land (Smith), 8
VOTE (Voter Organization through Education), 141, 174, 175–77
Voting Rights Act (1965), 167f, 241
VTN Los Angeles firm, 87

W. R. Company, 174
War on Poverty, 10, 20–26 *passim*, 31, 39–44, 147, 217
Watkins, Ted, 28–29, 33
Watts Labor Community Action Committee (WLCAC), 28–35, 37, 250
Watts riots, 77, 250
Welkos, Robert, 198, 202, 215
West Coast Businesswomen's Association, 115
Western Development Corporation, 262
West Virginia, 21
White House, 141
White Memorial Hospital, 164
Whitney Foundation, 161
Whittier (California), 189
Whittier Boulevard (East Los Angeles), 5; commercial revitalization project for, 126, 133, 137, 224–25, 234, 251–56 *passim*; riots on, 70–77 *passim*, 137
Whittier Boulevard Businessmen, 94
Wilmington barrio, 73, 75
Wilson High School, 57f
Winkler-Flexible Corporation, 130
Winner, Leslie, 175
Winner, Lovell, Taylor & Associates, 175–76

WLCAC, *see* Watts Labor Community Action Committee
Women (in TELACU), 109, 115, 179. *See also Names of specific women*
Woodland Hills, 121
Wyler, Leo, 174–76

Yaroslavzky, Zev, 237
Yeatman District Community Corporation (St. Louis), 41

Yñiquez, David, 154
Young, Andrew, 30, 140
Young Citizens for Community Action, 56. *See also* Brown Berets
Young Men's Christian Association, 225

Zócalo project, 97–98, 123–25, 224

Library of Congress Cataloging-in-Publication Data

Chávez, John R.
  Eastside landmark : a history of the East Los Angeles Community
Union, 1968–1993 / John R. Chávez
   p.   cm.
  ISBN 0-8047-3333-3 (cloth: alk. paper)
  1. Mexican Americans—California—East Los Angeles—Politics
and government. 2. East Los Angeles Community Union—History.
3. Mexican Americans—California—East Los Angeles—Social
conditions.   4. East Los Angeles (Calif.)—Politics and government.
5. East Los Angeles (Calif.)—Ethnic relations I. Title.
F869.E18C48   1998
979.4'94—dc21   97-49167
                                                                 CIP

This book is printed on acid-free, recycled paper.

Original printing 1998
Last figure below indicates year of this printing:
07 06 05 04 03 02 01 00 99 98